The Friars Club
2069 Rather Naughty Jokes

• •

Also from the Friars Club

The Friars Club Encyclopedia of Jokes

The Friars Club Bible of Jokes, Pokes, Roasts, and Toasts

How to Do It Standing Up

The Friars Club Private Joke File

* *

More Than 2,000 Very Naughty Jokes
from the Grand Masters of Comedy

Edited by Barry Dougherty

Introduction by Lewis Black

BLACK DOG
& LEVENTHAL
PUBLISHERS
NEW YORK

Library of Congress Cataloging-in-Publication Data on file at the office of the publisher.

Cover design by Jon Valk

Interior design by Martin Lubin

Manufactured in the U.S.A.

Published by

Black Dog & Leventhal Publishers, Inc.
151 West 19th Street
New York, New York 10011

Distributed by

Workman Publishing Company
 225 Varick Street
New York, New York 10014

g f e d c

ACKNOWLEDGMENTS

. . . .

It has taken a hundred years for the Friars to bite the bullet and admit they know more four-letter words than anybody—well, okay, Richard Pryor probably knew more. In any case, they figured it might be fun to pool their resources and come up with a few favorites. Then they got really daring and allowed me to rummage around in their archives and pull out a few Roast moments that are usually reserved for events held behind their huge oak doors. Must be the age thing creeping up on them—or maybe they just got tired of laughing their asses off in front of the same faces and wanted to share the wealth. Whatever the reason, the bottom line is they're at it again—corny, dirty, edgy, unorthodox, and always funny–that's what you get with the Friars.

I'm thrilled that these comedians took the time to talk to me about the art of telling this special genre of jokes—it adds a little credibility to such a silly topic: Joy Behar, Richard Belzer, Dick Capri, Susie Essman, Judy Gold, Gilbert Gottfried, Penn Jillette, Lisa Lampanelli, Samm Levine, Jackie Martling, Paul Provenza, Freddie Roman, Jeffrey Ross, and Stewie Stone.

A huge thanks to Lewis Black for providing the Foreword. It can't be easy to carry all that dirty/edgy/funny baggage around without a release every so often, and I'm so glad we reaped the benefit.

To Freddie Roman, the Dean of the Friars Club, and Jean Pierre Trebot, the Executive Director: thanks for giving me the keys to the joke closet. Entrusting me with that is akin to Frank Purdue handing over the rubber chicken to his son—a true honor.

I need to thank Michael Matuza for helping me get my dirty-joke fix. The poor guy sat through hours of Friars Club Roasts on tape, transcribing these filthy gems. When he's done washing his VCR out with soap maybe he'll have time to read the book and see the fruits of his labor. Don't tell his mother though.

Eve Burhenne outdid herself in helping me with research for this book. She's a walking Google page and my appreciation for her assistance is enormous.

I'm not really good at reliving the moment, as it were, so after sitting through a wonderful interview with a hilarious comedian I just don't want to hear it again. This is why I thank Luisa Buchell and Shannon Skelly for transcribing every word, from the four-letter ones to the multisyllabic ones. And speaking of four-letter words—thank you, David Smith and Roberto Estrada, for supplying me with one or two of them. Alison Grambs also deserves a thank-you for helping me sell the message that the world needs a dirty joke book!

Laura Ross, our editor, has once again proved that funny sells, especially outside of the Christian Science Reading Room.

Finally, I give a shout-out to all comics who have the *cojones* to liven things by thinking the unthinkable and saying the unmentionable. If it weren't for them, the only words you'd see on the next page would be "The End"—so thanks for giving me a book!

—BARRY DOUGHERTY

CONTENTS

• •

INTRODUCTION BY LEWIS BLACK

My parents are going to be beaming with pride when they find out that I have written an introduction to a book filled with dirty jokes. This is the moment they have been waiting for since I was born. "We were hoping he'd become a doctor, but since that didn't work out, this is a dream come true." But seriously, why in hell would I agree to add my name to this project? Well, it's a dirty job but someone had to do it. I guess everyone else turned them down. And you know what I think? There's nothing better than a good dirty joke. It takes you out of yourself for just a few moments and transports you into another space-time continuum, where silliness is the coin of the realm.

I can't remember the first dirty joke I ever heard. I do remember a moment of shock, a minor sense of panic that I was doing something wrong and that my parents would find out. I remember howling with laughter, laughing in a way that I never had at all of those idiotic knock-knock jokes of my childhood. I do know it was a life-changing experience, not a major one, but I knew that things would never be the same. A door had been opened and I would never want to close it. I had discovered the dark side and it was funny. And that's precisely what attracts us to such jokes: the fact that they are forbidden—that they are not jokes for everybody. This form of humor is called "profanity" for a reason. It is the opposite of the sacred. The sacred serves to remind us about what is important in our lives, while the profane reminds us not to take it too seriously. Pretty important, then, that profanity.

I have always wondered why these jokes upset some people. It's a joke, for crying out loud! It doesn't matter in the greater scheme. It's designed to help us blow off a little steam and then move on. These people who object to "blue humor"—how do they maintain such a state of innocence, where do they find the energy, and what is it that they do for fun?

Ultimately humor is a question of taste, of what makes you laugh. And as a comic who uses profanity, dirty makes me laugh. As you grow older, your brain gets cluttered with more and more shit, and you need a more screwed-up shovel to get the shit out. Sometimes, you just need to be shocked out of the nonsense that inundates you on a daily basis. It's good for the soul.

Can someone explain to me why certain words are considered dirty? These are the words we use to express our anger and outrage. What other words do we have at our disposal that do the job so well? (The word "fuck," uttered gutturally or shouted to the winds, releases all the pain, anguish, horror, and disgust one might feel in one great expulsion of air.) What words do people spontaneously use when they watch a horrifying event of epic proportions, such as a tsunami? When you're watching a body of water rise up and crush everything in its path, don't words like "Son of a bitch" or "Holy shit" cross your mind? Does anyone really think, "Aw, pshaw" or "pussyfeathers"?

There are a number of critics who believe that comedians can get easy laughs just by swearing. That isn't true. I am a comic who is considered "edgy," which means that I use profanity and tell jokes on topics that tend to make people uncomfortable—all the more reason that I have to know what I'm doing every second—because the audience isn't stupid. They know when you are not delivering the goods. And in that case, all of the "fucks" in the world won't save your ass. This book includes commentary from a number of comics whose work I admire. These geniuses help to illuminate what it's like to "work profane" and tell jokes that make people uncomfortable. You'll also find a discussion of The Aristocrats, the all-time classic Big Daddy of dirty jokes. One that comics have crafted to their own sense of humor. Reading about it offers real insight into the twisted recesses of the comic mind.

But let's face it—you didn't buy this book for the "commentary" any more than people buy Playboy for the articles. This is a book jam-packed with dirty jokes that the Friars have shared over the years (and mercilessly ripped off from one another), along with a nice big dose of some of the finest barbs ever flung at a Friars Roast.

This is definitely not a coffee-table book, especially if you have children. It's a book you keep in the bathroom—or the bedroom, even better.

So go ahead and enjoy the jokes that the Friars have honed over time and feel free to spread them around, but remember: don't tell these jokes to people who you know will be upset by them—it's not worth it. And they don't deserve them.

CHAPTER 1

Take My Spouse, Please

Lots of proof that you can't live with 'em . . .
but you're screwed if you leave 'em.

A woman asks her husband if he'd like some breakfast. "Bacon and eggs? Perhaps a slice of toast? Maybe a nice grapefruit and a cup of fresh coffee?" He declines. "It's this Viagra," he says. "It's really taken the edge off my appetite."

At lunchtime, she asks if he would like something. "A bowl of home-made soup, maybe, with a cheese sandwich? Or how about a plate of snacks and a glass of milk?" Again, he declines. "No, thanks, it's this Viagra. It's really taken the edge off my appetite."

At dinnertime, she asks if he wants anything to eat, offering to go out and buy him a burger. "Or would you rather I make you a pizza from scratch? Or, how about a tasty stir-fry? That'll only take a couple of minutes. . ." Once more, he declines. "Again, thanks, but it's this Viagra. It's really taken the edge off my appetite."

"Well, then," she says, "would you mind getting off me? I'm fucking STARVING!"

A woman is having an affair while her husband is at work. One wet and lusty day she's in bed with her boyfriend when, to her horror, she hears her husband's car pull into the driveway.

"Oh my God, hurry! Grab your clothes," she yells to her lover. "And jump out the window. My husband is home early!"

"I can't jump out the window!" comes the strangled reply from beneath the sheets. "It's raining out there!"

"If my husband catches us in here, he'll kill us both! He's got a very quick temper and a very large gun! The rain is the least of your problems!"

So the boyfriend scoots out of bed, grabs his clothes, and jumps out the window!

As he begins running down the street in the pouring rain, he quickly discovers he has run right into the middle of the town's annual marathon. So he starts running along beside the others, about three hundred of them. Being naked with his clothes tucked under his arm, he is trying to "blend in" as best he can. It isn't that effective.

After a little while, a few of the runners who have been studying him with some curiosity jog closer. "Do you always run in the nude?" one asks.

"Oh, yes" he replies, gasping. "It feels so wonderfully free having the air blow over your skin while you're running."

Another runner moves alongside. "Do you always run carrying your clothes under your arm?"

"Oh, yes," our friend answers breathlessly. "That way I can get dressed right at the end of the run and get in my car to go home!"

Then a third runner casts his eyes downward and queries, "Do you always wear a condom when you run?"

"Only if it's raining."

● ● ● ●

We're always looking for Miss Right. I found my Miss Right. I didn't know her first name was Always.

—MICKEY FREEMAN, SALUTE TO FREDDIE ROMAN, 2003

● ● ● ●

A man and his wife decide to go back to their honeymoon hotel for their twenty-fifth anniversary. As the couple reflects on that magical evening a quarter-century earlier, the wife asks her husband, "When you first saw my naked body in front of you, what was going through your mind?"

The husband replies, "All I wanted to do was fuck your brains out and suck your tits dry."

As the wife undresses, she asks, "What are you thinking now?"

"It looks as if I did a pretty good job."

T he newlyweds are in their honeymoon room and the groom decides to let the bride know where she stands right from the start of their marriage. He takes off his trousers and throws them at her, saying, "Put those on."

The bride says, "I can't wear your trousers."

He replies, "And don't forget that! I will always wear the pants in the family!"

The bride takes off her panties and throws them at him with the same vehemence, saying, "Try those on!"

"I can't get into your panties!"

"And you never will if you don't change your attitude."

Why doesn't Smokey the bear have any kids?

Because every time his wife gets hot, he covers her with dirt and beats her with a shovel.

• • • •

We all know Brett Butler was a little shaky, and during that time she had her breasts done. But the general rule of construction is you don't put a second floor on a house with a shaky foundation. I'm only kidding. I'm glad you are here and wish you luck in the future, though I kind of miss the old days when Brett would let you touch her tits for a Valium.

—ADAM FERRARA, ROB REINER ROAST, 2000

• • • •

Maria is a devout Catholic—no birth control for her! She gets married and has seventeen children and then her husband dies. She remarries two weeks later and has twenty-two children by her second husband. She dies.

At her wake, the priest looks tenderly at Maria as she lies in her coffin, looks up to the heavens, and says, "At last . . . they're finally together."

A man standing next to him says, "Excuse me, Father, but are you referring to her and her FIRST husband, or her and her SECOND husband?"

"Neither," the priest says politely. "I mean her LEGS."

● ● ● ●

Susie Essman is not your typical Jewish girl; she'll blow
you even if you don't have good credit.

—RICHARD BELZER, RICHARD BELZER ROAST, 2001

● ● ● ●

A guy walks into a sperm bank wearing a ski mask and holding
a gun. He goes up to the nurse and demands that she open the vault.

"But sir, this is a sperm bank! There's no money in there."

"I don't care, open it now!!!"

So she opens the door to the vault. The guy says, "Take one of those
sperm samples and drink it!" She looks at him, aghast.

"DO IT!" he says, so the nurse takes a deep breath and polishes it off.

"That one there, drink that one as well."

Once again the nurse drinks. After four more samples are consumed,
the man takes off his ski mask and says, "See, honey—it's not that
hard."

M rs. Schmidlap hires a maid with beautiful blond hair. The
first morning, the girl removes the hair and says, "I wear a wig because
I was born totally hairless. Not a hair on my body, not even...down
there."

That night, Mrs. Schmidlap tells her husband. He says, "I've never
seen anything like that. Please, tomorrow ask her to go into the bedroom and show you. I want to hide in the closet so I can have a look."

The next day, Mrs. Schmidlap does as her husband asked, and the two of them go into the bedroom. The girl strips and shows her. Then she confesses, "I've never seen one with hair on it. Can I see yours?" So Mrs. Schmidlap pulls off her clothes and shows her.

That night, Mrs. Schmidlap says to her husband, "I hope you're satisfied, because I was pretty embarrassed when that girl asked to see mine."

"You think YOU were embarrassed? I had my four poker buddies in the closet with me."

A man goes to the police station wishing to speak with the burglar who had broken into his house the night before. "You'll get your chance in court," says the desk sergeant.

"No, no, no!" insists the man. "I want to know how he got into the house without waking my wife. I've been trying to do that for years!"

• • • •

Don King knows the similarity between eggs benedict and a blow job. You never seem to get either one at home.

—Norm Crosby, Don King Roast, 2005

• • • •

A woman asks her husband, "Will you please fix the cabinet in the kitchen? It's been barely holding on to its hinges for weeks now."

He replies, "Does it say 'carpenter' on my forehead?"

Surprised, she lets it go and returns to her housework. As she is cleaning the bathroom, she notices that the lever on the toilet is getting stuck. She yells from the bathroom, "Honey, the toilet lever is stuck again! Can you fix it?"

He responds, "Do I have 'plumber' written on my forehead?"

The next day the husband comes home from work to find the cabinet fixed, the toilet fixed, and a chipper spouse making the bed in the master bedroom. "Who fixed everything?" he asks.

"A kind young gentleman came by today, said he was a handyman, and asked if I needed anything done around the house. When he finished, I told him I didn't have any cash in the house to pay him with. He said in that case, I could pay him by sucking his dick or cooking him a good meal."

"What did you cook for him?" asked the husband.

"Does it say 'chef' on my forehead?"

Becky is on her deathbed, with her husband Jake at her side. He holds her cold hand as tears silently stream down his face. Her pale lips move. "Jake…," she whispers.

"Hush," he quickly interrupts, "don't talk." But she insists.

"Jake," she says, "I have to talk. I must confess."

"There is nothing to confess," says the weeping Jake. "It's all right. Everything's all right."

"No, no. I must die in peace. I must confess, Jake, that I have been unfaithful to you."

Jake strokes her hand. "Now, Becky, don't be concerned. I know all about it," he sobs. "Why else would I have poisoned you?"

A pair of newlyweds, both virgins, are nervous about the wedding night. When the moment of truth comes, the wife quickly undresses and gets under the covers while the husband slowly sheds his clothes, one piece at a time. First, he takes off his socks, and his toes look strangely deformed. The wife asks, "What happened to your toes?"

"I had toelio."

"You mean polio?"

"No, toelio."

Then he takes off his pants and the wife sees that his knees are all discolored. The wife asks, "What happened to your knees?"

"I had kneasles."

"You mean measles?"

"No, kneasles."

Finally he takes off his underwear and she says, "Let me guess... smallcox?"

A couple is in bed getting busy when the girl places the guy's hand on her pussy. "Put your finger in me," she tells him. So he does, without hesitation, and she starts moaning.

"Put two fingers in," she says. So in goes another one.

She's really starting to get worked up when she says, "Put your whole hand in!"

The guy happily obliges, when she says, moaning aloud, "Put both your hands inside of me!!!" So the guy puts both of his hands in!

"Now clap your hands," commands the girl.

"I can't," says the guy.

The girl looks him straight in the eye and says, "See, I told you I had a tight pussy!"

A couple has just gotten married and on their honeymoon night, as they are about to make love, the wife tells the husband, "Please be gentle, I'm still a virgin." The husband, shocked, replies, "How is that possible? You've been married three times before."

"Well, my first husband was a gynecologist and all he wanted to do was look at it. My second husband was a psychiatrist and all he wanted to do was talk about it. And my third husband was a stamp collector and all he wanted to do was . . . oh, do I miss him!"

● ● ● ●

I was actually lucky enough to get invited to a party at the Playboy Mansion. I nearly came on the invitation. What a night. I got a hand job from Carrot Top.

—JEFFREY ROSS, HUGH HEFNER ROAST, 2001

● ● ● ●

A newlywed couple shares their first night together. The bride comes out of the bathroom showered and wearing a beautiful robe. The proud husband says, "My dear, we are married now, you can open your robe."

The beautiful bride opens her robe, and he is astonished. "Oh, oh, aaaahhh," he exclaims. "My God, you are so beautiful, let me take your picture.

"My picture?"

"Yes, my dear, so I can carry your beauty next to my heart forever."

She smiles and he takes her picture, and then he heads into the bathroom to shower. He comes out wearing his robe and the wife asks, "Why do you wear a robe? We are married now."

At that, the man opens his robe and she exclaims, "Oh, oh, oh my, let me get a picture."

He beams and asks why, and she answers, "So I can get it enlarged!"

What is the difference between a bachelor and a married man?

A bachelor comes home, sees what's in the refrigerator, and goes to bed.

A married man comes home, sees what's in the bed, and goes to the refrigerator.

"**A**nd will there be anything else, sir?" the bellboy asks, after setting out an elaborate dinner for two.

"No, thank you," the gentleman replies. "That will be all."

As the young man turns to leave, he notices a beautiful satin negligee on the bed. "Anything for your wife?" he asks.

"Yeah, that's a good idea," the fellow says. "Please bring up a postcard."

One day, Sara is at home alone and the doorbell rings. She opens the door and a guy says, "Hi, I'm Chris. Is Tony home?"

"No, he went to the store, but you can wait here if you want." So they sit down and after a few moments of silence Chris says, "You know, Sara, you have the greatest breasts. I'd give you a hundred bucks just to see one."

Sara thinks about it for a second and figures, what the hell—a hundred bucks! She peels back her robe and shows one to him for a few seconds. He promptly thanks her and throws a hundred bucks on the table.

They sit there a while longer and Chris says, "That was so amazing! I've got to see both of them. I'll give you another hundred dollars if I can just see them both together."

Sara, amazed by the offer, decides, what the hell, why not? So she opens her robe and gives him a nice, long look.

A while later, after Chris has gone, Tony comes home from the store. The wife says, "You know, your friend Chris came over."

"Did he drop off the two hundred bucks he owes me?"

●　●　●　●

My wife and I have been married for a wonderful forty-three years. And I can tell you honestly, in those forty-three years, I have never thought of another woman. I've slept with a few but afterwards I never thought of them. (It takes balls to do a joke like that in front of your wife!)

—FREDDIE ROMAN, SALUTE TO FREDDIE ROMAN, 2003

●　●　●　●

Wife: I dreamt they were auctioning off dicks. The big ones went for ten dollars and the thick ones went for twenty dollars.

Husband: How about the ones like mine?

Wife: Those, they gave away.

Husband: I had a dream too . . . I dreamt they were auctioning off cunts. The pretty ones went for a thousand dollars and the little tight ones went for two thousand.

Wife: And how much for the ones like mine?

Husband: That's where they held the auction.

A FEW DIRTY WORDS
FROM SUSIE ESSMAN

My father had a filthy mouth. He was always, "fuck this and fuck that," so I was never brought up with "I'm going to wash your mouth out with soap." I was always a little edgy.

Very early on, I realized you could always get a laugh with a dick joke but you needed to have a quality dick joke. I didn't want to get away with just saying "fuck" and getting a laugh or just saying "dick" and getting a laugh, so I developed some quality dick jokes that were acceptable to me.

The language is not gratuitous; it has a reason for being. Like, when I talk about the Connecticut WASPs and how they crunch their teeth with lockjaw—what are they protecting? It's almost as though they're afraid a wandering dick might fly by and just pop into their mouth at any given moment. To me, that's a quality dick joke.

I seem to talk about sex a lot onstage because it's one of our most base impulses and instincts and for some reason there's some taboo around it. Even the words "dirty joke"—I always felt like I wanted to talk about it.

I think that because I'm a woman I get away with things that a man wouldn't get away with. I remember in the late eighties, during the comedy boom years, the male comics would get so annoyed watching me because I could get away with stuff that they could never get away with. An example: I'll turn to a guy in the audience and say, "Did I fuck you?" A guy saying that would be considered sexist.

People will tell me the most intimate details of their lives when I'm onstage, in the same way that they'll go on Jerry Springer. It's amazing. If I can create an atmosphere where they feel safe, they will bare all. They will be sitting there with the girlfriend, and the wife is at home. They'll admit to strange sexual peccadilloes and weird kinds of things in front of an entire audience of strangers.

Women love me because I'm giving them freedom. There are men that I think are a little bit frightened of me. Gay men are my best audiences. I think I'm the woman they want to be. Gay men always love a bawdy woman.

The first time I saw Richard Pryor, I thought, that's what I want to do, because he had everything. He had that warmth and accessibility. He could tell stories, he could do characters, and he could tell jokes. He was as funny as you're going to get as a stand-up comic. He knew how to craft bits, long bits, short bits—he just had everything. He was so real, and you felt there was a vulnerability, too. To me, he was possibly the greatest stand-up comic of all time.

I think there are boundaries, but they're specific to each person. I don't think that there's a set of rules that everyone has to follow. There are things I don't want to talk about, that I don't find funny, that someone else can talk about and make funny. I might think they went over the edge; I'm sure people find that about me sometimes.

Mel Brooks made the Holocaust hilarious. There are a lot of people that would be afraid to talk about it. His point of view is, you take their power away by ridiculing these people. So, in a certain way, comedy and humor should not have boundaries. There's taste, and everybody should have their own comfort level of what they like to talk about. I don't know that I personally could make a rape joke funny.

What happens sometimes with audience members is that I'll get very flirtatious onstage and they'll take me seriously. Like a guy will think that I am really coming on to him and I'm not. I'll say something about a blow job, and they think I'm going to give them one. No! It's an act!

If I'm comfortable with the material, the audience is going to feel comfortable. If I'm feeling this material is not comfortable for me, the audience is going to feel uncomfortable. I have no problem talking about blow jobs and getting them to accept it. I'm just in conversation and telling them something, the way I would if I were with my girlfriends—believe me, women talk dirty when they're with their girlfriends—and that's always what I've tried to do, just turn it into a coffee klatch.

"Fucks" can be very funny, but they have to be used judiciously. "Did I fuck you?" is different than just fuck this and fuck that. There's a reason for saying it. I'll never turn to some big strapping, gorgeous guy and ask that question. It's usually some schleppy, unassuming guy. The relationship then becomes funny because, of course, I'm never going to have sex with this man. Then again, at the Jerry Stiller Roast, I said to Chris Noth, "You're the only fuckable guy on this entire dais," so, it's all context and you have to use the language judiciously, otherwise it loses its power and its shock value.

Sex in general is funny. Here is this biological need that we all have, without which the species would not exist. That's just a reality—yet we've created so much mishegos around it. There's so much misinformation out there that I feel that it's my job to free it up for everybody.

A n office manager arrives at his office to find an employee totally stressed out. He gives him some advice: "I was going through a tough time at work so I went home every afternoon for two weeks and had myself pampered by my wife. It was fantastic and it really helped. You should try it, too!"

Two weeks later when the manager gets to work, he sees the same employee looking happy and full of energy, typing away at his computer full speed.

"I see you followed my advice?"

"I did and it was great! By the way, I didn't know you had such a nice house!"

A man tells his wife that he's going out to buy cigarettes, but when he gets to the store he finds it closed. So he goes to the bar next door to use the vending machine. While he's there, he has a few beers and begins talking to this beautiful girl. He has a few more beers, and the next thing he knows he's in this girl's apartment having wild sex. The next thing he knows it's 3:00 a.m.

"Oh my god, my wife is going to kill me! Quick, give me some talcum powder!"

The girl shrugs and gets him some. He rubs it all over his hands and dashes out the door.

When he gets home his wife is up waiting for him and she's furious. "Where the hell have you been?"

"Well, to tell you the truth, I went into a bar, had a few drinks, went home with this blonde, and slept with her."

"Let me see your hands!"

He shows his wife his powdery hands.

"Damn liar, you were out bowling again!"

A husband comes home to find his wife in the living room with her suitcases packed. "Where the hell do you think you're going?" he says.

"I'm going to Las Vegas. You can earn $400 for a blow job there and I figured that I might as well earn money for what I do to you for free."

The husband thinks for a moment, goes upstairs, and comes back down with his suitcase packed as well.

"Where do you think you're going?" the wife asks.

"I'm coming with you . . . I want to see how you survive on $800 a year!!!"

As a painless way to save money, a young couple decides that every time they have sex, the husband will put his pocket change into a china piggy bank on the bedside table. One night, while being unusually athletic, he accidentally knocks the piggy bank onto the floor, where it smashes. To his surprise, among the masses of coins, there are handfuls of five- and ten-dollar bills.

"What's up with all the notes?" he asks his wife.

"Well, not everyone is as cheap as you are."

A beautiful woman walks into a shoe store, and the clerk can't stop staring at her. While helping her try on a pair of shoes he glances up her skirt to find she isn't wearing any panties. Uncontrollably, he blurts, "I'd like to fill your pussy with ice cream and lick it all out!"

Shocked, the woman runs out and says to her husband, "Honey, the shoe salesman in there said he'd like to fill my pussy up with ice cream and lick it all out! Now go kick his ass!"

The husband replies, "Dear, anyone who can eat that much ice cream, I ain't fuckin' with!"

A widow has her late husband cremated and brings home the urn containing his remains. Picking up the urn, she pours him out on the counter. While tracing her fingers in the ashes, she starts talking to him.

"Irving, you know that fur coat you promised me? I bought it with the insurance money!" And after a minute, "Irving, remember that new car you promised me? Well, I also bought it with the insurance money!" Another pause and then, "Irving, that emerald necklace you promised me? I bought it, too, with the insurance money."

Finally, still tracing her finger through the ashes, she says, "Irving, remember that blow job I promised you? Here it comes."

• • • •

A guy gets into bed with his wife and he's real horny. She says, "Not tonight. I'm going to the gynecologist tomorrow and I want to be fresh." He says, "Well, you're not going to the fucking dentist are you?"

—JACKIE MARTLING, FRIARS CLUB COMEDY MARATHON FOR POLICE AND FIREFIGHTERS, 2001

• • • •

A young husband and wife are sunning on a nude beach when a wasp buzzes into the woman's vagina. She screams! Thinking quickly, the husband covers her with a coat, pulls on his shorts, carries her to the car, and makes a dash to the hospital.

After examining her, the doctor explains that the wasp is too far in to be reached with forceps. He suggests that the husband try to entice it out by putting honey on his penis, penetrating her, and withdrawing as soon as he feels the wasp.

The man agrees to try right there and then, but because he is so nervous, he can't rise to the occasion.

"If neither of you objects," the doctor says, "I could give it a try."

The woman is clearly suffering, so both agree. The doctor quickly undresses, slathers on some honey, and mounts the woman.

The husband watches with increasing annoyance as the doctor's thrusts continue for several long minutes. "Hey, what do you think you're doing?"

"Change of plans," the physician pants. "I'm going to drown the little bastard!"

A guy comes home from work, walks into his bedroom, and finds a stranger fucking his wife.

"What the hell are you two doing?"

The wife turns to the stranger and says, "I told you he was stupid."

G ary and Mary go on their honeymoon, and the first night Gary spends six hours eating Mary's pussy. The next afternoon, they go to an Italian restaurant. Suddenly, Gary starts to freak out. He screams, "Waiter! Waiter! Come over here!"

The waiter says, "Can I help you, sir?"

Gary yells, "There's a hair in my spaghetti! Get it the fuck out of here!"

The waiter apologizes up and down as he quickly takes the spaghetti away.

Mary looks over at Gary, shaking her head, and whispers, "What a hypocrite you are. You spent most of last night with your face full of hair."

"Yeah? Well, how long do you think I'd have stayed if I'd found a piece of spaghetti in there?"

A woman pregnant with her first child pays a visit to her obstetrician's office. After the exam, she stammers, "My husband wants me to ask you..."

"I know... I know... " says the doctor, placing a reassuring hand on her shoulder. "I get asked this all the time. Sex is fine until late in the pregnancy."

"No, that's not it," the woman confesses. "He wants to know if I can still mow the lawn."

Two deaf people get married. During their first week as man and wife, they find that they are unable to communicate in the bedroom after they've turned off the lights because they can't use sign language in the dark. After several nights of fumbling around and misunderstandings, the wife comes up with a solution.

"Honey," she signs. "Why don't we agree on some simple signals? For instance, if you want to have sex with me, reach over and squeeze my left breast one time. If you don't want to have sex, reach over and squeeze my right breast one time."

The husband likes this plan and signs back to his wife, "Great idea, now if you want to have sex with ME, reach over and pull on my penis one time. If you don't want to have sex, reach over and pull on my penis . . . fifty times."

One fall day Bill is out raking leaves when he notices a hearse slowly drive by. Following the first hearse is a second hearse, which is followed by a man walking solemnly along who in turn is followed by a dog. Then comes about two hundred men walking in single file. Intrigued, Bill goes up to the man and asks him who is in the first hearse.

"My wife," the man replies.

"I'm sorry," says Bill. "What happened to her?"

"My dog bit her and she died."

Bill then asks the man who is in the second hearse.

"My mother-in-law. My dog bit her and she died as well."

Bill thinks about this for a while. He finally asks the man, "Can I borrow your dog?"

"Get in line."

A fifty-four-year-old accountant leaves a letter for his wife one Friday evening:

Dear Wife,

I am 54 and by the time you receive this letter I will be at the Grand Hotel with my beautiful and sexy 18-year-old secretary."

When he arrives at the hotel there is a letter waiting for him:

Dear Husband,

I, too, am 54 and by the time you receive this letter I will be at the Breakwater Hotel with my handsome and virile 18-year-old boy toy. AND you, being an accountant, will appreciate that 18 goes into 54 many more times than 54 goes into 18."

● ● ● ●

It's so easy to make racial jokes in front of this crowd, but Ice-T has become a good friend of mine. Does he hate Jews? Of course. But we all hate them. Susie Essman, for example.

—RICHARD BELZER, RICHARD BELZER ROAST, 2001

● ● ● ●

Two men waiting at the pearly gates strike up a conversation. "How'd you die?" the first man asks the second.

"I froze to death."

"That's awful, how does it feel to freeze to death?"

"It's very uncomfortable at first, you get the shakes, then you get pains in all your fingers and toes. But eventually, it's a very calm way to go. You get numb and you kind of drift off, as if you're sleeping. How did you die?"

"I had a heart attack. You see, I knew my wife was cheating on me, so one day I showed up at home unexpectedly. I ran up to the bedroom and found her alone, knitting. I ran down to the basement but no one was hiding there. I ran out to the garden but no one was hiding there either. I ran as fast as I could to the attic and just as I got there, I had a massive heart attack and died."

The second man shakes his head. "That's so ironic," he says.

"What do you mean?"

"If you had only stopped to look in the freezer, we'd both still be alive."

R oger's wife knows that he is a hard worker and spends most of his nights bowling or playing volleyball. One weekend, she decides that he needs to relax a little and take a break from sports, so she takes him to a strip club. The doorman at the club spots them and says, "Hey, Roger! How are you tonight?"

Surprised, the wife asks her husband if he has been here before.

"No, no. He's just one of the guys I bowl with."

They are seated and the waitress approaches, sees Roger, and says, "Nice to see you, Roger. A gin and tonic as usual?"

His wife's eyes widen. "You must come here a lot!"

"No, no," says Roger. "I just know her from volleyball."

Then a stripper walks up to the table. She throws her arms around Roger and says, "Roger! A table dance as usual?"

His wife, fuming, collects her things and storms out of the bar. Roger follows her and spots her getting into a cab, so he jumps in beside her. She looks at him, seething with fury, and lets Roger have it with both barrels.

At this, the cabby leans over and says, "Sure looks like you picked up a bitch tonight, Roger!"

As an ultimate test of his will power, a man decides to give up sex for Lent. Although not thrilled with the idea, his wife agrees to support him in this effort. The first few weeks aren't too difficult. Things get tougher as time goes on, though, so the wife starts wearing her dowdiest nightclothes and chewing on garlic before going to bed. The last couple of weeks are extremely hard for the husband, so the wife starts locking the bedroom door and forcing her husband to sleep on the couch.

Easter morning finally comes and there's a knock on the bedroom door where the wife is still sleeping.

"Guess who?"

"I know who it is!"

"Guess what I want?"

"I know what you want!"

"Guess what I'm knockin' with?"

● ● ● ●

My first wife died of natural causes, my second wife wouldn't.

— ROSS BENNETT, SALUTE TO JACKIE GREEN, 2003

● ● ● ●

A husband and wife decide to take golf lessons at a local country club. They meet the pro and all head onto the driving range. The man goes up to hit first. He swings and hits the ball a hundred yards. The golf pro says, "Not bad. But now hold the club as firmly as you hold your wife's breasts."

The man follows instructions and hits the ball three hundred yards. The golf pro says, "Excellent!"

Now, the woman takes her turn. Her ball goes thirty yards. The pro says, "Not bad, but now try holding the club like you hold your husband's dick."

She swings again and this time the ball goes ten yards.

"Not bad, but now try taking the club out of your mouth before you hit the ball."

A fter the rowdy annual office Christmas party, John wakes up with a pounding headache, cotton-mouthed and utterly unable to recall the events of the preceding evening. After a trip to the bathroom he is able to make his way downstairs, where his wife puts some coffee in front of him. "Louise," he moans, "tell me what went on last night. Was it as bad as I think?"

"Even worse," she assures him in her most scornful tone. "You made a complete ass of yourself, succeeded in antagonizing the entire board of directors, and insulted the chairman of the company to his face."

"He's an arrogant, self-important prick, piss on him!"

"You did. All over his suit, " Louise informs him. "And he fired you."

"Well, fuck him, then."

"I did. You're back at work on Monday."

A man asks his girlfriend to marry him and she insists that he prove his love to her by getting her name, Wendy, tattooed on his penis. He obliges, and the tattoo is a beautiful thing. When it is erect it says "Wendy" and when it is limp it says "WY."

The two lovebirds get married and go to Jamaica to a nude beach for their honeymoon. Wendy asks her husband to go and get her a drink, and while he is waiting at the bar, he notices that the bartender also has a "WY" on his penis. He says, "Excuse me, that's an interesting tattoo. Do you have a wife named Wendy?"

"No, my tattoo says, 'Welcome to Jamaica, have a nice day!!!'"

A husband and wife who have been married twenty years are doing some yard work. The man is working hard cleaning the barbecue grill while his wife is bending over, weeding the flower bed. He says, "Your rear end is almost as wide as this grill."

She ignores the remark.

A little later, the husband takes his measuring tape and measures the grill, then he goes over to his wife, still bending over the garden, and measures her rear end. He gasps, "Geez, it really IS as wide as the grill!"

She ignores this remark as well.

Later that night while in bed, the husband starts to feel frisky. The wife calmly responds, "If you think I'm gonna fire up the grill for one little wiener, you are sadly mistaken."

A couple decide to fly to Alaska for a romantic weekend. When they get to the rustic cabin it is frigid, so the wife asks her husband to go chop some wood for the fireplace. He comes in after five minutes and tells his wife that his hands were too cold to finish, so she says, "Put them between my thighs to warm them." He does this, and when he feels better, he goes back outside to finish chopping wood.

He comes in after another five minutes and says, "Honey, my hands are cold again." So they repeat the process.

When he comes in again five minutes later, complaining again, she says, "Damn, don't your ears ever get cold?"

I t is the mailman's last day on the job after thirty-five years of carrying the mail through all kinds of weather to the same neighborhood. When he arrives at the first house on his route he is greeted by the whole family, who congratulates him and sends him on his way with a big gift envelope. At the second house they present him with a box of fine cigars. The folks at the third house hand him a selection of terrific fishing lures.

At the fourth house a strikingly beautiful blonde in a revealing negligee meets him at the door. She takes him by the hand and gently leads him into the house and up the stairs to the bedroom, where she makes love to him, the most passionate love he has ever experienced. When he has had enough they go downstairs, where she fixes him a giant breakfast: eggs, potatoes, ham, sausage, blueberry waffles, and fresh-squeezed orange juice. When he can't eat another bite, she pours him a cup of steaming coffee. He notices a dollar bill sticking out from under the cup's bottom edge.

"All this was just too wonderful for words," he says, "but what's the dollar for?"

"Well," she says, "last night, I told my husband that today would be your last day and that we should do something special for you. I asked him what to give you. He said, 'Fuck him. Give him a dollar.' The breakfast was my idea."

A farmer is lying in bed with his wife when he turns to her, grabs her tits, and says, "Honey, if you could get milk out of these, we could get rid of the cow." Then he grabs her pussy and says, "Honey, if you could get eggs out of here, we could get rid of the chickens."

She turns to him, smiles, grabs his dick, and says, "Honey, if you could get this up I could get rid of your brother."

• • • •

There's been a lot of jokes about Hugh Hefner saying he takes Viagra. Let me tell you something, Hugh Hefner doesn't need Viagra. He needs cement. . . . The only way Hugh Hefner can get stiff is rigor mortis.

—GILBERT GOTTFRIED, HUGH HEFNER ROAST, 2001

• • • •

Three hillbillies are sitting on the porch. The first hillbilly says, "My wife is so dumb, yesterday she drug home a brand-new washer and dryer, and we isn't even got electricity!"

The second hillbilly says, "My wife is stupider than yers. Yesterday she brung home a new dishwasher and we isn't even got runnin' water!"

The third hillbilly says, "My wife is even stupider! Yesterday I was in the kitchen and I saw her purse on the table. Everything was spilled out of it and there was a bunch of rubbers layin' there . . . and she isn't even got a dick!"

A new bride goes to her doctor for a checkup. Lacking knowledge of the male anatomy, she asks him, "What's that thing hanging between my husband's legs?"

The doctor replies, "We call that the penis."

"Well, what's that reddish-purple thing on the end of the penis?"

"We call that the head of the penis."

"Uh-huh. Then, what are those two round things about fifteen inches from the head of the penis?"

"Lady, on him I don't know, but on me they're the cheeks of my ass!"

A man takes his pregnant wife to the hospital. The doctor looks her over and tells them it will be a rather difficult delivery. He offers to let the couple try an experimental procedure. The woman would be connected to a machine that would transfer part of the pain to the father of the baby, thus reducing her own. The man quickly agrees. The doctor warns him, though, that there is a slight bug in the machine that causes it to amplify the pain sent to the father by ten times, and that if the pain became too much for the husband to bear, he should let the doctor know.

The doctor turns on the machine and watches the man, who says he feels absolutely fine and could take more. The doctor turns the dial up to 40, 60, 80, and finally 100 percent of the pain—times ten! The woman delivers the baby painlessly and the doctor stares at the man, astonished that he did not even flinch in spite of the prolonged and difficult childbirth.

The couple takes the new baby home. There, on the front step, the mailman lies dead.

A man and his wife get into bed for the night. The wife curls up and closes her eyes, ready for sleep. The husband puts on his bed lamp, to read a book. As he reads, he reaches over and fondles his wife's pussy for a minute or two.

The wife rolls over with a smile and starts taking off her nightgown. The husband confusedly asks, "What the hell are doing?"

"You were playing with my pussy. I thought it was foreplay."

"Hell, no! I was just wetting my fingers so I could turn the pages."

Once there were twin brothers by the name of Jones. John Jones was married, and Joe Jones was single. The single brother, Joe, was the proud owner of a dilapidated rowboat. It happened that John's wife died the same day that Joe's rowboat filled with water and sank.

A few days later, a kindly old lady met Joe and, mistaking him for John, said, "Oh, Mr. Jones, I am sorry to hear of your great loss, you must feel terrible."

Joe smiled and said, "Well, I am not a bit sorry. She was rather old from the start. Her bottom was all chewed up and she smelled of dead fish. Even the first time I got into her, she made water faster than anything I ever saw. She had a bad crack and a pretty big hole in her front, and that hole got bigger every time I used her. It got so I could barely handle her, but if anyone else used her she leaked like anything. The thing that finished her was four guys from the other side of town. They came down looking for a good time and asked if I could lend her to them. I warned them she wasn't so hot, but they could take a crack at her if they liked. Well, the result was the crazy fools tried to get inside her all at once and it was too much for her. She cracked right up the middle."

Before he could finish, the old lady fainted!

A married couple was in a terrible accident where the woman's face was severely burned. The doctor told the husband that they couldn't graft any skin from her body because she was too skinny. So the husband offered to donate some of his own skin. However, the only skin on his body that the doctor felt was suitable was on the husband's buttocks. The couple agreed that they would tell no one about where the skin came from, and requested that the doctor also honor their secret.

After the surgery, everyone was astounded at the result. The woman looked more beautiful than she ever had before! All her friends and relatives just went on and on about her youthful appearance. One day, when she was alone with her husband, she was overcome with emotion at his sacrifice. She said, "Dear, I just want to thank you for everything you did for me. There is no way I could ever repay you."

"My darling," he replied, "Think nothing of it. I get all the thanks I need every time I see your mother kiss you on the cheek."

A married couple has been stranded on a desert island for many years. One day another man washes up on shore. He and the wife are attracted to each other right away, but realize they must be creative if they are to engage in any hanky-panky.

For his own reasons, the husband is also very glad to see the second man. "Now we can have three people doing eight-hour shifts in the watchtower, rather than two people doing twelve-hour shifts."

The newcomer is only too happy to help and, in fact, volunteers to take the first shift. He climbs up the tower to stand watch. Meanwhile, the couple on the ground is placing stones in a circle to make a fire to cook supper. The second man yells down, "Hey, no screwing!" They yell back, "We're not screwing!"

A few minutes later they start to put driftwood into the stone circle. Again the second man yells down, "Hey, no screwing!" Again they yell back, "We're not screwing!" Later, as they are putting palm leaves on the roof of their shack to patch leaks, the second man once again yells down, "Hey, I said no screwing!" They yell back, "We're not screwing!"

Eventually the shift is over and the second man climbs down from the tower to be replaced by the husband. He's not even halfway up before the wife and her new friend are hard at it. The husband looks out from the tower and says, "Son-of-a-gun. From up here it DOES look like they're screwing."

A woman and her boyfriend are necking on the couch when the phone rings. The woman gets up to answer it and is back in a few seconds.

"Who was it?" he asks.

"My husband," she replies.

"Uh-oh! I better get going! Where was he?"

"Relax. He's downtown playing poker with you."

A man is feeling ill so he goes to the doctor. The doctor examines him, shakes his head, and says, "You know, you should have come to see me sooner. You have a grave illness and, unfortunately, you are going to die this evening."

The man is distraught. He goes home and gently breaks the news to his wife, who takes it pretty well.

"Honey, we're going to make this the best night of your life. I am going to treat you like a king." She prepares a scrumptious gourmet dinner with wine, candles, the works. After dinner she slips away and returns in the most incredible negligee the man has ever seen. She leads him into their bedroom, where they make passionate love—the best ever. The man is beside himself. The wife rolls over to go to sleep, knowing she kept her promise.

Well, the husband is wide-awake watching the clock. He knows that he is doomed. He taps her, "Honey?" he whispers. She rolls over and again they make love. Again when they are done she rolls over—but again he taps her. She is getting cranky, but under the circumstances she grants her husband's dying wish. Finally, the wife rolls over and begins to snore. But the amorous husband strikes again.

"Honey?" he whispers.

She rolls over and yells, "Look, buster! YOU don't have to get up in the morning!!"

A wife arrives home after a long shopping trip and is horrified to find her husband in bed with a young, lovely thing. Just as she is about to storm out of the house, her husband stops her and says, "Before you leave, I want you to hear how this all came about. Driving home, I saw this poor young girl, looking very tired, and I offered her a ride. She was hungry, so I brought her home and fed her some of the roast you had left in the refrigerator. Her shoes were worn out so I gave her a pair of your shoes that you didn't wear because they were out of style. She was cold so I gave her that new birthday sweater you never wore even once because the color didn't suit you. Her slacks were worn out so I gave her a pair of yours that don't fit you anymore. Then, as she was about to leave the house, she paused and asked, 'Is there anything else that your wife doesn't use anymore?' And so, here we are!"

A married man keeps telling his wife, "Honey, you have such a beautiful butt." And you know what? He's right. His birthday is coming, so she decides to take a trip to the tattoo parlor and get the words "Beautiful Butt" tattooed on her ass.

She walks in and tells the tattoo artist that her husband thinks she has a beautiful butt. He looks and says, "You do have a beautiful butt." She tells him she wants "Beautiful Butt" tattooed on her ass.

The artist says, "I can't fit that on your ass, it takes up too much space. But I tell you what, I will tattoo the letters BB, one on each cheek, and that can stand for Beautiful Butt."

She agrees and gets it done.

On the man's birthday she is waiting for him when he comes home from work, wearing only a robe. She stands at the top of the stairs and when he opens the door she says, "Look, honey!" She takes off the robe, bends over, and the man yells, "WHO THE FUCK IS BOB?"

A couple is invited to a swanky masked Halloween party but she gets a terrible headache and tells him to go to the party alone. Being a devoted husband, he protests, but she insists that she is going to take some aspirin and go to bed, and there is no reason he shouldn't go ahead and have a good time. So he takes his costume and off he goes. The wife, after sleeping soundly for one hour, awakens without pain and decides to go to the party after all. Since her husband won't recognize her in her costume, she thinks she might have some fun watching him in secret.

She soon spots her husband cavorting on the dance floor, dancing with every pretty girl he can, copping a little feel here and a little kiss there. Being a rather seductive babe herself, the wife ventures onto the dance floor to entice her own husband away from his current partner.

She lets him go as far as he wishes, naturally, since he is, after all, her husband. Finally he whispers a little proposition in her ear and she agrees. Off they go to his parked car for a little bang. Just before midnight, when the party guests are planning to unmask and reveal their identities, she slips away, goes home, stashes her costume, and gets into bed, wondering what his husband will report about the evening.

She is sitting up reading when he comes in.

"How was it?" she asks, nonchalantly.

"Oh, the same old thing. You know I never have a good time when you're not there."

"Did you dance much?"

"I never even danced one dance. When I got there I met Pete, Bill Brown, and some other guys, so we went into the den and played poker all evening. But I'll tell you . . . the guy I loaned my costume to sure had a real good time!"

Do I wish that I could be further along in show business by this point? Of course. I'm not making excuses, but just think how far I could have gone with two balls. Look what Rosie O'Donnell has accomplished.

—RICHARD BELZER, RICHARD BELZER ROAST, 2001

● ● ● ●

An escaped convict breaks into a house and ties up a young couple who had been sleeping in the bedroom. As soon as he has a chance, the husband turns to his voluptuous young wife, bound up on the bed in a skimpy nightgown, and whispers, "Honey, this guy hasn't seen a woman in years. Just cooperate with anything he wants. If he wants to have sex with you, just go along with it and pretend you like it. Our lives depend on it."

"Dear," the wife hisses, spitting out her gag, "I'm so relieved you feel that way because he just told me he thinks you have a really nice, tight-looking ass!!!"

An upstanding young man is looking for a pure wife, so he starts to attend church in hopes of meeting one. Sure enough, he meets a woman right away who seems very nice, so he takes her home. When they get there, he whips out his manhood and asks, "What's this?" She replies, "A cock." He decides that she is not pure enough.

A couple of weeks later, he meets another girl and soon takes her home. Again, he pulls out his manhood and asks the question. She replies, "A cock." He is annoyed because she had seemed more pure than the first but, oh well.

A couple of weeks later, he meets yet another girl—and this one seems really pure. She won't go home with him for a long time, but eventually he gets her to go to his house. He once again whips it out and asks, "What is this?" She giggles and says, "A pee-pee." He decides that he has finally found his woman.

They get married, and on the wedding night, when he reveals himself, she giggles and says, "That's your pee-pee."

He says, "Look, you're a married woman now, and you should know. This is not a pee-pee, it is a cock."

She laughs. "No it's not, silly! A cock is ten inches long and black!"

● ● ● ●

I have a big penis, Paul Shaffer, and I will fuck you. I swear to God I am a horny white bitch. I will bang you like a dinner bell on the Ponderosa. I don't care if you're three feet tall, if I bang you, you will get stuck in the crack of my ass. I can't help it, it's that bald head. Every time I see you on TV it reminds me I have to clean my dildo.

—LISA LAMPANELLI, CHEVY CHASE ROAST, 2002

● ● ● ●

An old man is lying on his deathbed. With only hours to live, he notices a wonderful smell coming from the kitchen. With his last bit of energy the old man pulls himself out of bed, across the floor to the stairs, and down the stairs to the kitchen—only to find his wife baking chocolate chip cookies.

Summoning his flagging strength, the old man reaches for one of the steaming, fresh-baked treats. His wife quickly smacks his hand away. "Leave them alone, they're for the funeral!"

A FEW DIRTY WORDS
FROM FREDDIE ROMAN

Being the head of the Friars Club, I've been around dirty all my life and I head up one of the dirtiest events in the history of the world. It was never my personal style, but at Friars Roasts I've been as risqué as the next guy. I'll be honest, I enjoy working blue whenever I do it. I laughed about *The Aristocrats,* looking at the list of people they got to tell that joke in the movie. There were a lot of people there that I would never assume would tell it.

The Roasts used to be all male, so when women started attending after 1988 it made me a little uncomfortable at first. But then I just said to myself, "Well, if they want to be there to hear it, it's certainly not going to offend them, they know what to expect." Now it's just a matter of course, it's nothing out of the ordinary anymore.

Comics have to get bluer because of what's going on. You watch cable and you see them doing as dirty an act as can be done, and these guys that have been working blue all their lives are suddenly considered mainstream. They have to lower the bar, and sometimes it's been lowered quite a bit. It's like a limbo dance where you can't get much lower. For example, there's a show on HBO called *The Bad Boys of Comedy,* P. Diddy hosting the edgiest new comedians. They say it's comedy like you've never heard before—so it will probably be much bluer than anything that went before it.

When Richard Pryor worked blue and edgy, it wasn't just for the shock value, it was funny. But when I hear these guys just using words for the shock value, I don't find anything funny about that.

The most memorable of the early Roasts were the ones with people like Joey Bishop, who really prepared. Dick Capri gets dirty on these Roasts, but he does it in a way that's clever, not just the blatant use of words. The Roast is a strange vehicle, it really is. Interestingly enough, Dean Martin's producer stole the Roast idea and put it on *The Dean Martin Show*. He proved you didn't have to be dirty to be funny. Some of those Martin roasts were hysterical and so well done.

If I'm sitting in a club through five or six comedians and they've all used "fuck" constantly, by the third one I'm bored to death, I want to get out of there. I don't even care what they're saying. It just gets to the point where it's meaningless, it's not important. I watch young people's faces in the audience and, yeah, they may laugh the first time, but by the fourth time they get that there's no point, it's just rambling.

Susie Essman knows what she's doing out there. She'll use dirt but there are times when she knows not to do it. I had her with me on a show in a theater in Jersey a couple of years ago and she knew she couldn't get away with what she gets away with in a club. She cleaned it up—and she was hilarious. Instead of saying, "Did I fuck you in Hoboken?" she said, "Did I sleep with you?" and it got the same reaction and nobody got offended.

Nothing is taboo if there's humor involved. It happened that the Hugh Hefner Roast was scheduled just three weeks after 9/11, and I just didn't want us to look like we had no sensitivity toward it. On the other hand, what Hefner said was, "Well, maybe that's the way to get out of the funk of what happened and get people to laugh." It turned out he was right. The audience was laughing. When Gilbert Gottfried said, "I have to catch a flight to California. I can't get a direct flight. They said they have to stop at the Empire State Building first," it was a shock—but he has balls of steel, he really does. Then when he told the Aristocrats joke the audience bought it, absolutely. (It didn't air on Comedy Central, though—it was a little too rough for them.)

There was an old-timer by the name of Davey Starr; he came out of burlesque and throughout his whole career they only booked him at stags, at men's dinners, because he did dirty material. He never got anywhere in the mainstream of comedy but he was a wonderful comedian. And look at Lenny Bruce. What people now consider genius, in those days they hated. He was wonderful but

America wasn't ready. Yet he did it anyway, got prosecuted for it, became a drug addict, and still continued to do it.

Early in Buddy Hackett's career, when he became hot, he was clean as a whistle. His routines were gems—the Chinese waiter routine, the ski instructor at the Concord—there was no dirt, no sexual innuendo at all. I once asked him what made him switch to doing this other kind of material and he said, "It got to the point where there was no more challenge for me. I knew I was going to make them laugh so I got bored. I decided to shock them and get them to dislike me and see how long it took me to win them back." That seems very bizarre and perverse, yet he loved talking to young comedians about comedy.

Someone once said to me, "I watch some comedians and they'll say 'shit' onstage, I'm terribly offended; and yet, Freddie, when you say it, it's adorable." So in other words, persona has a lot to do with it. Hackett's persona was this cutie pie and you couldn't get mad at him; whereas Alan King, when he'd use a dirty word, which he did later on in life, the audience didn't like it. They wanted to hear his anger and his vitriol against the airlines and the doctors but they didn't want to hear him cursing about it.

Guys that do very well, not super superstars but the Richard Jenis and the Dom Irreras, rarely get blue. Dom gets a little blue but not terribly offensive. Then, on the other hand, you have a girl like Lisa Lampanelli who is quite offensive yet people like her onstage. She has that likeability factor. I watch the reaction to Lisa and to Kathy Griffin, who insults all the stars, but they're just so adorable doing it. Basically, this art of telling jokes, blue or otherwise, comes down to one thing—it's all in the personality, that smile at the end of the punch line.

Two women are having a friendly lunch when the subject turns to sex. "You know, John and I have been having some sexual problems," Linda tells her friend.

"That's amazing! So have Tom and I!" Mary replies.

"We're thinking of going to a sex therapist," says Linda.

"Oh, we could never do that! We'd be too embarrassed!" responds Mary. "But after you go, will you please tell me how it went?"

Several weeks pass, and the two friends meet for lunch again. "So how did the sex therapy work out, Linda?" Mary asks.

"Things couldn't be better! We began with a physical exam, and afterward the doctor said he was certain he could help us. He told us to stop at the grocery store on the way home and buy a bunch of grapes and a dozen donuts. He told us to sit on the floor nude and toss the grapes and donuts at each other. Every time a grape went into my vagina, John had to get it out with his tongue. Every donut that I ringed his penis with, I had to eat. Our sex life is wonderful; in fact it's better than it's ever been!"

With that endorsement, Mary talks her husband into an appointment with the same sex therapist. After the physical exams are completed the doctor calls Mary and Tom into his office. "I'm afraid there is nothing I can do for you," he says.

"But doctor, you did such good things for Linda and John, surely you must have a suggestion for us! Please, please, can't you give us some help? Any help at all?"

"Well, okay," the doctor answers. "On your way home, I want you to stop at the grocery store and buy a sack of apples and a box of cheerios."

A man phones home from his office and says to his wife, "I have the chance to go fishing for a week. It's the opportunity of a lifetime. I have to leave right away. Pack my clothes, my fishing equipment, and especially my blue silk pajamas. I'll be home in an hour to pick them up." The man rushes home to grab everything. He hugs his wife, apologizes for the short notice, and then hurries off.

A week later, the man returns and his wife asks, "Did you have a good trip, dear?" The man replies, "Yep, the fishing was great . . . but you forgot to pack my blue silk pajamas."

His wife smiles and says, "Oh, no I didn't . . . I put them in your tackle box!"

T wo married buddies are out drinking one night when one turns to the other and says, "You know, I don't know what else to do. Whenever I go home after we've been out drinking, I turn the headlights off before I get to the driveway. I shut off the engine and coast into the garage. I take my shoes off before I go into the house, I sneak up the stairs, and I get undressed in the bathroom. I ease into bed and my wife STILL wakes up and yells at me for staying out so late!"

His buddy looks at him and says, "Well, you're obviously taking the wrong approach. I screech into the driveway, slam the door, storm up the steps, throw my shoes into the closet, jump into bed, rub my hands on my wife's ass and say, 'How about a blow job?' . . . and she's always sound asleep."

• • • •

Henny Youngman created that great line, "Take my wife, please." Little did he know everybody did.

—MILTON BERLE, STEVEN SEAGAL ROAST, 1995

• • • •

A woman is in a coma. A male nurse is giving her a sponge bath, and as he washes her private area he notices that there is a response on the monitor. He goes immediately to her husband and explains what happened. "Crazy as this sounds," he says, "maybe a little oral sex will bring her out of the coma."

The husband is skeptical, but the nurse assures him that he'll close the curtains for privacy. The hubby finally agrees. After a few minutes of activity, the woman's monitor flat-lines... no pulse... no heart rate. The nurse runs into the room. The husband is standing there, pulling up his pants. "I think she choked."

A wealthy couple is preparing to go out for the evening. The woman of the house gives their butler, Jervis, the night off, saying that they intend to return home very late and she hopes he'll enjoy his evening.

A little while later, the wife isn't having a good time at the party so she decides to come home early, alone. Her husband stays on, socializing with important clients. As the woman walks into her house, she finds Jervis by himself in the dining room. She calls him to follow her into the master bedroom.

In the voice she knows he must obey, she says, "Jervis, I want you to take off my dress." This he does, hanging it carefully over a chair. "Jervis," she continues, "take off my stockings and garter belt." Again, Jervis silently obeys. "Now, Jervis, I want you to remove my bra and panties." Eyes downcast, Jervis obeys. By this point, both are breathing heavily, the tension mounting between them. She looks sternly at him and says, "Jervis, if I ever catch you wearing my stuff again, you're fired!"

Three women were sitting around throwing back a few drinks and talking about their sex lives. Karen said, "I call my husband 'the dentist,' because nobody can drill like he does."

Joanne giggled and confessed, "I call my husband 'the miner,' because of his incredible shaft."

Kathy quietly sipped her whiskey until Joanne finally asked, "Well, what do you call your boyfriend?"

Kathy frowned and said, "'The postman.'"

"Why the postman?" asked Joanne.

"Because, he always delivers late and half the time it's in the wrong box."

A couple makes a deal that whoever died first would come back and inform the other about the afterlife. The woman's biggest fear is that there is no heaven. After a long life, the husband is the first to go, and, true to his word, he makes contact. "Mary...Mary..."

Awestruck, Mary responds, "Is that you Fred?"

"Yes, I have come back like we agreed."

"Well, what is it like?"

Fred excitedly tells his tale: "Well, when I get up in the morning I have sex, then I have breakfast, then I have sex again, then I bathe in the sun, then I have sex twice more, then I have lunch, then I have sex all afternoon and into the early evening, until bedtime. And, then, I start all over again the next day."

This sounds great to Mary. "Oh Fred, you surely must be in heaven!"

"Hell no, Mary. I'm a rabbit in Kansas."

Jennifer suspects her husband is cheating on her. One day while she's at work, she dials her home and a strange woman answers. "Who is this?" Jennifer demands.

"This is the maid," answers the woman.

"We don't have a maid," says Jennifer.

"I was hired this morning by the man of the house."

"Well, this is his wife. Is he there?"

"He's upstairs in the bedroom with someone I figured was his wife."

Jennifer is fuming. "Listen, would you like to make $50,000?"

"What would I have to do?"

"I want you to get my gun from the desk and shoot the jerk and the bitch he's with."

The maid puts the phone down; Jennifer hears footsteps and two gunshots. The maid comes back to the phone and asks, "What do I do with the bodies?"

"Throw them in the swimming pool." Puzzled, the maid answers, "But...there's no pool here."

A long pause. "Is this 555-6897?"

●　●　●　●

Two Albanian women were shopping in the market. One picked up a sack of potatoes and said, "This reminds me of my husband's testicles." The other woman said, "So big?"
"No, so dirty."

— NORM CROSBY, DANNY AIELLO ROAST, 1997

●　●　●　●

What's the difference between your wife and your job?

After five years, your job still sucks.

"That wife of mine is a liar," says the angry husband to a sympathetic pal seated next to him in the bar.

"How do you know?" the friend asks.

"She didn't come home last night, and when I asked her where she'd been, she said she'd spent the night with her sister Shirley."

"So?"

"So, she's a liar. I spent the night with her sister Shirley!"

It's very appropriate that I've been asked to be here tonight to honor Jerry Stiller. He's been on TV, I've been on TV; he's been on Broadway, I've been on Broadway; he's been on Anne . . . .

— FREDDIE ROMAN, JERRY STILLER ROAST, 1999

I wouldn't say Jimmy Kimmel is a hairy guy, but Jeff Ross told me it took twenty minutes to find his anus. Jimmy's asshole has more hair around it than Santa's mouth.

—ADAM CAROLLA, HUGH HEFNER ROAST, 2001

A young girl gets married and a few days later her mother comes to visit. When she arrives, she is shocked to find her daughter standing naked at the front door. "What are you doing!" shrieks the mother.

"Mom, it's my love dress! Don't you like it?"

"I'll come back in a few weeks when the honeymoon is over," replies her mother, as she flees for the car.

A few weeks later, the mother returns to her daughter's house and once again, she is shocked when her daughter answers the door stark naked.

"Mom, it's my love dress! It keeps the marriage spicy!"

"I'll give you a few more weeks," replies her mother, as she retreats.

Later that night, the mother decides to try it for herself. When her husband arrives home, she greets him at the front door in the nude.

"Honey, what the hell are you doing!" exclaims the husband.

"It's my love dress, dear! What do you think of it?"

"Well, to be perfectly honest, I think you should have ironed it first!"

J on leaves for a two-day business trip to Chicago. He is only a few blocks away from his house when he realizes he's left his plane ticket on the dresser. He turns around and heads back to the house and enters quietly through the kitchen. He sees his wife washing the breakfast dishes, wearing her skimpiest negligee.

She looks so good that he tiptoes up behind her, reaches out, and squeezes her left tit. "Leave only one quart of milk," she says without turning around. "Jon won't be here for breakfast tomorrow."

A husband and wife visit a marriage counselor. First, the counselor speaks to the wife alone: "You say you've been married twenty years, so what seems to be the problem?"

"It's my husband—he's driving me crazy! I'm going to leave him if he continues!"

"How does he drive you crazy?"

"For twenty years he's been doing these stupid things. First, whenever we go out, he's always looking at the floor and refuses to go near anyone. It's very embarrassing."

The marriage counselor nods. "Is that it?"

"He picks his nose all the time! Even in public!"

"Hmm. Anything else?"

The wife hesitates. "When we're making love, he NEVER lets me be on top! Once in a while, I'd like to be in control!"

"Ah," says the counselor. "I think I'll talk to your husband now."

So the wife goes out of the room and the husband enters. The counselor tells him, "Your wife says that you've been driving her crazy. She might even leave you."

The husband looks shocked. "WHAT? For twenty years I've been a loving and considerate husband and I've always given her everything she wants! I never lie, I never cheat . . . what could possibly be the problem?"

"She says that you've got these habits that are driving her crazy. First, you're always acting strange in public—looking at the floor and never going near anyone else."

The husband looks concerned, "Oh, you don't understand! It's one of the few things my father told me to do on his deathbed and I swore I'd obey everything he said."

"Really? What exactly did he say?"

"He said that I should never step on anyone's toes!"

The counselor smiles. "Actually, that means that you should not do anything that would cause anyone else to get angry."

The husband looks sheepish, "Oh. Okay."

The counselor continues. "But there's more. Your wife says you pick your nose in public."

"That's another thing my father specifically commanded me to do! He told me always to keep my nose clean."

The counselor is getting a little impatient at this point. "Don't you understand? That just means that you shouldn't get involved in any criminal activity."

"Oh," says the husband, feeling stupid.

"And finally, she says that you never allow her to be on top during your lovemaking."

"This," says the husband seriously, "is the last thing my father talked to me about on his deathbed, and it's the most important thing."

"What did he say?"

"With his dying breath he said, 'Don't screw up!'"

After hearing a couple's complaints that their intimate life wasn't what it used to be, the sex counselor suggests they vary their positions. "For example," he says, "you might try the wheelbarrow. Lift her legs from behind and off you go."

The eager husband is all for trying this new trick as soon as they get home.

"Well, okay," the hesitant wife agrees, "but on two conditions. First, if it hurts you have to stop right away. And second..." she continues, "You have to promise we won't go past my parents' house."

A businessman and his secretary, overcome by passion, go to his house for an early-afternoon quickie. "Don't worry," he assures her, "my wife is out of town on a business trip, so there's no risk."

As things get hot and heavy, the secretary reaches into her purse and suddenly gasps, "We have to stop! I forgot to bring birth control!"

"No problem," he replies, "I'll get my wife's diaphragm." After a few minutes of searching, he returns to the bedroom in a fury. "That witch!" he exclaims. "She took it with her! I always knew she didn't trust me!"

● ● ● ●

I had only met Rob Reiner once before tonight and when I met him he did most of the talking. It was really hard for me to talk with my mouth full.

—BRETT BUTLER, ROB REINER ROAST, 2000

● ● ● ●

When Harry passed away, his wife Elaine put the usual death notice in the newspaper, but added that he had died of gonorrhea. Once the daily newspapers had been delivered, a good friend of the family phoned and chided, "You know very well that he died of diarrhea, not gonorrhea."

Replied the widow, "Yes, I know, but I thought it would be better for posterity to remember him as a great lover rather than the big shit that he really was."

A woman comes home to find her husband in bed with another woman. With superhuman strength borne of fury, she drags him down the stairs to the garage and puts his penis in a vise, securing it tightly and removing the handle. Next she picks up a hacksaw. The husband, terrified, screams, "Stop! Stop! You're not going to...to...cut it off are you?"

With a gleam of revenge in her eye, the woman hands him the hacksaw and says, "Nope. I'm just going to set the garage on fire."

Three guys and a woman are sitting at a bar talking about their professions.

The first guy says, "I'm a Y.U.P.P.I.E. You know... Young Urban Professional Peaceful Intelligent Ecologist."

The second guy says, "I'm a D.I.N.K.Y. You know... Double Income No Kids Yet."

The third guy says, "I'm a R.U.B. You know... Rich Urban Biker."

One of them turns to the woman and asks her, "So, what are you?"

"I'm a W.I.F.E. You know... Wash, Iron, Fuck, Etc."

Three women are sitting around talking about their husbands' performance. The first one says, "My husband works as a marriage counselor. He always buys me flowers and candy before we make love. I like that."

The second woman says, "My husband is a motorcycle mechanic. He likes to play rough and slaps me around sometimes. I kinda like that."

The third woman just shakes her head and says, "My husband works for Microsoft. He just sits on the edge of the bed and tells me how great it's going to be when I get it."

Afarmer and his wife are lying in bed one evening. She is knitting and he is reading the latest issue of Animal Husbandry. He looks up from the page and says to her, "Did you know that humans are the only species in which the female achieves orgasm?"

She looks at him wistfully, smiles, and replies, "Oh, yeah? Prove it."

He frowns for a moment, then says, "Okay." He gets up and walks out, leaving his wife rather confused.

About a half-hour later, he returns all tired and sweaty and proclaims, "Well, I'm sure the cow and sheep didn't, but the way that pig is always squealing, how can I tell?"

Awoman confides to her best friend, "My sex life stinks."

Her friend says, "Have you ever watched your husband's face while you're making love?"

"Well, only once, and I saw rage."

"Why would he be angry during sex?"

"Because he was looking through the window at us."

One day a man notices that his co-worker is wearing an earring. This man knows his co-worker to be a somewhat conservative fellow, so naturally he's curious about the sudden burst of fashion daring. He says, "I didn't know you were into earrings."

"Don't make such a big deal, it's only an earring," the other guy replies sheepishly.

"Well, I'm curious. How long have you been wearing an earring?"

"Er, ever since my wife found it in our bed."

• • • •

If you've never seen his show, Kevin James plays a loving husband to a woman whose tits are smaller than his.

—JASON ALEXANDER, JERRY STILLER ROAST, 1999

• • • •

Jim is complaining to Fred. "I had it all—money, a magnificent house, a fast car, the love of a beautiful woman...then, poof! It was all gone!"

"What happened?" asks Fred.

"My wife found out."

When Ralph first noticed that his penis was growing larger and staying erect longer, he was delighted, as was his wife. But after several weeks it had grown to nearly twenty inches—it extended past his knees! This was a little alarming, so the couple went to see a prominent urologist. After an initial examination, the physician explained that, though rare, Ralph's condition could be cured through corrective surgery. "How long will Ralph be on crutches?" his wife asked anxiously.

"Crutches? Why would he need crutches?" responded the surprised doctor.

"Well," said the wife, "you are planning to lengthen Ralph's legs, aren't you?"

• • • •

(To Beverly D'Angelo) You're with Al Pacino. I don't know what it's like to be in bed with Al Pacino, but I imagine there is a lot of overacting.

—AL FRANKEN, CHEVY CHASE ROAST, 2002

• • • •

A man is out shopping and discovers a new brand of Olympic condoms. Clearly impressed, he buys a pack. When he gets home, he tells his wife about the purchase.

"Olympic condoms?" she blurts. "What makes them so special?"

"There are three colors, gold, silver, and bronze."

"What color are you going to wear tonight?" she asks cheekily.

"Gold, of course!"

"Why don't you wear silver? It would be nice if you came second for a change!"

W hat's the difference between your paycheck and your cock?

You don't have to beg your wife to blow your paycheck!

A guy got married, but unfortunately his dick was too small, so every time he had sex with his wife he secretly used a pickle on her instead. For seven years he did that, until one night his wife got suspicious, so while they were doing it, she threw the covers off and turned on the lights! "What the hell is THAT?" she shrieked. "Are you using a pickle on me? Do you mean to tell me that for seven years you have been doing that, you piece of shit?"

"Shut the fuck up!" the man shoots back. "It's been seven years and I never asked where the hell those kids came from!"

A newly married sailor is informed by the navy that he will be stationed a long way from home, on a remote island in the Pacific, for a year. Tearfully, the newlyweds part. A few weeks later, he really begins to miss his wife, so he writes her a letter. "My love, we are going to be apart for a very long time. Already I'm starting to miss you and there's really not much to do here in the evenings. Young, attractive native girls constantly surround us. Do you think a hobby of some kind would keep me from being tempted?"

His wife immediately sends him back a harmonica saying, "Why don't you learn to play this?"

Eventually his tour of duty comes to an end and he rushes back to his wife. "Darling," he says, "I can't wait to get you into bed so we can make passionate love!"

She kisses him and says, "First, let's see you play that harmonica."

A husband and wife are out playing golf. They tee off and one drive goes to the right and one drive goes to the left. The wife finds her ball in a patch of buttercups. She grabs a club and takes a mighty swing at it, hitting a beautiful second shot, but in the process she hacks the hell out of the buttercups. Suddenly an ethereal female figure appears out of nowhere. She blocks the woman's path to her golf bag and says, "I'm Mother Nature, and I don't like the way you treated my buttercups. From now on, you won't be able to stand the taste of butter. Each time you eat butter you will become physically ill to the point of total nausea." The mystery woman then disappears as quickly as she appeared.

Shaken, the wife calls out to her husband, "Hey, where's your ball?"

"It's over here in the pussy willows."

"DON'T HIT THE BALL!!! DON'T HIT THE BALL!!!"

● ● ● ●

When Richard Belzer met his wife he fell in love with her at first sight and had to marry her immediately. Basically because he was running out of quarters.

—SUSIE ESSMAN, RICHARD BELZER ROAST, 2001

● ● ● ●

Two old friends are just about to tee off at their local golf course when a guy carrying a golf bag calls out to them, "Do you mind if I join you? My partner didn't turn up."

"Sure," they say, "no problem." So the three start playing and they're enjoying the game. Part way around the course, one of the friends asks the newcomer, "What do you do for a living?"

"I'm a hit man."

"You're joking!"

"No, I'm not," he says, reaching into his golf bag and pulling out a sniper's rifle with a large telescopic sight. "Here are my tools."

"That's a beautiful telescopic sight," says the other friend. "Can I take a look? I think I might be able to see my house from here." So he picks up the rifle and looks through the sight in the direction of his house. "Yeah, I can see my house all right. This sight is fantastic. I can see right in the window. Wow, I can see my wife in the bedroom. Ha-Ha, I can see she's naked! What the...! Wait a minute, that's my neighbor in there with her. He's naked as well!" He turns to the hit man. "How much do you charge for a hit?"

"For you, one thousand dollars every time I pull the trigger."

"Can you do two for me now?"

"Sure, whatever you want."

"First, shoot my wife. She's always been mouthy, so shoot her in the mouth. Then blast the neighbor, he's a buddy of mine, not a bad guy really, so just shoot his dick off to teach him a lesson."

The hit man takes the rifle, aims, then stands perfectly still for a few minutes.

"Are you going to do it or not?" says the wronged husband impatiently.

"Just wait a minute, be patient," says the hit man. "I think I can save you a thousand dollars here."

My husband came home with a tube of KY jelly and said, "This will make you happy tonight." He was right. When he went out of the bedroom, I squirted it all over the doorknob. He couldn't get back in.

Charlie marries a virgin. On their wedding night, he's on fire! He insists they get naked as soon as they get to the hotel, carries her into bed, and immediately begins groping her.

"Charles, I expect you to be as mannerly in bed as you are at the dinner table."

Charlie folds his hands in his lap and says, "Is this better?"

"Much better!" she replies with a smile.

"Okay, then . . . Now, will you please pass the pussy?"

● ● ● ●

I do a lot of work for Donald Trump, or, as his ex-wife calls him, The Donald. And I can relate to that, my ex-wife calls me The Dick. That name has killed my career. I lost my own cooking show on the Food channel. They were going to call it *Cooking with Dick*.

—DICK CAPRI, FRIARS FROLICS IN HONOR OF PAT COOPER, 1998

● ● ● ●

"Have you ever thought of getting married?" Harry asks his friend Tom.

"Yeah. A couple of times."

"Well, what happened?"

"The rabbits recovered!"

A young couple is on the way to Vegas to get married. Before they arrive, the girl says she has a confession to make. The reason that they have not yet been intimate is that she's very flat chested. "If you want to cancel the wedding, I'll understand," she says.

The guy responds, "I don't mind that you're flat, and sex is not the most important thing in a marriage anyway."

Several miles down the road, he turns to her and says that he, too, has a confession to make. There's another reason that they haven't been intimate. He is just like a baby below the waist.

The girl responds, "I don't mind that you're like a baby below the waist, and sex is not the most important thing in a marriage anyway."

So the happy couple continues on to Vegas and gets married. On their wedding night, the girl takes off her clothes and, true to her word, she is as flat as an ironing board. Then the guy gets naked. After one glance, the girl faints dead away. When she regains consciousness, the guy says, "I warned you before we got married, so what's the problem?"

"You told me it was just like a baby!"

"It is! It's eight pounds and twenty-one inches long!"

A man says to his wife, "I feel like some kinky sex! How about I blow my load in your ear?"

"No, I might go deaf!"

"I've been shooting my wad in your mouth for the last twenty years and you're still fucking talking, aren't you?"

A couple is married for twenty years. It is a happy, wonderful marriage, except that the wife is constantly unfaithful. The husband finally gets so tired of her infidelity that he makes her promise never again to be untrue to him. One day he comes home and finds her in bed with a midget. He cries out, "After you made all those promises, I find you in bed with another man, and a midget at that!"

"Don't you understand? I'm tapering off!"

● ● ● ●

A couple's in the living room. He says, "You're dry tonight."
     She says, "You're licking the rug."

— JACKIE MARTLING, FRIARS CLUB COMEDY MARATHON FOR POLICE AND FIREFIGHTERS, 2001

● ● ● ●

Two guys are discussing sex, marriage, and values. Stuart says, "I didn't sleep with my wife before we got married, did you?"

Leroy replies, "I'm not sure—what was her maiden name?"

Why was the virgin queen disappointed on her honeymoon?

She thought all rulers had twelve inches!

Sam and Becky are celebrating their fiftieth wedding anniversary. Sam says, "Becky, I was wondering, have you ever cheated on me?"

"Oh Sam, why would you ask such a question now? You don't want to ask that question."

"Yes, Becky, I really want to know. Please."

"Well, all right. Yes, three times."

"Three? When were they?"

"Well, Sam, remember when you were thirty-five and you really wanted to start that business on your own and no bank would give you a loan? And then one day the bank president himself came over to the house and signed the loan papers, no questions asked?"

"Oh, Becky, you did that for me? I respect you even more than ever, to do such an unselfish thing. So, when was number two?"

"Well, Sam, remember when you had that last heart attack and you needed that very tricky operation, and no surgeon would touch you? And then suddenly the best doctor in town announced that he'd do the surgery himself, and then you were in good shape again?"

"I can't believe it! Becky, you saved my life! I couldn't have a more wonderful wife. You must really love me, darling. So . . . when was number three?"

"Well, Sam, remember a few years ago, when you really wanted to be president of the golf club and you were seventeen votes short?"

● ● ● ●

The only time Chevy has a funny bone in his body is when I fuck him in the ass.

—RICHARD BELZER, CHEVY CHASE ROAST, 2002

● ● ● ●

A woman accompanies her husband to the doctor's office. After his checkup, the doctor calls the wife into his office alone and says, "Your husband is suffering from a very severe stress disorder. If you don't do as I instruct, he will surely die.

"Each morning, fix him a healthy breakfast. Be pleasant at all times. For lunch make him a nutritious meal. Later prepare an especially nice dinner for him. Don't burden him with chores. Don't discuss your problems with him—it will only increase his stress. No nagging. And most important, make love with your husband several times a week. If you can do this for the next ten months to a year, I think your husband will regain his health completely."

On the way home, the husband asks his wife, "So what did the doctor say?"

"He said you're going to die."

A young guy is playing golf when a golf ball hits him in the groin and he passes out. His friends take him to the doctor. When he regains consciousness, he asks, "Well, doc, what do you think?"

"We're going to have to put in a support for about a week."

He then takes four tongue depressors, positions them around the man's penis, and ties the whole bundle together with string.

The man is devastated. "But tomorrow is my wedding!" he tells the doctor.

"I'm afraid you're just going to have to cope."

The next night, the man and his new bride are in bed. She takes off her bra and caresses her breasts. "No one has ever seen these before," she says, seductively.

At which point the man drops his pants and says, "Well, mine's still in the crate!"

● ● ● ●

There is some hot meat up here, like Brett Butler. Brett overcame her drinking problem. She is the only person who has had her head in more toilets than me. We started out together, Brett and me. Here's something we are both used to hearing: Roll over. Come on, who are we kidding? She has had more bones buried in her than Forest Lawn.

—TRIUMPH THE INSULT DOG, ROB REINER ROAST, 2000

● ● ● ●

Two guys are walking down the street and one says to the other, "I think my wife died."

"You THINK she died?"

"Well, the sex is the same but the dishes are piling up."

Two blondes are talking about their sex lives. One says, "Do you and your husband have mutual orgasms?"

"No," answers her friend. "We have State Farm."

What's the difference between a girlfriend and wife?

Forty-five pounds.

A husband and wife are sound asleep at two a.m. when the phone rings. The husband picks it up sleepily, and says, "Hello?...How the hell should I know?...What am I, the fuckin' Weather Bureau???" He slams the phone down and tries to get comfortable again.

"Who was that?" asks his wife.

"I don't know, some jerk wanted to know if the coast was clear."

A middle-aged couple goes to a spouse-swapping party. They meet a Martian couple and think it would be interesting to switch partners with them for the night. When the woman sees the male Martian's penis she says, "Well, that's nice but it's kind of short, isn't it?"

The Martian reaches up and pats his head, and as he does, his penis gets longer and longer.

The woman is impressed—but then she says, "That's nice, but it's not very fat is it?"

At that, the Martian pulls on his ears, and as he does, his penis gets fatter and fatter.

The woman has a grand time that night.

In the morning, the earth couple compare their experiences. The woman says, "I really enjoyed myself! We should swap again."

The man says, "I enjoyed it, too, but I just can't figure out why she kept patting my head and pulling my ears!"

A sex researcher phones one of the participants in a recent survey to check on a discrepancy. He says to the guy, "In response to the question on frequency of intercourse you answered 'twice weekly.' Your wife, on the other hand, answered 'several times a night.'"

"That's right," replies the husband. "And that's how it's going to stay until our second mortgage is paid off."

A young couple has been married for a couple of weeks, and the man is constantly after his wife to quit smoking. One afternoon, she lights up after they make love and he says, "You really ought to quit."

Getting tired of his nagging, she says, "Look. I really enjoy a good cigarette after sex."

"But they stunt your growth."

She asks if he ever smoked, and he replies that he never has. She looks at his groin and sweetly inquires, "So, what's your excuse?"

The president steps out for a breath of air in the dead of winter. Right in front of him, on the White House lawn, he sees "The President Must Go" written in urine across the snow. He's pretty ticked off and storms into the office of his security staff. "Somebody wrote a threat in the snow on the front damn lawn!" he yells. "And they wrote it in urine! Sonofabitch had to be standing right on the porch when he did it! Where were you?!"

The security guys stay stare ashamedly at the floor.

"Well, dammit, don't just sit there! Get out and FIND OUT WHO DID IT! I want an answer, and I want it TONIGHT!"

The entire staff jumps up and races for the exits.

Later that evening, the chief security officer approaches the president and says, "Well, sir, we have some bad news and we have some really bad news. Which do you want first?"

"Oh hell, give me the bad news first."

"Well, we took a sample of the urine and tested it. The results just came back, and it belongs to the vice president."

"Oh my god, I feel so betrayed! My own vice president! Damn. Well, what's the really bad news?"

"Well, sir, it's in the First Lady's handwriting."

●　●　●　●

Let's talk about the bunnies. I think that they should be role models in today's society, especially for the girls—if only because they wax their assholes. I don't have the guts to do that. The closest I ever came to waxing my asshole, once I got it washed and styled.

—SARAH SILVERMAN, HUGH HEFNER ROAST, 2001

●　●　●　●

Mr. Hudson comes home to find his wife sitting naked in front of the mirror, admiring her breasts. "What do you think you're doing?" he asks.

"I went to the doctor today and he said I have the breasts of a twenty-five-year-old."

Mr. Hudson laughs. "Oh yeah? And what did he have to say about your fifty-year-old ass?"

"Nothing," she replies. "Your name didn't come up at all."

Bill and Valerie have been married for forty years. When they first got married, Bill said, "I am putting a box under the bed. You must promise never to look in it." In all their forty years of marriage, Valerie never looked. But on the afternoon of their fortieth anniversary, curiosity got the best of her, and she lifted the lid and peeked inside. In the box were three empty beer cans and $1,874.25 in cash. She closed the box and put it back under the bed. She was baffled and incredibly curious as to what this might mean.

That evening they went out for a special anniversary dinner. Afterward, Valerie could no longer contain her curiosity and she confessed, saying, "I am so sorry. For all these years I kept my promise and never looked into the box under our bed—but today the temptation was too much, and I gave in. Why do you keep those empty cans in the box?"

Bill thought for a while and said, "I guess after all these years you deserve to know the truth. Whenever I was unfaithful to you, I put an empty beer can into the box to remind myself not to do it again."

Valerie was shocked. "I am very disappointed and saddened, but I guess after all those years away from home on the road, temptation was bound to get the better of you a few times. Three cans is not that bad over forty years." They hugged and made their peace.

"So . . . why do you have all that money in the box?"

"Um . . . whenever the box filled up with empties, I cashed them in."

• • • •

Anne Meara says that, to this day, when Jerry makes love it's an art form. She says he's the LeRoy Neiman of nookie, the Picasso of poontang, he's the Gauguin of the G-spot and DaVinci of da vagina!

—DICK CAPRI, JERRY STILLER ROAST, 1999

• • • •

One bright, beautiful Sunday morning everyone in the tiny town of Johnson got up early and went to the local church, as they always did. They were sitting in their pews waiting for the preacher when, in a puff of green smoke, the Devil himself appeared at the altar. Everyone started screaming and running for the doors, trampling one another in a frantic effort to get away from Satan.

Soon the church was empty, except for one elderly gentleman who sat calmly in his pew, seemingly oblivious to the fact that he was in the presence of the Antichrist. This confused Satan a bit, so he said to the man, "Don't you know who I am?"

"Yep, sure do."

"Aren't you afraid of me?"

"Nope, sure ain't," said the man.

Satan was a little perturbed. "Why aren't you afraid of me?"

"Been married to your sister for over forty-eight years."

• • • •

Rob Reiner is a big homo. Not that that's a bad thing, unless of course you are me and in order to get a role in *A Few Good Men* you have to let this Jewish Paul Bunyan ride your rectum around the room like a Shetland pony.

— KEVIN POLLACK, ROB REINER ROAST, 2000

• • • •

Every time Sam brought home a paycheck his wife went right out and spent it. So one day he went to the tattoo parlor and asked to have a hundred-dollar bill tattooed on his penis. He then went home and when his wife walked in the door he pulled down his pants and said, "I want to see you blow THIS money!"

A husband suspects his wife is having an affair. He's going on a business trip for several days so he decides to set a trap for her. He puts a bowl of milk under the bed. From the bedsprings, he suspends a spoon. He has it calibrated so that her weight on the bed will not drop the spoon into the milk. But, if there is any more weight than that, the spoon will drop into the milk and he will detect it upon his return home.

He comes home several days later and the first thing he does is reach under the bed and retrieve the bowl. It's full of butter.

A woman goes to her parish priest all upset. "Father, how am I going to tell my husband that I am still a virgin?"

"My child, you have been a married woman for many years. You have had three husbands! Surely that cannot be."

"Well, Father, my first husband was a psychologist and all he wanted to do was talk. The next one was in construction and he always said he'd get to it tomorrow. The last one was a gynecologist and all he did was look. But this time, father, I'm marrying a lawyer and I'm sure I'm going to get screwed."

A couple is doing yard work and the wife goes in to take a shower. Her husband is looking for the rake and can't find it. He yells up to his wife, "Where's the rake?"

From the bathroom window she shakes her head and cups her hand behind her ear to show that she can't hear him. So he points to his eye (I), hits his knee (need), then makes raking motions.

She replies by pointing to her eye, grabbing her left breast, slapping her ass, then rubbing her crotch.

He runs upstairs and says, "What!?"

She says, "I left tit behind the bush."

● ● ● ●

Hugh's been called a visionary, a genius, a pioneer of free speech, but when I think of Hugh Hefner what comes to mind is rubbing my dong until it squirts.

—JIMMY KIMMEL, HUGH HEFNER ROAST, 2001

● ● ● ●

A policeman sends his wife and child to a sea resort for a vacation. After a week he joins them at the hotel. As soon as he gets to the room he wants to make love to his wife.

"No, darling, we can't do it here, our kid is watching us," she tells him.

"Yeah, you're right," he says, "let's go do it on the beach."

They take a long walk and start to make love on the deserted beach. But soon a policeman comes along and says, "Put your clothes on immediately! Shame on you, you can't do that in public!"

"You're right," says the husband, "but it was a moment of weakness. We haven't seen each other for a week. By the way, I am a policeman, too, and it would be very embarrassing if you fined me."

"Oh, don't worry about it. You're a fellow officer and it's your first time. But this is the third time I caught this bitch screwing somebody here in the last week, and she'll have to pay for it!"

CHAPTER 2

The Doctor Will See You Now

He can't cure you—
and you might die laughing.

A doctor walks into a bank. Preparing to endorse a check, he pulls a rectal thermometer out of his shirt pocket and tries to write with it. Realizing his mistake, he looks at the thermometer with annoyance and says, "Well, that's great, just great . . . some asshole's got my pen."

A well-known, much-married movie star says to her doctor, "I have a new boyfriend and he's eighteen, so I want you to tighten my vagina. This has to be our secret—no tabloids, definitely no leaks."

Her doctor is standing there when she wakes up after the operation. She looks at the table next to her bed and sees three bouquets of flowers. She says angrily to the doctor, "How could you do this to me? I told you this was to be a secret."

The doctor says, "Relax. The first bouquet is from me. The second is from the anesthesiologist who worked with me on your operation. He's gay and very trustworthy. He won't tell a soul. And the third bouquet is from Eric in the burn unit, who wanted to thank you for his new pair of ears."

● ● ● ●

I am a doctor but people don't believe me anymore. The other day I had this young lady in the office and I said, "May I recommend that I perform a pap smear and a breast exam immediately?" And she said, "Is that really necessary?" I said, "Who's the chiropractor, me or you?"

—DR. HOWIE GOODMAN, SUNSHINE COMMITTEE RAFFLE NIGHT, 2005

● ● ● ●

A woman is in the delivery room giving birth and the doctor tells her to push. She does and the baby's head pops out. The doctor says, "Oh! Your baby has slanted eyes."

She replies, "Yeah, I heard Chinese men were pretty good, so I decided to give them a try."

The doctor shrugs it off and tells her to push again. This time the baby's body comes out. "Holy shit, your baby has a white body," the doctor says.

"Yeah, I heard white men were pretty good, so I decided to give them a try," she says.

The doctor shrugs it off again and tells her to push hard one more time. So she does and the legs come out. "Holy shit! Your baby has black legs," the doctor says.

"Yeah, I heard black men were pretty good, so I decided to give them a try," she says.

The doctor ties the umbilical cord and slaps the baby on the ass until it starts to cry. He can't help asking the woman, "How are you going to deal with a baby who has slanted eyes, a white body, and black legs?"

"I'm just glad it didn't bark!"

A man goes to the doctor for some medicine and when he gets there the doctor tells him that he has to take it rectally, because if he takes it by mouth he'll vomit it up. The man asks the doctor to insert the first dose, since he's unfamiliar with the procedure.

So the doctor sticks the suppository in and the man yells, "OW!" The doctor nods sympathetically and advises the man that it is natural for this procedure to cause a little pain.

The next day, the man's wife inserts the medicine for him and, as she puts it in, he screams at the top of his lungs and lunges forward. She is taken by surprise, as she has inserted the suppository very gently.

He says, "When the doctor put it in, he had both hands on my shoulders!"

A doctor is leading a royal tour through his hospital. Upon passing a room where a man is masturbating, he leans in toward the Queen and explains, "I'm sorry your Highness, this man has a very serious condition where the testicles rapidly fill with semen. If he doesn't do that five times a day, they will explode and he will most likely die instantly."

"Oh, I am sorry," says the Queen.

On the next floor they pass a room where a young nurse is giving a patient a blow job.

"Oh, my God," gasps the Queen. "What on earth is happening in there?"

"Same problem, better health plan."

• • • •

How should I put this? Freddie Roman has not been blessed with classic leading-man looks. The other night I was watching the news and I thought they were showing Freddie's 8 x 10. It turns out it was a slide of the SARS germ.

—PAUL SHAFFER, SALUTE TO FREDDIE ROMAN, 2003

• • • •

A woman walks into a doctor's office and she is so breathtakingly beautiful that the doctor is bowled over. All his professionalism goes right out the window. He tells her to take off her pants, she does, and he starts rubbing her thighs.

"Do you know what I am doing?" asks the doctor.

"Yes, checking for abnormalities," she replies.

He tells her to take off her shirt and bra, which she does. The doctor begins rubbing her breasts and asks, "Do you know what I am doing now?"

"Yes, checking for cancer."

Finally, he tells her to take off her panties, lays her on the table, gets on top of her, and starts having sex with her. He says to her, "Do you know what I am doing now?"

"Yes, getting herpes—that's why I am here!"

A man is having problems with his dick, which has certainly seen better times. He consults a doctor who, after a couple of tests, says, "Sorry, but you've overdone it the last thirty years. Your dick is burned out. You only have thirty erections left in your penis."

The man walks home, deeply depressed. His wife is waiting for him at the front door and asks him what the doctor said concerning his problem.

He tells her what the doc told him. "Oh no! Only thirty times! We shouldn't waste that! We should make a list!"

"I already made a list on the way home, and I'm afraid you're name isn't on it."

A woman goes to her doctor with a problem but when she gets there she says, "I like to be...ohh...ah...ummm...I'm sorry, doctor, but I'm too ashamed to talk about it."

"Come, come, my dear. I'm a doctor. I've been trained to understand these problems. What's the matter?"

So the woman again tries to explain, but she gets so embarrassed that she turns bright red and looks as though she might faint. It is then that the doctor has an idea.

"Look," he says, "I'm a bit of a pervert myself. So if you show me your perversion, I'll show you mine. Okay?"

The woman considers the offer and agrees that it seems fair. So, after a slight pause, she says, "Well, my perversion...ohh...I like to be kissed on my ass!"

"Shit, is that all!" says the doctor. "Look, go behind that screen, take all your clothes off, and I'll come around and show you what my perversion is! Hee hee!"

So the woman does as she is told and undresses behind the screen. She gets down on all fours, thinking, "Hmm, perhaps he might kiss me on my ass."

Fifteen minutes pass and nothing has happened. So the woman peers around the side of the screen to see the doctor sitting behind his desk, his feet up on the table, reading a newspaper, and whistling to himself.

"Hey!" shouts the woman, "I thought you said you were a pervert!"

"Oh, I am," says the doctor. "I just jerked off in your handbag."

● ● ● ●

Al Sharpton has marched more than anyone in the history of the country—and he still weighs 280!

—COLIN QUINN, DON KING ROAST, 2005

● ● ● ●

Four surgeons are taking a coffee break and discussing their work.

The first says, "I think accountants are the easiest to operate on. You open them up and everything inside is numbered."

The second says, "I think librarians are the easiest to operate on. You open them up and everything inside is in alphabetical order."

The third says, "I like to operate on electricians. You open them up and everything inside is color coded."

The fourth says, "I like to operate on lawyers. They're heartless, spineless, gutless, and their heads and their asses are interchangeable."

Comedy has always been in my blood—the hepatitis is brand new.

—Tom Cotter, Sunshine Committee Variety Show, 2002

• • • •

What do Disneyland and Viagra have in common?

They both make you wait for two hours for a two-minute ride.

Mr. Jones gets a call from the hospital telling him that his wife has been in a terrible car accident. He rushes to the emergency room to find her.

They tell him that Dr. Smith is handling the case, and they page the doctor.

Doc comes out to the waiting room to find a terribly upset Mr. Jones. "Mr. Jones?" the doctor asks.

"Yes, sir, what's happened? How is my wife?"

"I'm afraid it's not good news. Your wife's accident resulted in two fractures of her spine."

"Oh, my God," says Mr. Jones. "What's her prognosis?"

"Well, her vital signs are stable but her spine is inoperable. She won't be able to move at all. You will have to feed her."

Mr. Jones begins to sob.

"And you'll have to turn her in her bed every two hours to prevent pneumonia."

Mr. Jones begins to wail.

"And, of course, you'll have to diaper her, as she'll have no control over her bladder or bowels. These diapers must be changed at least five times a day."

Mr. Jones begins to shake uncontrollably. He is a pitiful, wretched mess.

Just then, Dr. Smith reaches out his hand, pats Mr. Jones on the shoulder, and says, "Hey, relax. I'm just messing with you, dude! You don't have to do all that stuff—she's dead!"

A patient's family gathers to hear what the specialists have to say. "Things don't look good. The only chance is a brain transplant. This is an experimental procedure. It might work, but the bad news is that brains are very expensive, and you will have to pay the costs yourselves."

"Well, how much does a brain cost?" ask the relatives.

"For a male brain, $500,000. For a female brain, $200,000."

The patient's daughter is incensed by this. "Why the difference in price between male brains and female brains?"

"A standard pricing practice," says the head of the team. "Women's brains have to be marked down because they have actually been used."

"I understand you want to be a proctologist?" says the doctor to the young intern.

"Yes," says the intern.

"Well," advises the doctor, "I hear there are a lot of openings but it's kind of tight."

"Oh, that's all right," responds the intern. "Butt I hear you've got to put up with a lot of assholes all day."

"Yes, and you will be up to your elbows in work sometimes. Why, I've lost four Rolexes since I started five years ago. It's a real pain in the ass."

● ● ● ●

A guy goes to the doctor and says, "Doctor, I have this terrible problem—I can't hold my water, I don't know when I'm gonna pee. What should I do?" Doctor says, "Get off my carpet."

—FREDDIE ROMAN, SOUPY SALES STOP ME IF YOU'VE HEARD IT!, 2003

● ● ● ●

One day, Pete complains to his friend, "My elbow really hurts. I guess I should see a doctor."

His friend says, "Don't do that. There's a computer at the drugstore that can diagnose anything, and it's quicker and cheaper than a doctor. You just put in a sample of your urine, and the computer diagnoses your problem and tells you what you can do about it. And it only costs ten dollars."

Pete figures he has nothing to lose, so he fills a jar with urine and goes to the drugstore. Finding the computer, he pours in the sample and deposits the ten bucks. The computer starts making noises, and various lights start flashing. After a brief pause, out pops a small slip of paper, which reads:

1. You have tennis elbow.

2. Soak your arm in warm water; avoid heavy labor.

3. It will be better in two weeks.

That evening, while thinking about how amazing this new technology is and how it will change medical science forever, Pete begins to wonder if this computer could be fooled. He decides to give it a try. He mixes together some tap water, a stool sample from his dog, and urine samples from his wife and daughter. To top it off, he masturbates into the concoction.

He goes back to the drugstore, pours the sample into the computer, and deposits the money. The machine again makes some noises, flashes its lights, and prints out the following analysis:

1. Your tap water is too hard—get a water softener.

2. Your dog has ringworm—bathe him with antifungal shampoo.

3. Your daughter is using cocaine—put her into rehab.

4. Your wife is pregnant...twin girls. They aren't yours. Get a lawyer.

5. And if you don't stop masturbating, your elbow will never get better.

Young Bill is courting Mabel, who lives on an adjoining farm. One evening, as they are sitting on Bill's porch watching the sun go down over the hills, Bill spies his prize bull fucking one of his cows. He sighs in contentment at this idyllic rural scene and figures the omens are right for him to finally ask Mabel to have sex with him. He leans in close and whispers into her ear, "Mabel, I'd sure like to be doing what that bull is doing."

"Well, then, why don't you?" Mabel whispers back. "It is YOUR cow."

An anxious woman goes to her doctor and asks him nervously, "Doctor, can you get pregnant from anal intercourse?"

"Certainly," replies the doctor. "Where do you think lawyers come from?"

A man walks into a drugstore and quietly asks the pharmacist, "Do you sell Viagra here?"

The pharmacist answers kindly, "Yes, sir. We certainly do."

"Do you think I could get it over the counter?"

The pharmacist looks him over, thinks for a moment, and says, "Perhaps, if you took five or six pills at once, you could."

●　●　●　●

It's an honor to be here on this dais. There's hundreds of years of show business history up here and that's just Alan King. You know, Alan wanted to donate a kidney but nobody can use one that runs on steam.

—ADAM FERRARA, ROB REINER ROAST, 2000

●　●　●　●

A veterinarian is feeling ill and goes to see her doctor, who takes an extensive medical history and then inquires about her symptoms and complaints.

She interrupts him: "Hey, look, I'm a doctor myself, a vet, and I don't need to ask my patients all these questions. I can tell what's wrong just by looking. Why can't you?"

The doctor nods and says, "Okay, I'll take your challenge." He quickly performs a physical exam, being careful not to ask any questions, and then picks up a pad, writes a prescription, and hands it to her. "There you are. Take these pills four times a day for ten days. If this doesn't work, come back and we'll put you to sleep."

T hree guys go to see a witch doctor, hoping he can solve their problems. One is a smoker, one is an alcoholic, and one is gay but wants to change. The doctor puts a curse on them, stating that if any of them indulge in their habits even one more time they will die.

Two days later the alcoholic is dead because he gave in to temptation and had a drink.

The next day the gay guy and the smoker are walking down the street together. The smoker sees a cigarette lying on the ground and stops to stare at it.

The gay guy says, "If you bend over to pick that up, we are both fucked."

A man of a certain age goes to the doctor asking for a prescription for Viagra. He requests a large dose of the "strongest" variety. The doctor asks why he needs so much and the guy tells him that two young nymphomaniacs are spending a week at his place. The doctor fills the prescription.

Later that week, the same guy goes back to the doctor asking for painkillers.

The doctor asks, "Why? Is your dick in that much pain?"

"No," says the guy, "it's for my wrists. The girls never showed up!"

Two men are discussing how much trouble their wives give them about having sex. The first guy says, "My wife's so cold I can put a glass of water in bed with her and the next morning it's turned to ice."

The second guy says, "Hell, every time my old lady spreads her legs the furnace kicks in!"

● ● ● ●

I want to keep it short because I have a lot of friends coming out and let's face it, last year's show was more stretched out than Dr. Ruth's pussy. Which, by the way, is where they are holding next year's Roast.

—JEFFREY ROSS, ROB REINER ROAST, 2000

● ● ● ●

A woman goes to the doctor complaining of excruciating pain in her knees. After the diagnostic tests show nothing, the doctor questions her. "There must be something you're doing that you haven't told me. Can you think of any activity that might be causing harm to your knees?"

"Well," she says a little sheepishly, "my husband and I have sex doggy-style on the floor every night."

"That's got to be it," says the doctor. "There are plenty of other positions and ways to have sex, you know."

"Not if we both want to watch TV, there aren't."

Debbie got her vibrator stuck inside her, so she went to her gynecologist. "To remove that vibrator," said the doctor, "I'm going to have to perform a very long and delicate operation."

"I don't think I can afford that," said Debbie. "Could you just replace the batteries?"

A guy goes into a drugstore to buy condoms. The girl behind the counter asks, "What size?"

"I don't know."

She holds up a finger and says, "That big?"

He says, "Bigger."

She holds up three fingers and says, "That big?"

He says, "Smaller."

She holds up two fingers and he says, "That's it."

She puts the two fingers in her mouth, thinks, and says, "Medium."

John graduates with a degree in clinical psychology and opens his first office. After some advertising he is astounded to have nearly 300 people who want to be in group therapy. John decides to rent a big hall and invite the entire group. To break the ice and get the therapy started, he asks for a show of hands as to how often the attendees have sex.

He first asks that everyone who has sex almost every night raise his or her hand. A modest number of hands go up.

He then asks how many have sex about once a week? This time a larger number of hands are raised.

John then asks how many have sex once or twice a month. A few hands go up. After John has polled his group several more times, he notices one guy sitting off to the side who has never raised his hand. He has a huge, beaming grin on his face. John asks the man how often he has sex.

"Once a year!" the man replies.

"I'm sorry, but why are you so happy, if you have sex only once a year?"

"Tonight's the night!"

"I've got some good news and some bad news," says the doctor.

"What's the bad news?" asks the patient.

"The bad news is that unfortunately you've only got three months to live."

The patient is shocked. "Well . . . what's the good news then, Doctor?"

The doctor gestures toward his receptionist. "You see that blonde with the big breasts, tight ass, and legs that go all the way up to heaven?"

The patient nods.

"I'm fucking her."

• • • •

As far as Chevy's abilities as an artist are concerned, there's probably much more natural comic talent in Milton Berle's last fart. In fact, one would be hard-pressed to actually rationalize how Chevy has come this far on so little natural talent if it weren't generally known that in the egregiously blatant promotion of his career his tongue has claimed the ridges of more rectums than anyone since Troy Donahue won the lead in *Adventures in Paradise*.

—DAN AYKROYD, CHEVY CHASE ROAST, 1990

• • • •

I t was just announced on CNN that the list of ingredients found in Viagra has been released. It's made up of 2 percent aspirin, 2 percent ibuprofen, 1 percent filler, and 95 percent Fix-a-Flat.

I f a man overdoses on Viagra, how do they get the casket lid shut?

A man and a woman are sitting in a doctor's waiting room.

Man: "What are you doing here today?"

Woman: "Oh, I'm here to donate some blood. They're going to give me $5 for it."

Man: "Hmm, that's interesting. I'm here to donate sperm, myself. But they pay me $25."

The woman looks thoughtful for a moment and they chat some more before going their separate ways. A couple of months later, the same man and woman meet again in the same waiting room.

Man: "Oh, hi there! Here to donate blood again?"

Woman [shaking her head with mouth closed]: "Unh unh."

A guy can't get an erection so he goes to the doctor. The doctor tells him that the muscles at the base of his penis are damaged, and there's nothing to be done—except possibly some very experimental surgery.

The guy asks what the surgery is, and the doctor explains that they take the muscles from the base of a baby elephant's trunk, insert them in the base of his penis, and hope for the best. The guy says that sounds pretty scary but the thought of never having sex again is even scarier—so he decides to go ahead.

The doctor performs the surgery and about six weeks later gives the man the go ahead to "try out his new equipment."

The guy takes his girlfriend out to dinner. While at dinner he starts feeling an incredible pressure in his pants. It gets unbearable and he figures no one can see him so he undoes his pants. No sooner does he do this than his penis pops out, creeps across the table, grabs a dinner roll, and disappears back into his pants. His girlfriend stares in shock—then gets a sly look on her face.

"That was pretty cool! Can you do that again?"

With his eyes watering and a painful expression on his face, he says "Probably, but I don't know if I can fit another dinner roll up my ass!"

A doctor is having an affair with his nurse. Shortly after this starts, she tells him she is pregnant. Not wanting his wife to know, he gives the nurse a large sum of money and asks her to go to Italy and have the baby there.

"But how will I let you know the baby is born?" she asks.

"Just send me a postcard and write 'spaghetti' on the back."

Not knowing what else to do, the nurse takes the money and flies to Italy. Six months go by and then one day the doctor's wife calls him at the office and says, "Dear, you received a very strange postcard in the mail today. I don't understand what it means."

"Just wait until I get home. I'll read it and explain it to you."

Later that evening the doctor comes home, reads the postcard, and falls to the floor in a dead faint. So the wife picks up the card and reads, "Spaghetti, spaghetti, spaghetti, spaghetti—two with sausage and meatballs, two without."

A guy goes to a doctor and says, "Doc, you've got to help me. My penis is orange." The doctor pauses to think and asks the guy to drop his pants so he can check. Damned if the guy's penis isn't orange.

The doc says, "This is very strange. Sometimes things like this are caused by a lot of stress in a person's life."

Probing as to the causes of possible stress, the doc asks the guy, "How are things going at work?"

The guy responds that he was fired about six weeks ago.

The doctor tells him that this must be the cause of the stress.

"No. The boss was a real asshole, I had to work twenty or thirty hours of overtime every week and I had no say in anything that was happening. I found a new job a couple of weeks ago where I can set my own hours, I'm getting paid double what I got on the old job and the boss is a really great guy."

So the doc figures this isn't the reason. He asks the guy, "How's your home life?"

The guy says, "Well, I got divorced about eight months ago."

The doc figures that maybe this is the source of the stress.

But the guy says, "No. For years, all I listened to was 'nag, nag, nag.' God, am I glad to be rid of that old bitch."

Now the doc is baffled. He inquires, "Do you have any hobbies or a social life?"

The guy replies, "No, not really. Most nights I sit home, watch some porno flicks, and munch on Cheetos."

● ● ● ●

I went to see the doctor,

to get a Viagra pill,

and now I'm on the run with a loaded gun,

and can't find nuthin' to kill.

—Nipsey Russell, Soupy Sales Stop Me If You've Heard It!, 2003

● ● ● ●

A lady is having a bed-wetting problem, so she goes to the doctor. He asks her to get undressed and wait for him in the other room. When he enters the room he tells the lady to stand on her head facing the mirror.

It seems strange, but she figures he is a doctor, so she does what he asks. The doctor goes over to her, rests his chin between her legs, and looks in the mirror. After a few minutes he tells the lady to go ahead and put her clothes back on and he will talk to her when she is dressed.

When she is all dressed and sitting across the desk from the doctor, she asks him if he now knows what is wrong with her.

He tells her that she needs to quit drinking before she goes to bed.

"I don't understand—why did I have to get upside down and naked in front of a mirror?

"I wanted to see how I would look with a beard."

Frank's doctor tells him that masturbating before sex often helped men last longer during the act, so he decides, "What the hell, I'll try it." He spends the rest of the day thinking about where to do it. He couldn't do it in his office. He thinks about the restroom, but that is too public. He considers an alley, but figures that would be too risky. On his way home, he hits upon the answer. He pulls his truck over to the side of the highway, gets out, and crawls underneath as if he is examining the truck. Satisfied with the privacy, he undoes his pants and starts to masturbate.

He closes his eyes and thinks of his lover. As he grows closer to orgasm, he feels a quick tug at the bottom of his pants. He keeps his eyes shut and says, "What?"

"This is the police. What's going on down there?"

"I'm checking out the rear axle, it's busted."

"Well, you might as well check your brakes, too, while you're down there, because your truck rolled down the hill five minutes ago."

A beautifully put-together young woman goes in for her annual checkup. The doctor asks her to disrobe and climb onto the examining table.

"Doctor," she replies shyly, "I just can't undress in front of you."

"All right," says the physician. "I'll turn off the lights. You undress and tell me when you're through."

In a few moments, her voice rings out in the darkness, "Doctor, I've undressed. What shall I do with my clothes?"

"Put them on the chair, on top of mine."

● ● ● ●

Jerry Stiller is not the only one full of himself tonight; his colostomy bag is also full of himself.

—JIMMY KIMMEL, JERRY STILLER ROAST, 1999

● ● ● ●

A man tries everything he can to stop stuttering, but he just can't. Finally, he goes to a world-renowned doctor for help. The doctor examines him and says, "I've found your problem. Your penis is twelve inches long. It weighs so much it is pulling on your lungs, causing you to stutter."

So the man asks, "What's the cure, doctor?"

"We have to cut off six inches."

The man thinks about it and, eager to cure his stuttering, agrees to the operation, which is a great success—he stops stuttering. Two months later, he calls the doctor and tells him that since he had the surgery, all of his girlfriends have dumped him and his love life has gone down the toilet. He wants the doctor to put back the six inches. Not hearing anything on the line, he repeats himself, "Hey doc, didn't you hear me? I want my six inches back!"

Finally, the doctor responds, "F-f-f-f-f-f-uck y-y-you!"

A guy walks into his local pharmacy, where a female pharmacist is filling prescriptions. When she finally gets around to helping him he says, "I'd like ninety-nine condoms please."

"Ninety-nine condoms?" she repeats, shocked. "Fuck me!"

"Make it a hundred, then."

The FDA has been looking for a generic name for Viagra. They announced today that they have settled on Mycoxafloppin.

A FEW DIRTY WORDS
FROM GILBERT GOTTFRIED

I never denied being a hypocrite and I will say out loud now, I should be allowed to say anything, and everyone else should be censored!

When I work in clubs, for the most part, I work very clean. I never really made any conscious decision to tell dirty jokes. I once opened for Belinda Carlisle and one of the managers said, "Now, there's a lot of children here with their parents so don't do anything dirty." I attempted to work clean for about ten minutes and then I launched into every dick joke I knew. Now, here I am saying I normally work clean . . . oh well, I guess we are discovering how I'm destroying my career in leaps and bounds.

The main reason that my act is clean is that I tend to avoid any kind of dirty word. If I'm talking about sex, I'll say "sex," rather than "fuck" because I'm always wondering, "Did I come up with something funny or did I just say fuck and that made people laugh?"

Sometimes when a comedian on a TV show tells a joke where the punch line is something like " . . . and the dinner tasted like dirt," and it doesn't get that big a laugh, I know that when he first did it in a club it was probably ". . . . and the *fucking* dinner tasted like *shit*." What happens so often is the comedian hears the laugh and says, "Oh, that's a great joke." But they forget what the audience was actually laughing at. So they figure, "Oh, I'll just clean it up a little for TV." But if the joke was great the way it was, then it's not going to work when it's cleaned up.

Right after Pee-Wee Herman got arrested for masturbation, I was at the Emmy Awards that aired on Fox. They said, "Just go onstage and have fun." So I figured, "What's more fun than masturbation?" I went on and said, "I just want to get it off my chest. I can really sleep easier now that Pee-Wee Herman has been arrested. If masturbation's a crime, I should be on death row. Right now my right hand is like Superman. I could hold a piece of charcoal and crush it into a diamond. I don't know how they prove that you masturbated, maybe they dust for prints." I got a very big reaction from the audience—they were laughing. I didn't know anything was wrong until later on in the evening when someone told me, "Oh, you know they're going to censor that. They're cutting you out of the West Coast."

By censoring it, more people saw it. Every news show and enter-tainment show ran the story, "Horrible Stuff Unfit for Family Consumption." As long as they say that, then they can advertise it twenty times and show bits of it in their ads, and show it during family viewing hour at, like, five in the evening.

Shortly after that, there was an entire *Seinfeld* episode devoted to masturbation. People now refer to it as a classic episode. Since then, what's gotten on TV is amazing.

When reporters were interviewing me after that incident they referred to me as "dirty-mouth comic Gilbert Gottfried." Like that's what I was famous for. In fact, one television interview I did for some news show purposely bleeped every other word to make it sound like, "Wow this guy is uncontrollable, look how much he curses." I wasn't even saying anything dirty, but when you hear a bleep, you assume.

See, what bothered me the most when I'd see them print up my joke was that they were all quoting me as saying, "Masturbation's a crime, I should be on death row." And it was "IF masturbation's a crime, I should be on death row." That bothered me because one word can change the feeling of a joke. Not that it makes it clean or dirty, it's still the same joke, but it's important they get it right.

Shortly after that Emmy show I did an HBO special and one critic brought up that when I was on network TV, I caused this controversy and then once I'm on HBO, where anything goes, I work perfectly clean. Right after that whole thing with the Emmys and Fox, I did a voiceover for the animated film *Aladdin*. So I guess I was too dirty for Fox but clean enough for Disney.

One time I did something kind of dirty and somebody yelled out, "Hey, I have my kids in the audience!" I said, "Oh, well, it's very nice of you to bring your kids to a place where they drink alcohol and smoke. 'Hey kids, let's go to a nightclub. Let's breathe in cigarette smoke and hang around drunks.'" He just sort of shut up after that.

I think my favorite review was when someone called me the most unpleasant thing to happen to show business since the snuff film. It was quite an accomplishment.

I always worry a little that the fewer restrictions there are, the less excitement there will be. I've had fun being in situations, like on *Hollywood Squares*, where I can see how far I can go with the punch line and still get across on the air. That used to be fun, and the audience would really like it. Because there are restrictions and censorship, it stays exciting. If there's no censorship then it could take away some of that excitement, some of the creativity of trying to work around saying something without saying it.

I think the censors spin a wheel blindfolded, throw a dart, and whatever it hits, it's too dirty. Sometimes I think, "They will definitely cut that out"—but they don't. Other stuff that seems perfectly clean, they get offended by. Once on the *Tonight Show with Jay Leno,* during a rehearsal, I said, "Take that and shove it up your ass." Of course the censor said, "You can't say that," and I thought, "Well, obviously." But then he says, "If you want, you can say, 'Take that and stick it up your ass.'" So he wasn't concerned about putting something in your ass, it was basically how violently you do it.

On *Hollywood Squares*, Robert Klein once tried to do an imitation of me and it didn't come across, and he goes, "I'm trying to do a Gilbert Gottfried imitation, but I can't get it down." So I said, "And I can't get it up," and that they allowed on the air. But then I get a question, "This weighs ten tons and gets blown a few times a day," and I said, "A very happy whale." That one they cut out.

Someone I know, some comic, was at a restaurant and George Burns was there. He went over and Burns invited him to sit down. They talked about comedians working dirty. Burns said that back then, his generation had respect for the audience, would never do anything filthy. After dinner, Burns is standing up, he's putting on his jacket and the waiter walks over and he goes, "Are you leaving Mr. Burns?" He says, "Yeah, I gotta hurry home. I hired a teenage faggot to punch me up the ass." He just said this to the waiter, almost like everything he'd said about working clean was a build-up to that.

A man walks into a therapist's office looking very depressed. "Doc, you've got to help me. I can't go on like this."

"What's the problem?" the doctor inquires.

"Well, I'm thirty-five years old and I still have no luck with the ladies. No matter how hard I try, I just seem to scare them away."

"My friend, this is not a serious problem. You just need to work on your self-esteem. Each morning, I want you to get up and run to the bathroom mirror. Tell yourself that you are a good person, a fun person, and an attractive person. Say it with real conviction. Within a week you'll have women buzzing all around you."

The man nods thoughtfully and walks out of the office. Three weeks later, he returns with the same downtrodden expression on his face.

"Didn't my plan work?" asks the doctor.

"Oh, it worked all right. For the past several weeks I've had great sex with the most fabulous women."

"So, what's your problem?"

"I don't have a problem," the man replies. "My wife does."

• • • •

My proctologist won't even see me anymore, he's so sensitive. The last time he saw me, I moaned the name of another doctor.

—DICK CAPRI, FRIARS FROLICS IN HONOR OF PAT COOPER, 1998

• • • •

A dwarf goes into her doctor's office complaining of an irritated crotch. After an examination, the doctor says, "I can't find anything wrong with you. Does it get better or worse at any time?"

"Yeah, it's really bad whenever it rains," she replies.

"Well, then, next time it rains, get in here at once and we'll take another look at it."

Two weeks later, it's raining really hard and the little lady shows up at the doctor's office. "Doctor, it's really bad today. Please, you have to help me!"

"Well, let's have a look," he says, as he lifts her up onto the table. "Oh, yes, I think I see the problem. Nurse, bring me a surgical kit. Don't worry, ma'am, this won't hurt a bit."

The lady closes her eyes in painful anticipation. The doctor begins snipping away and finishes a few minutes later. "There you go, ma'am, try that."

She walks back and forth around the office and exclaims, "That's great, Doc, what did you do?"

"I just took a couple of inches off the tops of your rain boots."

A man goes into a pharmacy and asks to talk to a male pharmacist. The woman behind the counter replies that she is the pharmacist, that she and her sister own the store, and that there are no males employed there. "But surely I can help you," she says.

"This is embarrassing for me, but I have a permanent erection that causes me a lot of pain and severe embarrassment. I was wondering what you could give me for it?"

"Just a minute, I'll go talk to my sister."

When she returns, she says, "The best we can offer is one-third ownership in the store and three thousand a month in living expenses."

A man goes to a doctor and says, "What should I do? I've just been raped by an elephant!"

The doctor tells him to bend over so he can have a look at his ass. "That's odd," he says. "Your asshole is ten inches wide! I thought elephants had long, thin dicks?"

"Yeah, but he fingered me first!"

A gay man goes into the doctor's office and takes off his clothes for examination. The doctor sees that he's wearing a nicotine patch at the end of his penis and says, "Hmmm, that's interesting. Does it work?"

"Sure does. I haven't had a butt in three weeks!"

Richard Pryor is truly the "hottest" man in show business. A man who is not only bigger than Milton Berle, but is hickory smoked.

—ROBIN WILLIAMS, RICHARD PRYOR ROAST, 1991

A doctor says to his patient, "Joe, the good news is I can cure your headaches. The bad news is that it will require castration. You have a very rare condition that causes your testicles to press on your spine, and the pressure creates one hell of a headache. The only way to relieve the pressure is to remove the testicles."

Joe is shocked and depressed. He wonders if he has anything to live for. But ultimately, he decides that he has no choice but to go under the knife.

When he leaves the hospital after the surgery, he is headache free for the first time in twenty years—but he feels as if he is missing a vital part of himself. It is as if he is a different person. He can make a new beginning and live a new life. He sees a men's clothing store and thinks, "That's what I need, a new suit."

He enters the shop and tells the salesman, "I'd like a new suit."

The elderly man eyes him briefly and says, "Let's see, size 44 long."

Joe laughs. "That's right, how did you know?"

"Been in the business sixty years!"

Joe tries on the suit and it fits perfectly. As he is admiring himself in the mirror, the salesman asks, "How about a new shirt?" Joe thinks for a moment and says, "Sure, why not?"

The salesman eyes him again and says, "Let's see, 34 sleeve and 16½ neck."

Again, Joe says, "That's right, how did you know?"

"Been in the business sixty years!"

Joe tries on the shirt, and it fits perfectly. As he is adjusting the collar, the salesman asks, "How about new shoes?"

Joe is on a roll now, and says, "Sure."

The salesman eyes Joe's feet and says, "Let's see. 9½E."

"That's right, how did you know?"

"Been in the business sixty years!"

Joe tries on the shoes and they fits perfectly. As he's trying them out by walking around the shop the salesman asks, "How about some new underwear?" Joe says, "Sure, why not?"

The salesman steps back, eyes Joe's waist and says, "Let's see . . . size 36."

Joe laughs. "Ah ha! I got you! I've worn size 34 since I was eighteen years old."

"You can't wear a size 34. Size 34 underwear would press your testicles up against the base of your spine and give you one hell of a headache."

What does the receptionist at the sperm clinic say to clients as they are leaving?

"Thanks for coming."

A woman goes to her dentist and after he is through examining her, he says, "I am sorry to tell you this, but I am going to have to drill a tooth."

The woman says, "Ooooohhhh, I hate the drill! The pain is so awful I'd rather have a baby!"

"Make up your mind," replies the dentist. "I have to adjust the chair."

• • • •

I was trying to tell all my homies I'm going to be working with Richard Belzer on *Law and Order* and they said I've never heard of that motherfucker. I said, "He looks like Bowser from Sha Na Na and Jerry Seinfeld after a bad car accident."

—ICE T, RICHARD BELZER ROAST, 2001

• • • •

A handsome guy goes into the hospital for some minor surgery and, the day after the procedure, a friend stops by to see how he is doing. The friend is amazed at the number of nurses who come by the room with refreshments, offers to fluff his pillows, make the bed, give him back rubs, etc.

"Why all the attention?" the friend asks. "You look fine to me."

"I know!" grins the patient. "But the nurses kinda formed a little fan club when they all heard that my circumcision required twenty-seven stitches."

A man goes to his doctor seeking help for his terrible addiction to cigars. The doctor is quite familiar with his very compulsive patient, so he recommends an unusual and quite drastic form of aversion therapy.

"When you go to bed tonight, take one of your cigars, unwrap it, and stick it completely up your asshole. Then remove it, rewrap it, and place it back with all the others in such a fashion as you can't tell which one it is. The aversion is obvious: you won't dare smoke any of them, not knowing which is the treated cigar."

"Thanks, doc, I'll try it." And he does. But three weeks later he comes back and sees the doctor again.

"What? My recommendation didn't work? It has been known to be effective even in the most addictive cases."

"Well, it kind of worked, doc. At least I was able to transfer my addiction."

"What the hell is that supposed to mean?"

"Well . . . I don't smoke anymore, but now I can't go to sleep at night without a cigar shoved up my ass."

A man goes to the doctor to pick up his wife's test results. The nurse at the desk asks him the family name, to which he replies, "Smith."

"Mr. Smith . . . hmmm . . . we have so many Smiths that I'm not quite sure which test results are your wife's. We've narrowed it down to two possibilities. Either she has Herpes or Alzheimer's Disease."

"Well, what should I do?"

"I suggest you take your wife into town and leave her there. If she finds her own way home, DON'T fuck her."

A woman goes to the gynecologist but won't tell the receptionist what's wrong with her, just that she must see a doctor. After hours of waiting, she gets in.

"Ma'am, what seems to be the problem?" the doctor asks.

"Well," she says, "my husband is a compulsive gambler and every nickel he can get his hands on he gambles away. I had five hundred dollars and in order to hide it from him, I stuffed it in my vagina—but now I can't get it out."

"Don't be nervous. I see this sort of thing all the time." He asks her to pull down her underwear, sits her down with her legs wide open, puts his gloves on and says, "I only have one question. What am I looking for? Bills or loose change?"

A doctor and his wife are having a big argument at breakfast. "You aren't so good in bed either!" he shouts, and storms off to work. By mid morning, he decides he'd better make amends, and calls home.

"What took you so long to answer?"

"I was in bed."

"What were you doing in bed this late?"

"Getting a second opinion."

A young couple goes to the doctor for their annual physical exams. Afterward, the doctor calls the young man into his office and tells him that he has some good news and some bad news. "The good news is that your fiancée has a particular strain of gonorrhea that I have only heard of once before."

The guy pales. "If that's the good news, then what the hell is the bad news?"

"Well... the bad news is that I heard about it just last week from my dog's vet."

●   ●   ●   ●

Danny Aiello had to lose some weight because it was interfering with his sex life. He couldn't get his mouth to his cock. Danny is a very macho guy. He got his first tattoo on his cock, which is a very macho thing to do, but it was a picture of another guy's mouth.

—RICHARD BELZER, DANNY AIELLO ROAST, 1997

●   ●   ●   ●

A lady goes to the doctor's office and tells him that she can't get her husband to have sex with her anymore. So the doctor hands her a bottle of pills and says she should give her husband one in his dinner whenever she wants to have sex. That night she gives him one and they have a pretty good night of sex.

The next night she decides to try four pills, and the sex is even better.

The following night she decides to pull out all the stops and she hides eight pills in his dinner. The sex is fantastic!

The next night she goes for broke, dumping the entire remainder of the bottle into her husband's dinner.

The following day her son shows up at the doctor's office and says, "Doctor! Doctor! What did you do to my dad? My mom's dead, my sister's pregnant, my butt hurts, and my dad's going around saying, 'Here kitty, kitty, kitty!'"

T his guy visits the doctor and says, "Doc, I think I've got a sex problem. I can't get it up for my wife anymore."

The doctor says, "Come back tomorrow and bring her with you."

The next day, the guy shows up with his wife.

The doctor says to the wife, "Take off your clothes and lie on the table."

She does it, and the doctor walks around the table a few times looking her up and down. He pulls the guy to the side and says, "You're fine. She doesn't give me a hard-on, either."

T hree women are sitting in the doctor's waiting room. The first one goes in to be examined, and the doctor notices a big Y-shaped tattoo on her chest.

"Why do you have a big Y on your chest?" he asks.

"Well, my boyfriend went to Yale and when we make love he likes to wear his college sweater."

The doctor nods and moves on to the next patient. When he examines her he notices a similar tattoo and asks, "Why do you have a big H on your chest?"

"My husband went to Harvard and when we make love he likes to wear his college sweater."

The doctor nods and moves on to the third patient. Once again, she has a tattoo, this time of the letter M. "Don't tell me," he says. "Your boyfriend went to Michigan?"

"No . . . but my girlfriend went to Wisconsin."

A young girl is feeling under the weather so she goes to her family doctor.

"Young lady," says the doctor, "you're pregnant."

"But that can't be. The only men I've been with are nudists, and in our colony we practice sex only with our eyes."

"Well, my dear," said the doctor, "someone in that colony is cock-eyed."

● ● ● ●

I'm a feminist. I wear a brassiere. Not for political reasons—it has more to do with Newton's laws of physics at this point. The last time I went for a mammogram, I just KICKED my tit into the machine. These nipples are facing Venezuela at this point.

—JOY BEHAR, BAD GIRLS OF COMEDY, 1998

● ● ● ●

Three women are in the waiting room of a gynecologist, and each of them is knitting a sweater for her baby-to-be. The first one stops and takes a pill.

"What was that?" the others ask her.

"Oh, it was vitamin C. I want my baby to be healthy."

A few minutes later, another woman takes a pill.

"What was that?" the others ask.

"Oh, it was iron. I want my baby to be big and strong."

They continued knitting. Finally the third woman takes a pill.

"What was that?" the others ask her.

"It's Thalidomide," she said. "I just can't get the arms right on this fucking sweater!"

A young woman is having a physical examination and is very embarrassed about her weight. As she removes her last bit of clothing, she blushes. "I'm so ashamed, Doctor." she says. "I guess I let myself go."

The physician is checking her eyes and ears. "Don't feel ashamed, Miss. You look just fine."

"Do you really think so, Doctor?"

"Of course," he says, brandishing a tongue depressor. "Now open wide and say 'Moo.'"

Do you know what a gynecologist is? A spreader of old wives' tails.

Two men are sitting in a doctor's office and one asks the other, "What are you here for?"

"I have a red ring around my pecker. What are you here for?"

"I have a green ring around my pecker."

The doctor calls the first man in and examines him. As the man is leaving, he tells him not to worry, it wasn't a serious problem.

The doctor then examines the second man. Looking alarmed, he says, "I'm sorry to say this but your penis will soon fall off and then you'll die."

"What? You told the man with the red ring he was perfectly okay, but I'm gonna die?"

"Yes, but there's a big difference between lipstick and gangrene!"

What's a practical nurse? One who marries a wealthy old patient.

• • • •

Today, for the first time ever, there are more lines on Richard Belzer's face than under his nose.

—Susie Essman, Richard Belzer Roast, 2001

• • • •

A man runs into his doctor's office looking very agitated, yelling, "I have something wrong with my pecker!"

The nurse reprimands him. "You can't just come screaming in here, yelling things about your private parts. I suggest you go outside, enter the office again, quietly this time, and say you have something wrong with, say, your ear."

Chastened, the patient goes out and returns calmly a minute later, saying, "Excuse me, but I have something wrong with my ear."

"And what exactly is wrong with you ear?"

"I can't piss out of it!"

A man who is having gas problems explains to his doctor that every time he farts it sounds like a Honda. The doctor does an examination and finds nothing wrong with the man. As a last resort he looks into the patient's mouth and finally spots the problem. "I'm sorry, you'll have to go to a dentist for your problem."

So the man goes to see his dentist and explains his gas problem. After a quick exam, the dentist announces that the man has an abscess. "Don't worry, I'll have you fit and back to normal in a jiffy," says the dentist.

Sure enough, the man's problem disappears and he no longer farts like a Honda. The next week the man calls up the dentist and thanks him. But before he hangs up he has to ask the dentist how he knew that an abscess caused the problem.

"It's easy. Everyone knows that an abscess makes the fart go Honda."

A doctor goes into his patient's room and says, "I've got some good news and some bad news. Which do you want to hear first?"

"The bad news," says the frightened patient.

"Well, during your hernia operation, the surgeon's knife slipped and cut off your penis."

" My God! Then what is the good news?"

"It wasn't malignant."

A woman goes to the doctor, and says, "Doctor, I've got a bit of a problem. I'll have to take my clothes off to show you."

The doctor tells her to go behind the screen and disrobe. When she emerges, he asks, "Well, what seems to be the trouble?"

"It's a bit embarrassing, but these two green circles have appeared on the inside of my thighs."

The doctor examines her and finally admits he has no idea what the cause is. Then a lightbulb goes on and he asks, "Have you been having an affair with a gypsy?"

The woman blushes and says, "Well, um, yes, actually I have."

"That's the problem! Tell him that his earrings aren't made of real gold!"

A woman golfer suffers a nasty bee sting and leaves the course to go see her doctor about it. "What happened?" asks the doctor.

"I got stung between the first and second hole," replies the woman.

"You must have an awfully wide stance!"

Howard was feeling terribly guilty. No matter how he tried to forget about what he'd done, or justify it, he just couldn't. His sense of guilt was overwhelming. Every once in a while he'd hear a soothing voice inside his head, trying to reassure him: "Howard, don't worry about it. You aren't the first doctor to sleep with a patient and you won't be the last."

But invariably, the other voice in his head would bring him back to reality: "Howard, you're a veterinarian."

●　●　●　●

Rob Reiner, you fat fuck. Look at you; you were so cute on *All in the Family*. What happened? Did you swallow Carroll O'Connor? You are like Orson Welles without all that genius baggage. Look at you. David Crosby thinks you've let yourself go.

—TRIUMPH THE INSULT DOG, ROB REINER ROAST, 2000

●　●　●　●

A middle-aged woman has a heart attack and is rushed to the hospital. While on the operating table she has a near-death experience. Seeing God, she asks if this is it. God says, "No, you have another forty-three years, two months, and eight days to live."

Upon recovering, the woman decides to stay in the hospital and have some cosmetic surgery. She has a facelift, liposuction, breast augmentation, and a tummy tuck. She even has someone come in and change her hair color. Since she has so much more time to live, she figures she might as well make the most of it. She finally leaves the hospital, and as she crosses the street she is struck and killed by an oncoming ambulance. Arriving in front of God, she demands, "I thought you said I had another forty-three years!"

"I didn't recognize you."

A man and his wife are having problems in their relationship, so they decide to seek counseling. They start seeing a psychologist but it doesn't seem to be helping. The woman complains that her husband isn't affectionate. The man says he doesn't understand what she is talking about.

After many sessions in which the psychologist tries to explain to the man his wife's need for affection, the psychologist loses his patience. He tells the wife to take off her clothes, has sex with her, and tells the man, "This is what your wife needs every day."

The man frowns, thinks for a moment. "Okay, what time do you want me to bring her back tomorrow?"

● ● ● ●

Chevy Chase looks great. He's tall. I love tall guys. I've dated little guys. In fact, I think I still have one inside me.

—LISA LAMPANELLI, CHEVY CHASE ROAST, 2002

● ● ● ●

A guy and a girl meet at a bar. They get along so well that they decide to go to the girl's place. A few drinks later, the guy takes off his shirt and then washes his hands. He takes off his pants and washes his hands again. The girl watches him and says, "You must be a dentist."

Surprised, the guy says, "Yes. How did you figure that out?"

"Easy, you keep washing your hands."

One thing leads to another and they make love. After they're done, the girl says, "You must be a great dentist."

Beaming, the guy, says, "Yes, actually I am a great dentist. How did you figure that out?"

"Easy. I didn't feel a thing!"

● ● ● ●

Hef has so much sex, every couple of years he checks into the hospital for a ball tuck and a cock lift.

—Jeffrey Ross, Hugh Hefner Roast, 2001

● ● ● ●

"**D**oc," says Steve, "I want to be castrated."

"What on earth for?" asks the doctor in amazement.

"It's something I've been thinking about for a long time and I want to have it done."

"But . . . that's a radical step. Have you thought it through properly? Once it's done, there's no going back. It will change your life forever!"

"I'm aware of that and you're not going to change my mind, so either you schedule the operation or I'll go to another doctor."

"Well, okay," says the doctor reluctantly, "but it's against my better judgment!"

So Steve has his operation and the next day he is up and hobbling gingerly down the hospital corridor. Heading toward him is another patient who is walking exactly the same way. "Hi there," says Steve. "It looks as if you've just had the same operation I had."

"Well," says the patient, "I finally decided after thirty-seven years of life that I would like to be circumcised."

Steve stares at him in horror and screams, "Shit! THAT'S the word!"

CHAPTER 3

Bottoms Up!

I love ya man, you're my beeeesst friennnnnd!!—
Drinks for everybody—HIC!

Two guys are drinking at a bar. The first says, "Do you ever start thinking about something, and when you go to talk, you say something you don't mean?"

The second guy says, "Yeah, I was at the airport buying plane tickets, and the chick behind the counter had these huge tits, and instead of asking her for two tickets to Pittsburgh, I asked for two tickets to TITSBURGH."

The first guy says, "Yeah, well I was having breakfast with my wife last week, and instead of saying 'Honey, can you please pass me the sugar?' I said, 'You've ruined my life, you FUCKING BITCH!'"

A guy goes up to a girl in a bar and says, "You want to play 'Magic'?"

"What's that?" she asks.

"We go to my house and fuck, and then you disappear."

Three gal pals go out on the town and party together until the wee hours, and then go home separately. They meet up the next day to compare notes. The first girl claims that she was the drunkest: "I drove straight home, walked into the house, and as soon as I got through the door, I blew chunks."

The second girl responds, "You think you were drunk? I got in my car, drove out of the parking lot, and wrapped my car around the first tree I saw. I don't even have insurance!"

The third proclaims, "I was by far the most drunk. I got home and started a big fight with my husband, knocked a candle over, and burned the whole house down!"

"Well, you win," says the second girl.

"Not so fast," the first girl says. "Ladies, Chunks is my dog."

● ● ● ●

My father is Jewish and my mother is Irish, so all my life I've had the urge to buy whiskey at wholesale prices.

—STEVEN "SPANKY" MCFARLIN, FRIARS NEW FACES OF COMEDY, 2002

● ● ● ●

A man and a woman are having drinks when they get into an argument about who enjoys sex more. The man says, "Men obviously enjoy sex more than women. We're completely obsessed with getting laid!"

"That doesn't prove anything," the woman countered. "Think about this...when your ear itches and you put your finger in it and wiggle it around, then pull it out, which feels better—your ear or your finger?"

W hy did God create alcohol?

So ugly people would have a chance to have sex.

T wo dwarfs decide to treat themselves to a vacation in Las Vegas. At the hotel bar they're dazzled by two women, and wind up taking them to their rooms.

The first dwarf is embarrassed to find that he can't get an erection. His discomfort is intensified by the sounds coming from his friend's adjoining room. All night long he hears cries of ONE, TWO, THREE...UH!

In the morning, the second dwarf asks the first, "How did it go?"

"It was so embarrassing. I simply couldn't get it up."

"You think that's embarrassing? I couldn't even get onto the bed!"

● ● ● ●

I met Richard Belzer twenty-seven years ago. That was when he still considered heroin one of the four basic food groups.

—Paul Shaffer, Richard Belzer Roast, 2001

● ● ● ●

A man says to a bartender, "I'll bet you $500 that I can piss in this cup from across the room."

The bartender looks at the man like he's nuts and says with a laugh, "Okay, buddy. You got a deal."

So the man walks over to the other side of the room, pulls down his zipper, and just lets it fly. Piss goes everywhere: on the bar, on customers, all over the bartender, but not a drop lands in the cup. He then walks back over to the bartender, who can barely control his laughter as he says, "Pay up!"

Without batting an eye, the man pays him, turns around, and breaks into a grin.

"You just lost $500, why are you smiling?" the bartender asks.

"Well, you see that man over there."

"Yeah."

"Well, I bet him $10,000 that I could piss all over you and your bar and that you'd just laugh about it!"

A guy walks into a bar and sees a gorgeous blonde sitting there all alone, so he sits down next to her and pulls a small box from his pocket. He opens it and there's a frog inside. The blonde says, "He's cute, but does he do tricks?" "Yeah, he licks pussy. Would you like to come to my place for a demonstration?"

After some thought, she decides, why not? When they get there, she takes her clothes off, gets on the bed, and spreads her legs. The guy sets the frog between her legs and it just sits there, not moving at all.

"Well? What's up?" says the blonde.

"I'm sorry, I don't know what's gotten into him. Let's give him a minute."

Still, the frog doesn't move a muscle.

So the guy leans over to the frog and says, "All right, I'm only going to show you how to do this one more time!"

A drunk walks into a bar, sits down, and happens to notice a twelve-inch-tall man standing on the bar. Astonished, the man asks the guy next to him, "What the hell is that?"

"He's a piano player!" the guy replies.

"No way. You're pulling my leg."

Without saying a word, the guy picks up the little man and sets him on a high stool in front of the piano. Sure enough, he starts hammering out all the patrons' favorite tunes.

Stunned, the drunk says, "Now I've seen everything. Where the hell did you get him?"

"Well, it's like this. I was walking through the alley out back and I came across an old bottle. When I started polishing it, out popped a beautiful genie, who granted me one wish..."

Before the guy can finish his story, the drunk lurches off his barstool and out into the alley, where he finds the bottle and starts rubbing it. Sure enough, a beautiful genie pops out and says, "For freeing me from the bottle, I grant you one wish."

In his excitement, the drunk slurs his words as he says, "I wish for a million bucks." In an instant, the sky turns black as a million ducks fly over his head, shitting all over him. Angrily, the drunk storms back inside, slams the door, and begins cursing, "You son of a bitch, I found that genie bottle and wished for a million bucks and instead I got a million *ducks* shitting all over my new suit!"

The guy starts laughing and shaking his head. "You don't really think I wished for a twelve-inch *pianist*, do you?"

A FEW DIRTY WORDS
FROM RICHARD BELZER

I was always provocative and I used so-called "body language," but it was always to serve a purpose. I don't think I ever swore just for effect, having grown up on Redd Foxx, and later Richard Pryor and Lenny Bruce, so there's a precedent for poetic swearing. It depends on who you're talking about—Chris Rock is poetry, and I don't mean to besmirch any of my fellow comics, but there are clearly comics who use certain words over and over again to the point where they lose their impact.

It's impossible now to push the envelope. That's why Sam Kinnison was kind of a revelatory act. You wonder how far you can go, and then someone comes along and just takes it further. I think because of cable television, because of Def Jam Comedy and other things, that it's virtually impossible to shock these days with language. It has to be subject matter, not necessarily language, which shocks people.

I've been censored for politics, not for language. I was supposed to do an interview on a radio station and it was abruptly canceled because, apparently, the Mormons own the station and they didn't want that "New York comic" on. New York comic is code for "Jew."

Another time I was doing a panel discussion for *Variety* in the eighties and I started talking about how the Reagan administration was suppressing free expression. Someone came right up the aisle and said, "Well, that's all, thank you," and just cut me off.

So I got in trouble for making fun of presidents, but never for language.

In the beginning of Reagan's presidency I would get booed; I got very few laughs. Then, as time went on, the same routine got more laughs, more recognition, and eventually applause breaks. So, I'm not saying I'm a hero, but I stuck with the material. I believe my obligation is to make the audience laugh but also I'm a bit of a provocateur and will do things that the whole audience doesn't like or get. One time, a critic said, "Richard Belzer is the only comedian that I've ever seen who the audience leaves wondering if *he* liked *them*." I love that review because I don't ever play down to or placate an audience. There have been times where I have talked about things that most of the audience didn't know about, but somehow I would make it entertaining and that's a challenge to me. It was just on principle that I felt these subjects had to be addressed. It was funny; it wasn't like there was dead silence when I did it—and the laughter did build over the years.

If audiences were reluctant to get what I was doing, I would make more of a point of admonishing them and lecturing them, but in an aggressive, funny way. I never back off when I'm onstage. I feel much more on a mission than I do when I'm offstage.

I began to develop my style when I started to emcee shows. Having to go on every night, five, six, sometimes seven nights a week from nine at night till two, three in the morning, bringing up twenty-five, thirty acts. After the first few, you run out of material pretty quick. So I had to improvise and talk to the audience, talk about that day's events. That was the best training ground I have ever had. That was the early seventies, and interacting with the audience was very rare. A lot of guys would just start with the same word, end with the same word, and not really address the audience.

I find the Roasts just a great, great tradition of filth and bawdiness. They bring to mind "Bodkins," filthy and scatological wedding performers from the tenth and eleventh centuries. They would get up at a wedding in an Eastern European village and say things like, "There's a penis under the groom's beard," or "The mayor's daughter is fucking the baker." They would just rip the entire village apart with this kind of in-rhyme Yiddish rap that was very dirty and very funny. There are transcripts of Bodkins' trials where one Bodkin would accuse another Bodkin of stealing his material and they would both have to perform in front of a judge. To this day, they fly in Bodkins from Israel to Brooklyn on private jets to do rich, Hassidic weddings. I've seen footage of a Bodkin at a wedding, standing on a table with hundreds of men with the *payes*, and the guy is just rapping and going crazy. You don't hear about it much; they've tried to suppress them because they're so filthy. But it's a thousand-year-old tradition that still exists and it's hysterical. I love the Roast, format. My whole act is roasting the audience and roasting political figures. I'm a Bodkin Roaster. I'm a Roasted Bodkin.

They've found filthy graffiti in Egypt like, "Cleopatra sucks." Ever since there's been humanity, there's been scatology and toilet humor and sex humor. Yet, this is a puritan country. It's worse now than any society: the anti-science, the anti-art, the anti-progressive, homophobic, racist—it's just despicable. Here's the most hypocritical thing in a long time: at a White House press dinner, Laura Bush told a joke about the president jerking off a horse. The joke was, "He's so stupid that he milked a horse." If Al Franken did that or if I did that at that dinner, we would be vilified on every right-wing talk show, we'd be on the front page of magazines, we would be reviled. If the president's wife does it, oh, it's good for his image, it makes her more human and it's okay—but if a Jew or a black comic had done it, they would have torn our flesh off.

Dirty jokes have been around ever since people have been able to talk; and then there are the categories: priest jokes, hooker jokes, and farmer jokes. I'm sure farmer jokes and farmer's daughter jokes must be centuries old. Steve Allen had an interesting theory: he felt that a lot of the dirty jokes started in prison and that's where jokes, for some reason, just happened. It's an interesting theory but my question is, how did the jokes get out, then?

As a kid I was always very contrarian, got in trouble, and challenged authority—so later, when I heard people like Lenny Bruce, Redd Foxx, and Groucho Marx, that kind of validated what I was doing naturally. Groucho Marx was master of the double entendre. Everybody has an uncle like Groucho doing racy, suggestive stuff.

Buddy Hackett was pretty raw and hysterical and filthy, and some of the stuff he did makes me cringe. Jack Benny was revelatory.

To hear Jack swear was a rare thing. That's why I think it was so explosively funny when he would do that stuff at the Roasts, like read a dirty telegram or something. You didn't expect it from him.

I try to do something at Roasts that no one else would think of, and that is find things that are already in existence about the person that are hilariously unflattering. I think that Roasts, by definition, are meant to cross the line.

●　●　●　●

I've been trying to get in shape. I've been doing the Fonda workout. The Peter Fonda workout—where I wake up in the morning, take a hit of acid, smoke a joint, and go over to my sister's house and ask for money.

—Kevin Meaney, Friars Frolics in Honor of Joy Behar, 1999

●　●　●　●

A very handsome man walks into a singles bar, gets a drink, and takes a prime seat. During the course of the evening he tries to chat with every single woman who walks into the bar, with no luck. Then a hideously ugly man walks in, sits at the bar, and within seconds he is surrounded by women. Minutes later he walks out with two of the most beautiful women you ever saw.

Disheartened by all this, the good-looking guy says to the bartender, "Excuse me, but do you know that man's secret? I mean, he's not what you'd call attractive—in fact, he's as ugly as sin—and yet the ladies adore him. I'm everything a girl could want but I haven't been able to score all night. What's going on?"

"Well," said the barman, "I don't know how he does it, but he does the same thing every night. He walks in, orders a drink, and just sits there licking his eyebrows."

A huge, muscle-bound guy walks into a bar and orders a beer. The bartender can't help but stare at him because, in contrast to his large muscles, the man has a head the size of an orange. The bartender hands the guy his beer and says, "I want to compliment you on your physique, it really is phenomenal! But I have to ask, why is your head so small?"

The big guy gives a half-smile. He's obviously fielded this question many times. "One day," he begins, "I was hunting and got lost in the woods. I heard someone crying for help. I followed the cries and they led me to a frog that was sitting next to a stream."

"No shit?" says the bartender, thoroughly intrigued.

"Yeah, so I picked up the frog and it said, 'Kiss me. Kiss me and I will turn into a genie and grant you three wishes.' I looked around to make sure I was alone, I gave the frog a kiss, and POOF! The frog turned into a beautiful, voluptuous, naked woman. She said, 'You now have three wishes.' I looked down at my scrawny, 115-pound body and said, 'I want a body like Arnold Schwarzenegger.' She nodded, snapped her fingers, and POOF, there I was, so huge that I ripped open my clothes and was standing there naked!

"She then asked, 'What will be your second wish?'

"I looked hungrily at her beautiful body and replied, 'I want to make crazy love to you right here by this stream.' She nodded, lay down, and beckoned to me. We made love for hours, the best sex I've ever had!

"Afterward, as we lay next to each other glowing, she whispered into my ear, 'You know, you do have one more wish. What will it be?'

"I looked at her and replied, 'How about a little head?'"

A couple of airplane mechanics are in the hangar at Logan; it's fogged in and they have nothing to do. One of them says to the other, "Man, have you got anything to drink?"

The other one says, "Nah, but I hear you can drink jet fuel, and that it will kinda give you a buzz."

So they drink it, get smashed, and have a great time. The following morning, one of them gets up and is surprised by how good he feels. In fact, he feels great—NO hangover!

The phone rings and it's his buddy, who says, "Hey, how do you feel?"

"I feel great!"

"I feel great too!! You don't have a hangover?"

"No. That jet fuel is great stuff, no hangover. We ought to do this more often."

"Yeah, we could, but there's just one thing."

"What's that?"

"Did you fart yet?"

"No."

"Well, DON'T, 'cause I'm in Phoenix!"

T he guys in a local bar were so sure that their bartender was the strongest man in town that they offered a standing thousand-dollar bet. The bartender would squeeze a lemon until all the juice ran into a glass, and then hand the lemon to a patron. Anyone who could squeeze out one more drop of juice would win the money. Many people had tried over the years—weight lifters, longshoremen, you name it—but nobody could do it.

One day, this scrawny little man comes into the bar wearing thick glasses and a polyester suit and says in a tiny, squeaky voice, " I'd like to try the bet." After the laughter dies down, the bartender shrugs, grabs a lemon, and squeezes away. Then he hands the wrinkled remains to the little man.

The crowd's laughter turns to astonished silence as the man clenches his fist around the lemon and six drops fall into the glass. As the other patrons cheer, the bartender pays the little man the thousand dollars and asks him, "What do you do for a living? Are you a lumberjack, a weight lifter, or what?"

"Oh no. I work for the IRS."

• • • •

The Smothers Brothers we honor today

Tom is the drunk, Dickie is gay

Stand-up bass and guitar they play

CBS was right, they should just go the fuck away

I'm surprised so many people came out to honor you

but don't forget that public hanging used to draw a big crowd, too

You've been in show business for forty-four years, at least that's what your bio said

If after forty-four years I'm only at your level please somebody put a fucking bullet in my head

You started out in San Francisco where the bright lights and theaters beckoned

You got your first laugh in 1962 perhaps today you'll get your second

You got your TV show in 1967 that brought you fame and money

Coincidentally that's the exact same year that Freddie Roman stopped being funny

You are more of my father's generation you were performing long before I was born

I'm the same age as some of your children and like them I'm addicted to porn

Dick is an exercise enthusiast he has a low body-fat ratio

He's even taken up yoga so he can give himself fellatio

Tom is a great golfer he can drive the ball pretty far

He also likes to show off his yo-yo skills, which is how he gets young children into his car

He thinks he's cool with his yo-yo tricks, he calls himself Yo-Yo Man, or so I'm told

Yesterday he showed us how to walk the dog by taking a stroll with Judy Gold

Dick attended San Jose State University; it's a wonder he knows how to spell

Tom went to Columbia and he worked for a cocaine cartel

Tom has three lovely children and a pretty wife named Marcy, too

Dick has eleven children—he married the old woman who lives in a shoe

Tom wants to retire to his vineyard but he'll never get the chance

See Dick has so many mouths to feed because he can't keep it in his pants

When people think of famous brothers from California it's surprising there are so many others

But you guys are ranked at number seventeen right behind the Menendez brothers

For forty years you used your hook and said Mom liked you the best

If I were your mom I'd make your dad pull out and come on my chest

It takes guts to sit where you are so I'll propose a toast

To Tom and Dickie Smothers for bringing dignity back to our Roast.

—TOM COTTER, SMOTHERS BROTHERS ROAST, 2003

● ● ● ●

A wino scraped together five dollars, bought and downed two bottles of Thunderbird, and passed out behind a hedge in a nearby park. Not long afterward a gay man strolled by and noticed him. "That's appealing," he thought to himself, and he rolled the wino over and fucked him. It was such a pleasant experience that he tucked five dollars in the drunk's pocket and went on his way.

When the wino woke up he was amazed to find that he still had money in his pocket. Hurrying over to the liquor store, he proceeded to spend it on wine and pass out in the same place, where the gay man found him on his way to lunch. Quite delighted, the man had another go at him and tucked another five-dollar bill in his pocket.

When he woke up this time, the wino could hardly believe his good fortune. Again he got drunk and passed out, and again the gay man found him and screwed him. But this time, in his enthusiasm, the grateful gay man tucked twenty dollars into the wino's pocket and went home.

When the wino came to, he pulled the twenty dollars out of his pocket. Clutching it tightly, he staggered to the liquor store and beckoned to the clerk. "Hey, buddy, get me some good wine off the shelf, cuz this cheap shit's killing my asshole."

"I remember the first time I used alcohol as a substitute for women."

"Yeah, what happened?"

"Well, um, I got my penis stuck in the neck of the bottle."

A man and a giraffe walk into a bar and they proceed to get blitzed. The giraffe drinks so much he passes out on the floor. The man gets up and heads for the door, at which point the bartender yells, "Hey! You can't leave that lyin' there!"

"That's not a lion! It's a giraffe."

● ● ● ●

Kelsey Grammer has been in and out of Betty Ford more times than Gerald Ford.

—Jeffrey Ross, Kelsey Grammer Roast, 1996

● ● ● ●

A woman walks into a bar with her five-pound Chihuahua and carefully places the little dog near her feet. She soon notices that the guy sitting next to her looks a little bit queasy. He's clutching his stomach and grimacing, and he's sweating profusely. After a few minutes the guy doubles over and vomits. Afterward, he notices the little dog struggling in the pool of vomit and says, "Whoa, I don't remember eating that!"

A guy walks into a bar with this really great shirt on. The bartender asks, "Where'd you get the great shirt?"

"David Jones."

A second guy walks into the bar with really good pants on and the bartender asks, "Where'd you get the great pants?"

"David Jones."

A third guy walks into the bar with really great shoes on. The bartender asks, "Where'd you get the great shoes?"

"David Jones."

Just then, some nut runs in naked. The bartender yells, "HEY! You can't come in here like that! Who the hell are you?"

"I'm David Jones!"

A FEW DIRTY WORDS FROM DICK CAPRI

I started out doing impressions. It took me years to learn to have a point of view and speak on a subject. And I find out I'm not speaking on one subject, I just get ten or twelve jokes and put them together and try to make a story out of them.

I never did blue jokes, I always did clean jokes. I only learned to do blue jokes when I would hear a joke and then tell it in a bar or at a golf tournament, where they expect to hear dirty jokes. That was weird for me because I went to the school of clean material. They would frown upon anybody who did anything dirty. So to break out of that and do a sex joke or a dirty joke, it was a little disconcerting.

If I did find a dirty joke I would try to clean it up for my act. But if you clean it up it doesn't work because there are certain words that you have to say to get the laugh. Instead of saying I fucked someone, I'd try "bedded." Well, bedded them is not as funny as when you fucked them.

But at a golf outing, I can safely tell a quadruple amputee joke. A quadruple amputee is lying on the beach. Now, the setup right there is funny to me, just the setup. Some people try to tell the joke and they say a paraplegic but a paraplegic in not funny, quadruple amputees are funny, I don't know why. So this quadruple amputee, he's lying on the beach and a woman walks over and she sees this poor guy lying there and she says to him, "Have you been hugged today?" And he says "No," and she gives him a hug and walks away. And then another woman walks over and sees this guy lying there and she says, "Have you been kissed today?" And he says, "No," so she kisses him and she walks away. Another woman walks by and she sees him lying there and she says, "Have you been fucked today?" And he says, "No," and she says, "Well, you're gonna get fucked because the tide comes in, in two minutes." Now, sometimes, if I think a crowd isn't ready for the word "fuck" I'll say, "Have you been screwed today?" And it still works.

At the Drew Carey Roast I said, "I envy Drew Carey, who's never had the horror of a divorce, because when I got divorced the first thing I did was put a tampon on top of the TV set to remind me of the cunt that took the VCR." Now, I told that joke to somebody and he said, "You've got to change it, you can't say VCR anymore." But DVD just didn't hit my ear. Besides they hear the other words in the joke and that's that, they're not listening for VCR or DVD or whatever. I never told that joke before and I was a little apprehensive about telling it in front of women. Then I rationalized it because they know it's going to be blue material at a Roast. Now I see some young guys, they're so used to going out there being really blue, but to me it's a novelty. "Cunt" is such a great word. They all remember that joke; it's become my signature joke. It makes me so proud. It's not what you can do for your country; it's what they can put in a joke book.

There are certain vulgarities that I don't do, like scatology for me is a little over the line. Incest is not funny to me at all. Not everyone can pull off telling dirty jokes; some people are more sensitive. They don't want the audience to think that that's the kind of person they are. But, you see, if you do it with a twinkle in your eye and they know that you're kidding around, then it's acceptable. You know I'm not serious; it's just jokes, ladies and gentlemen. There is a certain way to do it where they know you're only joking.

I did a joke: "My grandmother did all the cooking and she says to my grandpa, I'm not going to cook for you anymore, and he says if you don't cook for me you're not going to see me for three days. So she didn't cook for him and she didn't see him for three days. And after the fourth day she could see him a little bit out of her left eye."

I did that joke and women would come up to me and say that they didn't like that because the woman was beaten up. So I switched the joke around where the grandfather did all the cooking and HE says I'm not going to cook anymore and SHE says if you don't you won't see me for three days—it didn't hurt the joke.

I find my jokes all kinds of ways. Like the joke with the quadruple amputee, my dentist's secretary told me the joke. Usually it's an old crappy joke but that one I said, "That's a great joke, I'm gonna tell it, too." But I can hear them from anyplace.

Most comics talk about what they did, or "Did you ever notice this?" or "Did you ever notice that?" I don't do that. It doesn't work for me. I can't get a laugh on it, unless I'm sitting at a table with you and I have a drink and I tell you about what happened to me today, a personal thing like that, then I'll get a laugh. I want to tell a joke. The Friars is Roasting Don King, I don't want to talk about how big his dick is, everybody is going to talk about how big his dick is. I'll say I saw his dick and it looked like Gary Coleman's arm. I think that's funny.

I used to do a routine about a married priest. If I did it now it wouldn't mean anything because we have priests that leave and get married. But I did this routine on *The Merv Griffin Show.* I got tons of letters. It was about a married priest coming home after a tough day at the altar, and he calls to his wife, Trixie, and he asks, How's our son, Father Junior. He says, "I heard confessions today. People don't sin like they used to. It used to be so much fun to listen to." Things a husband says to his wife when he comes home from work, and here's a priest coming home and talking about his day. A lot of letters came in about it. It didn't help that I called it the NACP: The National Association for Collared People. It was bad. I should try to update it since priests are hot again.

In order to stand out, you've got to do your stuff with a lot of power. You can't be wishy-washy, and you've got to go out with no fear. You've got to go out there and kick a little balls. My delivery is Jack Benny. I try to do a nice, slow, deliberate delivery. If you're slow then you can pose a little bit. Posing is good. I watch the young people at Comedy Central and they're reading what's on the paper, they always bend over toward the microphone— you just lose timing when you do that. When you know that punch line is strong you just wait and then lay it into them. That's the way I do it. Everybody does it different, though.

A FEW DIRTY JOKES FROM DICK CAPRI

This guy picks up this girl in a bar, takes her into the backseat of his car, and she's blowing him and he reaches under her dress and he feels a cock and balls. So he leans down and he says, "When you're finished, we're going to have to talk."

This woman is cleaning her son's bedroom and she finds an S & M magazine. She runs to her husband and says, "I was cleaning our son's bedroom and I found an S & M magazine in his room. How are we going to discipline him?" And the father goes, "Well, we can't spank him."

● ●

This prospector comes down from the Klondike after prospecting for a year and a half in the mountains of Alaska. He comes into town and parks his donkey outside a bar. He goes into the bar and says to the bartender, "I'd like two bottles of beer and the toughest whore you got in Alaska!" The bartender puts the two bottles of beer in front of him and says, "Go up to room fourteen, knock on the door, and ask for Tilly. She's the toughest whore we got in Alaska." He takes his two bottles of beer and walks up the stairs, knocks on the door, door opens up, and this big woman says, "Yes?" He goes, "Are you Tilly?" She says, "Yes, I am." "I understand you're the toughest whore in Alaska." She says, "Yes, I am. Come on in." He goes in and closes the door. She turns around, puts her dress over her head, bends over, and grabs her ankles. He says, "What makes you think I want it like that?" She says, "I thought you might want to open those bottles first."

● ● ● ●

They say nobody knows who Susie Essman is; I know who she is. I met her a long time ago in Las Vegas. We did an act out there, we had a few drinks, we got a little shaky, and it was late at night. I walked her back to her room and if you knew Susie, like I know Susie... I said, "Susie, nobody here but me and you, how 'bout a blow job?" And she looked around, she thought about it, and she said, "Okay." Well, I must've sucked her dick for, oh, about an hour and a half.

—GEORGE WALLACE, JERRY STILLER ROAST, 1999

● ● ● ●

Drunk in a bar: "Hey, how about you and me go somewhere and fuck? I've got a coupla dollars and it looks like you could use a little money."

Young Lady: "What makes you think I charge by the inch?"

A guy walks into a bar with a dog under his arm, puts the dog on the bar, and announces that the dog can talk and that he has a hundred dollars he's willing to bet anyone who says he can't. The bartender quickly takes the bet and the guy turns to his dog and asks, "What's the thing on top of this building that keeps the rain from coming inside?"

"ROOF," answers the dog.

"Who are you kidding?" says the bartender. "I'm not paying."

The dog's owner says, "How about double or nothing and I'll ask him something else?"

"Well...okay."

The guy then turns to his dog and asks, "Who was the greatest ballplayer of all time?"

"RUTH," replies the dog.

With that, the bartender picks them both up and throws them out the door. As they hit the sidewalk the dog looks at his owner and says, "Do you think I should've said DiMaggio?"

Barry Levinson. What can you say about the guy who launched Paul Reiser's career except, "What the fuck were you thinking?"

—RICHARD BELZER, RICHARD BELZER ROAST, 2001

• • • •

A preacher goes into a bar and says, "Anybody who wants to go to heaven, stand up." Everybody stands up except for a drunk in the corner. The preacher says, "My son, don't you want to go to heaven when you die?"

"When I die? Sure. I thought you were taking a load up now."

A man walks into a bar and sees a good-looking, smartly dressed woman perched on a barstool. He walks up behind her and says, "Hi there, good looking, how's it going?"

She turns around, faces him, looks him straight in the eye and says, "Listen, I'll screw anybody, anytime, anywhere, your place, my place, it doesn't matter. I've been doing it ever since I got out of college. I just flat out love it."

"No kidding? I'm a lawyer, too! What firm are you with?"

A man walks into a bar with a steering wheel in his pants. The bartender says, "Okay, I'll bite. Why do have a steering wheel in your pants?"

"I don't know, but it's driving me nuts."

A woman in a bar says that she wants to have plastic surgery to enlarge her breasts. After a few more drinks her husband tells her, "Hey, you don't need surgery to do that. I know how you can do it without surgery."

"Oh yeah? How do I do it without surgery?"

"Just rub toilet paper between them."

"How does that make them bigger?"

"I don't know, but it worked for your ass."

A guy walks into a bar and orders a drink. After a few more he needs to go to the can. He doesn't want anyone to steal his drink so he puts a sign on it saying, "I spat in this beer, do not drink!" He returns a few minutes later to find another sign saying, "So did I!"

This really hot chick walks up to a bartender and says in a sexy, seductive voice, "May I please speak to your manager?"

"He's not here right now. Is there anything I can help you with?"

"I don't know if you're the man to talk to . . . It's kind of personal."

Thinking he might get lucky, the bartender says, "I'm pretty sure I can handle your problem, miss."

She looks at him with a sexy smile and playfully puts two of her fingers in his mouth. He begins sucking them, thinking, "I'm in!!!" After a few minutes she says, "Can you give the manager a message from me?"

The bartender nods.

"Tell him there's no toilet paper in the ladies' restroom."

• • • •

I drink a lot. I don't even like alcohol but I know it's a poison and I'm trying to build up an immunity.

—TOM COTTER, FRESH FUNNY FACES, 1999

• • • •

Pete is new in town, so he decides to go down to the local bar and make some friends. He walks in and reads a sign hanging over the bar that says FREE BEER FOR THE PERSON WHO CAN PASS THE TEST! So Pete asks the bartender about it.

"First you have to drink that whole gallon of pepper tequila, the whole thing at once, and you can't make a face while doing it. Second, there's an alligator out back with a sore tooth. You have to remove it with your bare hands. Third, there's a woman upstairs who's never had an orgasm. You gotta make things right for her."

"Well, as much as I would love free beer, I won't do it. You have to be nuts to drink a gallon of pepper tequila—and then it gets crazier from there."

As the night goes on and Pete downs a few drinks, he asks, "Where's zat teeqeelah?" He grabs the gallon of tequila with both hands and downs it with a big slurp, tears streaming down his face.

Next, he staggers out back and soon all the people inside hear the most frightening roaring and thumping, then silence. The man staggers back into the bar, his shirt ripped and big scratches all over his body.

"Now," he says, "Where zat woman with the sore tooth?"

• • • •

To many people, Alan King's name is synonymous with stand-up comedy. To many others, it's synonymous with open bar.

—JOY BEHAR, FREDDIE ROMAN ROAST, 1999

• • • •

Two drunks get thrown out of a bar, so they're walking down the street when they come across a dog sitting on the curb, licking his balls. They stand there watching and after a while one of them says, "I sure wish I could do that!"

"Well, I think I'd pet him first."

George is standing outside of his favorite bar, Sally's Legs. He's a little early, so he is waiting for it to open. A cop sees him loitering there and gets a little suspicious. "What are you doing?" asks the cop.

"I'm waiting for Sally's Legs to open so I can get a drink."

Two old drunks are sitting in a bar when the first one says, "Ya know, when I was thirty and got a hard-on, I couldn't bend it, even using both hands. By the time I was forty, I could bend it about ten degrees if I tried really hard. By the time I was fifty, I could bend it about twenty degrees, no problem. I'm gonna be sixty next week, and now I can bend it in half with just one hand."

"So," says the second drunk, "what's your point?"

"Well, I'm just wondering how much stronger I'm gonna get!"

O ne night a man is getting very drunk in a pub. He staggers back to the men's room to take a piss, whipping out his prick as he goes in the door. The problem is, he has wandered into the ladies' room by mistake, and surprises a woman sitting on the can.

"This is for ladies!" she screams.

"SO'S THIS," cries the drunk, waving his dick.

O ne night a police officer is staking out a particularly rowdy bar for potential drunk drivers. At closing time the patrons stagger out. He notices one guy stumble a couple of times, trip on the curb, and try his keys on five different cars before he finds the right one. Finally, he manages to start his engine and begins to pull away. The police officer is ready to pounce. He stops the driver, and administers a Breathalyzer test. The results show a reading of 0.0! The puzzled officer demands an explanation.

The driver replies, "Simple. Tonight, I'm the Designated Decoy."

● ● ● ●

How long have the Smothers Brothers been around? When they began, Alan King was in the early stages of alcoholism. Alan King's liver is so black and bloated that at this point it's the spitting image of Star Jones.

—SUSIE ESSMAN, SMOTHERS BROTHERS ROAST, 2003

● ● ● ●

A comparison between the two things men treasure most, beer and pussy: A beer is always wet. A pussy needs encouragement. A beer tastes horrible served hot. A pussy tastes better served hot. Twenty-four beers come in a box. A pussy is a box you can come in.

If you come home smelling like beer, your wife may get mad. If you come home smelling like pussy, she will kill you. It is socially acceptable to have a beer in the stands at a football game. You are a legend if you have a pussy in the stands at a football game. Pussy can make you see God. Beer can make you see the porcelain god.

Peeling labels off of beers is fun. Peeling panties off of pussy is more fun. If you try to snag a beer at work, you get fired. If you try to snag a pussy at work, you get hit with sexual harassment.

A man walks into a bar, sits down, and orders a beer. As he sips it, he hears a soothing voice say, "Nice tie!" He looks around, but the bar appears to be empty except for himself and the bartender, who is at the other end of the bar. He shrugs and sips his beer. A few minutes later he hears the same voice saying, "Beautiful shirt."

Concerned that he must be drinking his beer too fast, the man decides he needs a smoke, so he goes over to the cigarette machine. As he drops in his coins he hears a harsh voice say, "You ugly bastard!" He looks but there's still no one around. Then the nasty voice says, "Fuck off you ugly cocksucker!"

At this, the man calls the bartender over. "Hey, I must be losing my mind," he says. "I keep hearing these voices, one saying nice things, and one being really offensive—and there's not a soul in here but us."

"Ah," answered the bartender. "The peanuts, they're complimentary, but the cigarette machine is out of order."

• • • •

Billy Crystal couldn't make it in person. He's blowing a guy who looks like Whitey Ford.

—PAUL SHAFFER, RICHARD BELZER ROAST, 2001

• • • •

A guy walks into a bar carrying an eighteen-inch alligator. The bartender says, "What do think you're doing? Get that goddamn thing out of here. I don't allow pets in my establishment!" The guy tries to explain, "Look he won't cause any trouble. He's well trained and I'll prove it."

He puts the alligator on the bar and says, "Open." The alligator opens its mouth and you can see all of its razor-sharp teeth. "Now watch this," he says, and proceeds to take his dick out of his pants and lay it gently inside the alligator's gaping mouth. He then orders a beer and proceeds to drink it. All the while the alligator keeps its mouth open and nothing happens. After finishing the beer, the man gently removes his dick and puts it back into his pants. He then says, "Close," and the alligator closes its mouth.

"You see? He is perfectly trained. Does anyone else want to try it?"

After a minute or two, a drunk sitting at the end of the bar says, "Sure, I'd like to try. But I don't know if I can keep my mouth open that long."

A waitress walks up to one of her tables and is shocked to see three blond men all masturbating violently. "What the hell do you think you're doing?" she screams. Says one, "Well, it says on the menu, First Come, First Serve!"

A guy walks into a bar located at the top of a very tall building. He sits down, orders a pint, chugs it, walks over to the window, and jumps out. Five minutes later, the guy walks into the bar again, orders another pint, chugs it, walks over to the window, and jumps out again. Five minutes later, he reappears and repeats the whole thing.

Finally, one of the other patrons stops the guy and says, "Hey, how the hell are you doing that?!"

"Oh, it's just simple physics. When you chug that much beer, it makes you all warm inside and since warm air rises, if you just hold your breath you become lighter than air and float down to the sidewalk."

"WOW!" exclaims the second man. "I gotta try that!" So he orders a pint, chugs it, goes over to the window, jumps out, and splats on the sidewalk below.

The bartender says to the first guy, "Superman, you're such an asshole when you're drunk."

S o this guy walks into a bar and says to the bartender, "Give me two single whiskeys."

"Sure," says the bartender. "Do you want them both now or one at a time?"

"Oh, both now," replies the guy. "One's for me and one's for my little friend here." The guy proceeds to pull a three-inch-tall man out of his shirt pocket.

The bartender looks at the little man in amazement and asks, "Can he drink?"

"Sure," replies the guy, and with that the mini-man slugs back his whiskey.

"That's amazing," says the bartender. "What else can he do? Can he walk?"

"Sure!" says the guy, and he flips a quarter down to the other end of the bar and the little fella immediately runs down the bar and retrieves the coin, then jogs back to the guy.

"Well, now I've seen everything," says the bartender. "Can he talk?"

"Of course," says the guy. "Hey Jim, tell him about that time we were in Africa and you called that witch-doctor a motherfucker."

• • • •

The Friars Club is just a gay bar without all the good-looking guys.

—JOY BEHAR, DANNY AIELLO ROAST, 1997

• • • •

W hile the bar patron nursed a double martini, an attractive woman sat down next to him. The bartender served her a glass of orange juice, and the man turned to her and said, "This is a special day. I'm celebrating."

"I'm celebrating, too," she replied, clinking glasses with him.

"What are you celebrating?" he asked.

"For years I've been trying to have a baby. Today my gynecologist told me I'm pregnant!"

"Congratulations," the man said, lifting his glass. "As it happens, I'm a chicken farmer, and for years all my hens were infertile. But today they're finally fertile."

"How did it happen?"

"I switched cocks."

"What a coincidence," she said, smiling.

A straight guy walks into a bar and instantly realizes it's a gay bar. But what the hell, he figures, a drink is a drink. The bartender approaches him and asks, "What's the name of your penis?"

"Look, I'm not into any of that. All I want is a drink."

"I'm sorry, but I can't serve you until you tell me the name of your penis. Mine, for instance, is called Nike, for the slogan 'Just Do It.' That guy down at the end of the bar calls his Snickers because 'It really Satisfies.'"

The customer looks dumbfounded so the bartender tells him he will give him a minute or two to think it over. So the guy says to the man sitting to his left, "Hey bud, what's the name of your penis?"

The man smiles and says, "Timex."

"Why Timex?"

"'Cause it takes a lickin' and keeps on tickin'!'"

A little shaken, the customer then turns to the guy on his right and asks, "So, what do you call your penis?"

"Ford. 'Have you driven a Ford, lately?'"

Suddenly, a light comes into the customer's eyes. He turns to the bartender and says, "Okay, the name of my penis is Secret. Now give me my beer."

The bartender begins to pour the beer, but he can't help asking, "Why Secret?"

"Because it's STRONG ENOUGH FOR A MAN, BUT MADE FOR A WOMAN!"

• • • •

You know what really offends me about being Irish? No Irish salad dressing. French, Italian, Russian . . . no Irish. You know why? Because we just pour beer right onto the lettuce.

—Tom Cotter, Fresh Funny Faces, 1999

• • • •

Four guys are sitting in a bar having a few drinks, and one of them has a question for the others: "So tell me, what do you do to drive your wife wild?"

"Well," says the first guy, "after we make love, I go out to the garden and pick some roses. Then I take the petals off and sprinkle them all over her body and I blow them off with my soft, warm breath. That drives her wild."

The second guy says, "After my wife and I make love, I get some baby oil and massage it gently all over her body, and that drives her wild!"

The third guy says, "When me and the old lady are through, I jump out of bed and wipe my cock on the curtains. Drives her nuts!"

A man walks into a bar with an ostrich and a cat. The bartender walks over to them and says, "What can I get for you?"

The man says, "I'll have a beer."

The ostrich says, "I'll have a beer."

The cat says, "I'll have half a beer and I'm not buying."

So the bartender says, "Okay, that will be $3.87."

The man reaches into his pocket, brings out the exact change, and pays him.

About an hour later the bartender goes back over to them and says, "What'll you guys have?" Once again, the man orders a beer, the ostrich does the same, and the cat says, "I'll have half a beer and I'm not buying."

The bartender gets them their beers and says, "That'll be $3.87."

The man reaches into his pocket, brings out the exact change, and pays him.

A couple of days later they come back into the bar and the bartender asks, "What do you guys want today?"

The man says, "I'll have a scotch."

The ostrich says, "I'll have a bourbon."

The cat says, "I'll have half a beer and I'm not buying."

So the bartender says, "Okay, that will be $7.53."

The man reaches into his pocket, brings out the exact change, and pays him.

The bartender's curiosity has finally gotten the best of him. "How is it that you always have the exact change in your pocket?"

"I found a bottle with a genie in it and she granted me three wishes. My first wish was that I always have the exact change in my pocket for anything I want to buy."

"That's a great wish, better than asking for a million dollars. A million dollars will run out but that never will. What were your other two wishes?"

"That's where I screwed up. I asked for a chick with long legs and a tight pussy."

• • • •

I'm not saying Richard Belzer is a junkie. I will say that the first snowfall every year Richard's gotta take a big shit.

—PAUL SHAFFER, RICHARD BELZER ROAST, 2001

• • • •

A young man sits down at the bar. "What can I get you?" the bartender inquires.

"I want six shots of bourbon," responds the young man.

"Six shots? Are you celebrating something?"

"Yeah, my first blow job."

"Well, in that case, let me give you a seventh on the house."

"No offense, sir. But if six shots won't get rid of the taste, nothing will."

F our farmers were seated at the bar in a tavern. At the table next to them sat a young girl. The first man said, "I think it's WOOMB."

"No, it must be WOOOOMBH," said the second.

"You both have it wrong, it's WOOM," said the third.

"No, it has to be WOOMMMMBBB," said the fourth.

At this, the young lady couldn't stand it any longer. She got up, walked over to the farmers and said, "Look, you hayseeds, it's WOMB. That's it, that's all there is to it." Then she left.

Eventually, one of the farmers broke the silence by saying, "Well, I don't know. A slip of a girl like that, I'll bet she's never even HEARD an elephant fart!"

A guy came into a bar one day and said to the barman, "Give me six double vodkas."

"Wow! You must have had one hell of a day," said the barman.

"Yes, I've just found out my older brother is gay."

The next day the same guy came into the bar and asked for the same drinks. When the bartender asked what the problem was this time, the guy said, "I've just found out that my younger brother is gay, too!"

On the third day the guy came into the bar and ordered another six double vodkas. "Jesus!" said the bartender. "Doesn't anybody in your family like women?"

"Yeah, my wife!"

T he police arrested Malcolm Davidson, a twenty-seven-year-old white male resident of Wilmington, North Carolina, in a pumpkin patch at 11:38 p.m. on Friday. Davidson will be charged with lewd and lascivious behavior, public indecency, and public intoxication at the county courthouse on Monday. The suspect stated that, as he was passing a pumpkin patch, he decided to stop.

"You know, a pumpkin is soft and squishy inside, and there was no one around here for miles. At least I thought there wasn't," he stated in a phone interview from the county jail. Davidson went on to state that he pulled over to the side of the road, picked out a pumpkin that he felt was appropriate for his purposes, cut a hole in it, and proceeded to satisfy his "needs." "I guess I was just really into it, you know?" he commented with evident embarrassment.

In the process of the act, Davidson apparently failed to notice the Wilmington Municipal police car approaching and was unaware that he was being observed until Officer Brenda Taylor approached him.

"It was an unusual situation, that's for sure," said Officer Taylor. "I walked up to [Davidson] and he's . . . just working away at this pumpkin. I just went up and said, 'Excuse me sir, but do you realize that you are screwing a pumpkin?' He got real surprised as you'd expect and then looked me straight in the face and said, "A pumpkin? Damn . . . is it midnight already?""

T wo drunk gay guys are walking home from a bar when one of them says, "You're not going to believe this, but I think I smell penis."

"That's because I just burped."

• • • •

Hugh Hefner has always been a sexual innovator. He was the first person to mix Viagra with prune juice. Now he doesn't know if he's coming or going.

—JEFFREY ROSS, HUGH HEFNER ROAST, 2001

• • • •

T hree vampires walk into a bar and order drinks. The first vampire asks for blood. The second vampire asks for blood. The third vampire asks for some hot water.

The bartender is baffled. "Why don't you want blood like everyone else?"

"Because," says the third vampire, pulling out a used tampon, "I'm making tea."

Two buddies are sharing drinks while discussing their wives. "Does your wife ever, well, you know, does she, well, let you do it doggy style?" asks one.

"Well, not exactly," his friend replies. "She's more into the trick dog aspect of it."

"Oh, I see. Kinky stuff, huh?"

"Um...no. Whenever I make a move, she tends to roll over and play dead."

Late one night, a guy runs into a pub and demands a glass of water. He drinks it in one gulp, then asks for a second glass. Six pints later, he has recovered enough to speak. "Thanks," he croaks.

"That's one hell of a thirst you've got," says the bartender.

"Any man would be as bad if they'd just had sex with the woman in my car. She's insatiable. She wants me to go right back out there and do it all again, but I can't."

"Where's your car?" the bartender asks.

"At the roadside," the guy gasps.

"Tell you what," says the bartender, "you watch the bar for me and I'll run out and take your place."

"Be my guest," the guy says. So the bartender goes outside and gets in the car. It's totally dark, so the woman doesn't realize she's with a different man and they get right down to it.

Five minutes later there's a knock on the window. It's a cop, and he shines his flashlight on the naked couple. "What's going on here?" he asks.

"It's all right, officer," explains the bartender, "She's my wife."

"Oh, sorry sir, I didn't realize."

"Neither did I—till you switched on that damned light."

I'm half-Irish and half-Scottish which means I like to get really drunk and wear a skirt.

—TOM COTTER, FRESH FUNNY FACES, 1999

• • • •

A man is sitting in a bar and he notices two lovely women across the way. He calls the bartender over and says, "I'd like to buy those two ladies a drink."

"It won't do you any good," replies the bartender.

"It doesn't matter, I want to buy those women a drink."

The bartender delivers the drinks to the ladies and they acknowledge the gift with a nod of their heads. About a half-hour later, the man approaches the women and says, "I'd like to buy you two another drink."

"It won't do you any good," they reply in tandem.

"I don't understand. What do you mean it won't do me any good?"

"We're lesbians," says the first lady.

"Lesbians? What are lesbians?"

"Lesbians," repeats the second. "You know—we like to lick pussies."

Says the man, "Bartender, three beers for us lesbians."

E very night after dinner Harry took off for the local watering hole. He would spend the whole evening there and arrive home drunk around midnight. He usually had trouble getting his key to fit the keyhole and couldn't get the door open. His wife would go to the door and let him in, and then proceed to yell and scream at him for his behavior and constant drunkenness.

One day, the distraught wife was talking to a friend about her husband's nocturnal activities. The friend listened sympathetically and said, "Why don't you treat him a little differently when he comes home? Instead of berating him, why don't you welcome him home with some loving words and a kiss? Then, he might change his ways."

The wife, willing to try anything, agreed that this might be a good idea.

That night, Harry took off again after dinner. And at about midnight, he arrived home in his usual condition. His wife heard him at the door, quickly opened it, and let Harry in. Instead of berating him as she had always done, she took his arm and led him into the living room. She sat him down in an easy chair, put his feet up on the footstool, and took his shoes off. Then, she sat on his lap and cuddled him a little. After a while, she whispered, "Honey, it's pretty late. I think we should go upstairs to bed now."

"Hell, I guess we might as well," Harry replied. "I'll get in trouble when I get home anyway!"

● ● ● ●

I love the Friars Roasts. They're the only place where someone can call me a cunt and it's a compliment.

—SUSIE ESSMAN, RICHARD BELZER ROAST, 2001

● ● ● ●

A woman walks into a tattoo parlor. "Do you do custom work?" she asks the artist.

"Why, of course!"

"Good. I'd like a portrait of Robert Redford on the inside of my right thigh, and a portrait of Paul Newman on the inside of my left thigh. And I want them both looking at my pussy."

"No problem," says the artist. "Strip from the waist down and get up on the table."

After two hours of hard work, the artist finishes. The woman sits up and examines the tattoos. "That doesn't look like them!" she complains loudly.

"Oh, yes it does," the artist says indignantly, "and I can prove it. Let's get an impartial observer to decide." With that, he runs out of the shop and grabs the first man off the street he can find; it happens to be the town drunk.

"Well, what do you think?" the woman asks the man, spreading her legs apart. "Do you know who these men are?"

The drunk studies the tattoos for a couple of minutes and says, "I'm not sure who the guys on either side are, but the fellow in the middle is definitely Willie Nelson!"

A guy had too much to drink at a party and, the following morning, he woke up on the sidewalk. The last thing he remembered about the party was that there had been a golden toilet. Determined to find out exactly where he'd been, the fellow knocked on the door of every home on the street, asking the homeowners if they had a golden toilet. Everyone said no and quickly shut the door.

Finally, he got to the house at the end of the block. "Excuse me, sir, but would you happen to have a golden toilet?" he asked.

The man at the door got angry. "I remember you! I threw you out on your ear last night, after you took a shit in my tuba!"

A man went into a bar after work one day, and after a beer or two, he noticed a man passed out in the corner. An hour later, the fellow was still very drunk and incoherent, so, being a nice guy, the first man decided to take him home. He looked up the drunk's name and address in his wallet, then started struggling to get the man out to his car. He tried to coax the man to walk, but to no avail—the man just could not stand up.

Dragging, heaving, and finally carrying the man, our hero finally reached his car. He drove to the man's house and then, again, lugged him to the front door. The Good Samaritan rang the bell, and the door was promptly opened by a pleasant-looking woman.

"Oh. Thank you so much for bringing him home," she said. "But, where's his wheelchair?"

T he town drunk staggered into the neighborhood whorehouse, threw some money on the table, and slurred, "Hey, barkeep! Gimme a hooker!"

All the prostitutes were busy with clients, but the owner of the establishment figured that this wino was too drunk to differentiate between a real girl and an inflatable doll. So he instructed one of his employees to blow up the inflatable love toy they kept in the back for emergencies, put it on an empty bed, and escort the drunk to the room.

A few minutes later the drunk staggered back to the lobby, looking completely confused.

"So, buddy, did you have a good time?" the owner asked with a wink.

"I dunno what happened!" the wino cried. "I bit her tit, she farted, and flew right out the window!"

What is the difference between a fox and a pig?

About five drinks.

• • • •

What kind of man reads *Playboy*? I don't know. My guess is whoever's shitting.

—ADAM CAROLLA, HUGH HEFNER ROAST, 2001

• • • •

What's the difference between a straight man and a gay man?

About six beers.

Two guys in a bar are chatting about what they do for a living. One says, "I've got this job in a circus where I have to clean up the elephant. You know, hose him down three times a day, clean up his shit all day long, stuff like that. The smell of that shit—phew! It's so bad, it really gets me down sometimes."

His companion says, "Well, if you can't stand the smell and the rest of the work, why don't you quit?"

"What? And leave show business?"

A guy is sitting in a bar getting bored, looking to strike up a conversation. He turns to the bartender and says, "Hey, about those Democrats in Congress..."

"STOP pal—I don't allow talk about politics in my bar!" interrupted the bartender.

A few minutes later the guy tries again: "You know what some people say about the pope?"

"NO religion talk, either," the bartender cuts in.

One more try to break the boredom: "This year, I really thought the Yankees would..."

"NO sports talk. That's how fights start in bars!" the barman says.

"Look, how about sex. Can I talk to you about sex?"

"Sure, that we can talk about any time," replies the barkeep.

"GREAT... GO FUCK YOURSELF!"

● ● ● ●

Hugh, if you lined up all the pussy you've ever had end to end, I figured this out, you would have a really long line of stinky pussy.

—SARAH SILVERMAN, HUGH HEFNER ROAST, 2001

● ● ● ●

A police officer pulls over a guy who's been weaving in and out of the lanes. He goes up to the guy's window and says, "Sir, I need you to blow into this Breathalyzer tube."

"Sorry, officer, I can't do that. I am an asthmatic. If I do that, I'll have a really bad asthma attack."

"Okay, fine. I need you to come down to the station to give a blood sample, then."

"I can't do that either. I am a hemophiliac. If I do that, I'll bleed to death."

"Well, then, we need a urine sample."

"I'm sorry, officer, I can't do that either. I am also a diabetic. If I do that, I'll get really low blood sugar."

"All right! Then I need you to come out here and walk this white line."

"I can't do that, officer."

"Why not?"

"Because I'm drunk."

A man who smells like a distillery flops on a subway seat next to a priest. The man's tie is stained, his face is plastered with red lipstick, and a half-empty bottle of gin is sticking out of his torn coat pocket. He opens up a crumpled newspaper and begins scanning the pages. After a few minutes he turns to the priest and asks, "Say, Father, what causes arthritis?"

"Mister, it's caused by loose living, being with cheap, wicked women, indulging in too much alcohol, and showing general contempt for your fellow man."

"Well, I'll be damned!" the drunk mutters, returning to his paper.

The priest, fearing that he'd been too harsh, nudges the man and apologizes. "I'm very sorry. I didn't mean to come on so strong. How long have you had arthritis?"

"I don't have it, Father. I was just reading here that the pope does."

Five guys are in a bar getting pretty sloshed when they start to discuss the size of their penises. Soon the conversation escalates into a full-blown argument, each man insisting that his penis is the biggest. "Put them on the bar so we can compare," suggests the bartender.

The drunks do just that. Shortly, a gay man comes in, looks around, and says to the bartender, "I think I'll have the buffet."

Young Billy the Kid wants to be the best, most feared gunfighter in the Old West, and when he spots Doc Holliday having a beer in a saloon, he asks if he could have a word with him.

"Sure, son, what's on your mind?" asks Doc, looking up at the young man.

"Sir, I want to be the best gunfighter there is, and I'd be in your debt if you'd give me a lesson or two," says Billy.

"Well, the first thing I'd do," says Doc, "is tie the bottom of your holster to your leg so your pistol don't get caught in it when you draw."

Billy does as suggested, whips out his pistol, and shoots the string tie off the guy playing the piano. "Hey, you were right, Doc," says Billy. "What else?"

"If you cut a notch in the top of your holster where the hammer hits, your gun will come out smoother," suggests Doc.

Billy does as Doc recommends, draws again and shoots a cufflink off the piano player. "This is great, Doc," says the delighted Billy. "Anything more?"

"One more thing," says Doc. "Get that tub of lard over there and rub it all over your pistol."

"You mean so it'll slide out of the holster faster?" says young Billy.

"No, so when Wyatt Earp gets done playing the piano and shoves your gun up your ass, it won't hurt as much."

T wo women friends are having a Girls' Night Out, and have been decidedly overenthusiastic on the cocktails. Weaving their way home, they realize that they need to pee. They're near a graveyard—so they decide to do their business behind a headstone.

The first woman has nothing to wipe with so she takes off her panties, uses them, and throws them away. Her friend, however, is wearing a rather expensive pair and doesn't want to ruin hers. She manages to salvage a large ribbon from a wreath on one of the graves and proceeds to wipe herself with that. Soon, they're heading for home.

The next day the first woman's husband phones the other husband and says, "These damn girls' nights out have got to stop. My wife came home last night without her panties."

"That's nothing," says the other husband. "Mine came back with a card stuck between the cheeks of her ass that said, "From All of Us at the Fire Station, We'll Never Forget You.""

A guy who owns a piano bar just can't find a decent piano player. He puts a "Help Wanted" sign in his front window, and on occasion someone auditions, but he never hears anyone he thinks is good enough to hire. Then one day, out of the blue, a disheveled man stumbles into the bar, sits down at the piano, and plays the most beautiful song imaginable. Flabbergasted, the bar owner exclaims, "That was amazing! What's the name of that song?"

The unkempt man shrugs his shoulders. "It's a little ditty I made up. It's called, 'I Fucked a Whore on Sunday and Came on Her Face.'"

The owner is shocked by the title, but before he can say anything the man plays another song—this one more beautiful than the last.

"What a wonderful song!" the owner says. "What's the name of that one?"

"I call it, 'I Took a Shit and Forgot to Wipe My Ass.'"

"Look, you're an amazing piano player and I'm going to hire you—but on two conditions. First, you must wear a tuxedo and second, don't tell anyone the names of your songs!"

The pianist agrees and, before too long, the piano bar is the hottest spot in town. Hundreds of people flock in nightly for a few drinks and some beautiful music. One day, during his break, the pianist goes to the bathroom and walks out having forgotten to zip his fly. As he gets ready to sit back down at the piano, one of the patrons taps him on the shoulder and says, "Hey, buddy, do you know you just took a leak and left your dick sticking out?"

"Know it?" the pianist exclaims. "I wrote it!"

A n extremely drunk man looking for a whorehouse stumbles into a podiatrist's office instead and weaves over to the receptionist. Without looking up, she waves him over to the examination bed and says, "Stick it through that curtain."

Looking forward to something kinky, the drunk pulls out his penis and sticks it through the crack in the curtains. "That's not a foot!" screams the receptionist.

"Holy shit, lady. I didn't know you had a minimum!"

CHAPTER 4

Animal Crackers

Beauties, beasts—
the animals are running the zoo.

Mr. Bear and Mr. Rabbit didn't like each other very much. One day, while walking through the woods, they came across a golden frog. They were amazed when the frog talked to them. The golden frog admitted that he didn't often meet anyone, but when he did, he always gave them six wishes. He told the bear and the rabbit that they could have three wishes each.

Mr. Bear immediately wished that all the other bears in the forest were females. The frog granted his wish. Mr. Rabbit, after thinking for a while, wished for a crash helmet. One appeared immediately, and he placed it on his head. Mr. Bear was amazed at Mr. Rabbit's wish, but carried on with his second wish, which was that all the bears in the neighboring forests were females as well. The frog granted his wish.

Mr. Rabbit then wished for a motorcycle. It appeared before him, and he climbed on board and started revving the engine. Mr. Bear complained that Mr. Rabbit had wasted two wishes that he could have had for himself. Shaking his head, Mr. Bear made his final wish, that all the other bears in the world were females as well, making him the only male bear in the world. "So let it be done," said the frog.

At that point they both turned to Mr. Rabbit, curious as to what his last wish might be. Mr. Rabbit revved the engine, thought for a second, then said, "I wish that Mr. Bear was gay!" and he rode off as fast as he could!

A dog, a cat, and a penis are sitting around a campfire one night. The dog says, "My life sucks—my master makes me do my business on a fire hydrant!"

The cat says, "You think that's bad? My master makes me do my business in a box of sand."

Outraged, the penis says, "At least your master doesn't put a bag over your head and make you do push-ups until you throw up!"

● ● ● ●

The shark must be the stupidest animal in the world. Can't he figure out to swim, like, a foot lower on the approach? When is he going to realize that that fin is tipping everybody off?

—RUSS MENEVE, TAX RELIEF COMEDY NIGHT, 2002

● ● ● ●

An army camp in India is assigned a new commander. During his first inspection everything checks out except one thing: there is a camel tied to a tree on the edge of the camp. The commander asks what it's for.

One of the soldiers who has been stationed there for a while explains that the men sometimes get lonely since there are no women in camp, so they have the camel.

The commander decides to let it go. After a few weeks he is feeling pretty horny himself, so he orders the men to bring the camel to his tent and he goes to work on it. After about an hour the commander comes out zipping up his pants and says, "So, is that how the other men do it?"

One of the men responds, "No, we usually just use the camel to ride into town."

Little Red Riding Hood was on her way to see her grandmother. Her mother warned her, "Don't walk through the forest; take the path, or else the Big Bad Wolf will catch you and suck your tits dry!"

Little Red started toward her grandmother's house but the path was so long and winding that she decided to take the shortcut through the forest, in spite of her mother's warning.

The turtle stopped Little Red and said, "Turn back and use the path, because if the Big Bad Wolf finds you, he'll suck your tits dry!"

But Little Red was almost there so she kept going through the forest. Sure enough, the Big Bad Wolf jumped out of nowhere and snarled, "Take off your shirt, Little Red Riding Hood—I'm gonna suck your tits dry!"

"Oh, no you don't!" yelled Little Red, as she pulled up her skirt. "You're gonna eat me just like the story says!"

This guy has a twenty-five-inch dick. He goes to a witch in the woods and asks her if she can make it smaller because he just can't please the ladies. It is just too big, and he hasn't found a lady yet who can stand it. He just can't get any pleasure. The witch tells him to go into the woods, find a frog, and ask the frog to marry him. If the frog says no, his cock will shrink five inches.

He goes into the woods and finds the frog. He asks, "Frog, will you marry me?"

The frog says "No," and his prick shrinks five inches. The guy thinks to himself, "Wow, that was pretty cool. But, it's still too big." So he goes back to the frog and again asks, "Frog, will you marry me?"

Frog says, "No, I won't marry you."

The guy's dick shrinks another five inches. But it's still fifteen inches, which is still just a little bit too big. Ten inches would be just great. So once again he asks the frog, "Will you marry me?"

Frog says, "How many times do I have to tell you, NO, NO, NO!!!"

A city doctor moved to the country to become a farmer. He figured, "Since I'm going to have a farm, I might as well have animals on it." So he got in his truck to go looking for animals. Along the way, he spotted a sign saying, "Cocks 4 Sale." He pulled over and asked the farmer what a cock was. "A cock is a rooster," the farmer replied. So the doctor bought a cock and put it in the back of his truck.

The doctor continued on his way until he saw a sign saying, "Pullets 4 Sale." He pulled over and asked the farmer what a pullet was. "A pullet is a hen," the farmer replied. "But sometimes a cock and a pullet will fight, so watch out."

The doctor thanked the farmer and went on his merry way. Down the road a bit, there was another sign saying, "Asses 4 Sale." So the doctor pulled over again to ask about it. "An ass is a donkey," the farmer told him. "But watch out, because this donkey is different. If he gets scared, he'll sit down and won't move until you scratch his belly."

The doctor thanked the farmer and turned around to head home. In the road was a broken bottle and the doctor ran his truck right over it. Pop!!! The sound made the cock and pullet start to fight, and the donkey sat on the spare tire. A lady just happened to be passing by and asked if the doctor needed help. The doctor, wanting to sound like a professional farmer, replied, "Yes, I need help. Will you please hold my cock and pullet while I scratch my ass?"

Two men and one woman, along with their dogs, are in a vet's waiting room. The first man's dog asks the second man's dog what he's there for.

"They are putting me down."

"Oh, no!" says the first dog. "Why?"

"Well, I've been chasing the postman for years. Yesterday, I finally caught him and bit him. So, I'm going to be put to sleep."

"Well, my master just completely remodeled the inside of his house. I didn't like it because my scent wasn't anywhere anymore. So, when he went to bed last night I pissed on everything I could find. This morning, he found out what I had done so he is putting me to sleep also."

The third dog says, "This is my master's new girlfriend. She runs around the house all the time without her clothes. This makes me very horny. So this morning, after she got out of the shower and was bending over to wipe up the water on the floor, I couldn't stand it anymore, so I jumped on her and gave it to her good!"

"So, that's why they are putting you to sleep?" asks the first dog.

"No, she just brought me in to get my toenails clipped!"

● ● ● ●

My neighbor was walking his dog this morning, it's the strangest-looking dog. He told me it's a combination of a pit bull and a poodle. Isn't that disgusting? I told him that's not a mixed breed, it's a rape.

—DEBBIE PEARLMAN, FRIARS NEW FACES OF COMEDY, 2002

● ● ● ●

A guy was riding through the desert on his camel. He had been traveling so long that he felt really horny. There were no women in the desert, so the man turned to his camel—but every time he tried to have sex with his camel, the animal ran away. The man had no choice but to run after the camel, get back on, and start to ride again.

After crossing the entire desert, still feeling frustrated, the man came to a road. There was a broken-down car sitting there with three voluptuous and beautiful blondes sitting in it. He asked the women if they needed any help.

The hottest girl said, "If you fix our car, we will do anything you want."

Luckily, the man knew a thing or two about cars and fixed it in a flash. When he finished, the three girls asked, "How can we ever repay you?"

After thinking it over for a few minutes, the man replied, "Could you hold my camel?"

One winter, two little fleas headed for the warm, sunny beaches of California to escape the cold. The first flea got there and started rubbing suntan lotion on his little flea arms and his little flea legs. Just then, the second flea arrived, shivering and shaking. The first flea asked, "What the hell happened to you?"

"I just rode out here on a biker's mustache and I'm so very colddddd!"

"Don't you know the special trick to getting here? You go to the airport, go straight to the ladies room, wait for a pretty young stewardess to come along, and when she sits down you climb right up in there where it's nice and warm."

The second flea agreed that this was a great idea. The next winter came along and it was time for the fleas to head for the sunny beaches again. The first flea arrived and began putting suntan lotion on his little flea arms and his little flea legs. About that time, the second flea arrived, again shivering and shaking, and mumbling about how cold he was. The first flea cried, "What happened? Didn't you try that trick I taught you about getting here nice and warm?"

"I did just as you said. I went to the ladies room and this pretty stewardess came in and sat down, so I climbed right up in there and it was so very warm. Next thing I knew, we stopped at a bar and I fell asleep. All of a sudden I woke and there I was, right back on that biker's mustache!"

A man is driving down an Alaskan road and his car breaks down. He phones the Alaskan Mobile Fixit Service and they arrive shortly after. The service man opens the hood and after a while says, "It looks like you've blown a seal."

The man replies, "No . . . that's just frost on my mustache."

Tarzan had been living alone in the jungle for thirty years with only apes for company and suitably shaped holes in trees for sex. Jane, a reporter, came to Africa in search of this legendary figure. Deep in the wilds she came to a clearing and discovered Tarzan vigorously thrusting into a jungle oak. She watched in awe for a while.

Finally, overcome by this display of animal passion, Jane came out into the open and offered herself to him. As she reclined on the wild grass, Tarzan ran up and gave her a big kick in the crotch. In pain, she screamed, "What the hell did you do that for?"

"Always check for squirrels."

Jerzy and Latvia are bored one day and decide to go to the zoo and taunt the gorillas. As they make faces at the apes, they don't notice that one of the animals is getting quite turned on by Latvia's tits. All of a sudden, the ape reaches through the bars, grabs hold of Latvia's blouse, and pulls her into his cage.

"What should I do!?" she screams at Jerzy, as the gorilla tears off her skirt and starts to fondle her.

"I dunno. Tell him what you tell me all the time, that you have a headache."

A male and a female whale are swimming off the coast of Japan when they notice a whaling ship. The male recognizes it as the same ship that had harpooned his father many years earlier. He says to the female, "Let's both swim under the ship and blow out of our air holes at the same time. This should make the ship turn over and sink."

They try it and, sure enough, the ship capsizes and quickly sinks. Soon, however, the whales realize that the sailors have jumped overboard and are swimming to the safety of shore. The male is enraged that they are going to get away and tells the female, "Let's swim after them and gobble them up before they reach the shore." But the female is reluctant to follow him.

"Look," she says, "I went along with the blow job, but I absolutely refuse to swallow the seamen."

Once upon a time in a faraway land, a beautiful, independent, self-assured princess happened upon a frog while contemplating ecological issues on the shores of an unpolluted pond in a verdant meadow near her castle. The frog hopped into the princess's lap and said, "Elegant lady, I was once a handsome prince until an evil witch cast a spell upon me. One kiss from you, however, and I will turn back into the dapper young prince that I am, and then, my sweet, we can marry and set up housekeeping with my mother in your castle, where you can prepare my meals, clean my clothes, bear my children, and feel forever grateful doing so."

That night, as the princess dined sumptuously on a repast of lightly sautéed frogs legs seasoned in a wine-and-onion cream sauce, she chuckled to herself and thought: I don't fucking think so.

● ● ● ●

Paul Shaffer, you look great tonight. You look like Doc Severinsen fucked a turtle.

—JEFFREY ROSS, RICHARD BELZER ROAST, 2001

● ● ● ●

A farmer has about two hundred hens but no rooster—and he wants chicks. So he goes down the road to the next farm and asks his neighbor if he has a rooster. The other farmer says, "Yeah, I've got this great rooster, named Randy; he'll service every chicken you've got. No problem."

Well, Randy the rooster is expensive, but the farmer decides the investment will pay off, so he buys Randy, takes him home, and sets him down in the barnyard. He gives the rooster a pep talk: "Randy, I want you to pace yourself now. You've got a lot of chickens to service here and you cost me a lot of money and I'll need you to do a good job. So, take your time and have some fun."

Randy seems to understand, so the farmer points towards the hen house and Randy takes off like a shot. WHAM—he nails every hen in there THREE or FOUR times, and the farmer is just shocked. Randy runs out of the henhouse and sees a flock of geese down by the lake. WHAM—he screws all the geese. Randy then visits the pigeon coop. He wanders down to the pasture to visit the cows. Randy is jumping on every animal the farmer owns.

The farmer is distraught, worried that his expensive rooster won't even last the day. Sure enough, the next day the farmer finds Randy dead as a doorknob in the middle of the yard. Buzzards are circling overhead.

The farmer, saddened by the loss of such a valuable and impressive animal, shakes his head and says, "Oh, Randy, I told you to pace yourself. I tried to get you to slow down, now look what you've done to yourself."

Randy opens one eye, nods toward the sky and says, "Shhh. They're getting closer."

O ne afternoon a farmer is telling his neighbor how to screw a sheep. "The trick," he whispers, "is to sneak up behind her, grab hold of her rear legs, spread 'em and lift 'em up to your dick."

"That sounds easy enough . . . but how do you kiss her?"

T here are three flies in a jar, two females and one male. One of the females asks the male, "Do you know a way to get out?"

"Suck my dick and I'll tell you."

So she does it, and the male fly tells her to fly up to the top of the jar and hit the lid real hard. She follows his directions and falls back down to the bottom of the jar, dead.

The second female fly then says to the male, "Please, you must tell me how to get out of here!"

"Suck my dick and I'll tell you."

She does as he asks, and the male fly tells her to fly up to the top of the jar and hit the lid two times, really hard. She does it and falls to the bottom of the jar, dead.

Want to know how the male fly got out? Suck my dick and I'll tell you.

A man is telling a story: I was playing golf, and even though I am usually a pretty good player, I was playing horribly that day. As I was about to tee off at the fourth hole I heard a voice say, "Three wood."

I looked around and no one was behind me so I took my stance. Then, once again, I heard, "Three wood."

I looked down and there was a frog at the corner of the tee box, and he was telling me to use my three wood. This seemed crazy, but I was playing so badly that I figured nothing could hurt me so I took out my three wood. It was a long par four and I hit the ball straight two hundred and fifty yards with that three wood! The frog seemed to be lucky, so I picked him up and took him along with me.

At the next hole he told me to use my five iron. It was a par three and I got my first hole-in-one ever. I made at least a birdie on all the rest of the holes, and all I had to do was listen to that frog.

That night I took the frog to the casino in my hotel. We played roulette. I put my money where the frog told me to and I won on every spin of the wheel. After that I was tired so I went up to bed. I took the frog out of my pocket and put it on the dresser. Suddenly it looked at me and said, "Kiss me."

Now, I'm not the type that goes around kissing frogs, but he said it again. So I kissed the frog and he turned into the most beautiful fifteen-year-old girl you have ever seen in your entire life. And that, your honor, is how that underage girl ended up in my hotel room.

A FEW DIRTY WORDS FROM STEWIE STONE

I had to work up to being blue because for years the only place you could be dirty was at a Roast. I come from the generation of comedians where you had to be ultraclean. You couldn't make a living if you were dirty. There were certain comics that were "blue comics." Redd Foxx was always a blue comic. They said Lenny Bruce was blue, but in the scheme of things he was never that blue. He talked about adult subject matter, but he wasn't technically blue.

Redd Foxx was always successful but when *Sanford and Son* hit he would work commercial venues and people were in shock when they heard his act. They expected a sweet little old man, a grandfather. They were walking out going, "Who is this guy?" They didn't know he had all of these X-rated albums. He would always do midnight shows, which were ultra-X-rated, and people mobbed to come in and see him.

It took me a lot of years to call somebody a cocksucker. It took a lot of years to say "fuck you" onstage because it wasn't in my repertoire. Alan King once told me, if you needed "fuck" at the end of a joke, you didn't have a joke. So I said to him, "Fuck you." But at a Roast, "fuck you" IS a joke. You can get away with it but you can't make a living doing Roasts.

I talk about the subject matter. For example, "If Donald Trump's father wasn't born first he'd be a fuckin' waiter at this affair." At the Smothers Brothers Roast I said, "Tommy Smothers looks like he should be on a ventriloquist's knee. If you can put your hand up his ass you can make him talk."

It was shocking to hear Jack Benny say "fuck you" to somebody at a Friars Roast, but now it's not shocking to hear anything. What makes the Roast great is to be able to say something to somebody that everybody would love to say. Everybody would love to tell the boss, "Go fuck yourself." Everybody would love to walk up to the president of the United States and say, "Hey Bush, you're a cocksucker." At a Roast you can do it and it's funny. All gloves are off. Everybody would love to tell Donald Trump, "You're an ass-hole," but you can't do it anywhere in the world but at a Roast. It's a great feeling. It's a great weapon. It's one of the great get-even things in life.

I bought my co-op from a very wealthy real estate guy and he screwed me out of twenty-three thousand dollars on the deal. I've always been mad at this guy and I couldn't get even with him because my wife wanted the co-op and I had to buy it and eat the twenty-three thousand dollars. Since the deal was made, I've done a lot of charity auctions and Roasts and he's always in the audience. I always work this guy over. "There's the rat bastard that screwed me out of twenty-three thousand dollars. This motherfucker, with all your money, stick it up your ass, you lying bastard," and the people laugh and they think it's so funny—but I'm being honest. He will come up to me and say, "When is this gonna end?" and I say, "When you give me the twenty-three thousand dollars back." So, isn't it a great weapon? Think about it. People will laugh when you're telling the truth.

I think it was Redd Foxx who said there was always integration but never during the day. The people that get uptight about this kind of humor are full of shit; they come in wanting to get uptight. I don't think they're insulted by it. One of the greatest comics ever was Richard Pryor. When I went to see Richard work, I never heard the dirty words because he was talking about his life and it was in context. He was saying the dirty words but I didn't hear them, it was him being Richard. Now, Bill Cosby wouldn't call somebody a motherfucker; it would have been dirty and shocking if he did, because it wasn't his lifestyle. I know that Andrew Dice Clay's biggest fans were women, not men—women. They loved it—"Suck my cock; I'll put my balls on your chin..."

The greatest one at a Roast was Milton Berle. He was sensational because he was rapid-fire; he was totally irreverent and funny. He was always considered edgy. When I first started working up in the mountains and watching Buddy Hackett, he was always wild but he became dirty later on in years. Somebody once asked him why he was dirty and he said, "I took shit and turned it into a million dollars." He liked shocking people; it was his fun. I think he had problems with that, I think a lot of people walked out and said, what does he need that shit for, but he was a star. The difference between being a star and an unknown is four seconds. When you're a star you have four seconds longer to get to the punch line. When you're an unknown they'll say, "Would you hurry this shit up, already?" Comedy is a very intellectual business.

Ten years ago I would do jokes about Reagan, they laughed, nobody gave a shit. Today, you do a line about Bush and four guys will boo you: "That's our president! You're talking about our president!" They want to change the laws, they want to censor television, they want to throw Janet Jackson in jail, and Howard Stern has to go on Sirius radio because he can't do whatever it is. Where's the First Amendment? Where's freedom of speech?

I walked out on stage at Brigham Young University and my opening joke was, "I want to give my impression of a Mormon comedian: 'Take my wife, take my wife, take my wife...'" They thought that was so unfunny and were so offended by it I could never get them back. It was one of the worst shows I ever did. They just said, "Who the fuck are you?" If a singer bombs he can say, well, the band sucked, but if a comic dies, it's 'They didn't like ME.' There's no cop-out as a comic. I think comedy is the only pure art form.

W hy do dogs lick their balls?

Because they can.

An old lady is rocking away the last of her days on her front porch, reflecting on her long life, when all of a sudden a fairy godmother appears in front of her and informs her that she will be granted three wishes.

"Well, now," says the old lady, "I guess I would like to be really, really rich." POOF—her rocking chair turns to solid gold.

She smiles and says, "Gee, I guess I wouldn't mind being a young, beautiful princess." POOF—she turns into a beautiful young woman.

"Your third wish?" asks the fairy godmother.

Just then the old woman's cat wanders across the porch in front of them. "Ooh . . . can you change him into a handsome prince?" she asks. POOF—there before her stands a young man more handsome than anyone could possibly imagine.

She stares at him, smitten. With a smile that makes her knees weak, he saunters across the porch and whispers in her ear, "Bet you're sorry you had me neutered!"

●　●　●　●

This is my first Roast, and I'm very nervous. This morning I could feel tension mounting. Tension is my dog.

—TOM COTTER, SMOTHERS BROTHERS ROAST, 2003

●　●　●　●

A guy is walking down the street with some chicken wire under his arm. His neighbor sees him and asks what he has. The guy replies, "It's chicken wire and I'm going to catch some chickens."

"You fool, you can't catch chickens with chicken wire."

Later that night, the neighbor sees the guy walking down the street dragging twelve chickens.

The next day he sees him walking down the street with some duct tape under his arm. Once again he asks what the guy is up to. The guy says he has some duct tape and he is going to catch some ducks.

"You fool, you can't catch ducks with duct tape."

Sure enough though, later that night, the neighbor sees the guy walking down the street dragging twelve ducks behind him.

The next day, he sees the guy walking down the street with something else under his arm. He asks what it is.

"It's pussy willow."

"Hold on, let me get my hat."

Two gophers are sitting on one side of the street, wondering what it is like across the way. So one gopher decides to dig a tunnel under the street to get to the other side. Once he gets there he decides to pop his head out of the tunnel. Just as he does this, a woman gets out of her car and starts to pee over the hole.

The gopher goes back to the other side of the street and his friend asks him what he saw. He says, "All I know is it rains so much over there that the birds build their nests upside down."

What did the elephant say to the naked man?

"How do you breathe through something so small?"

A man travels to Spain and goes to a restaurant in Madrid for a late dinner. He orders the house special and the waiter brings him a plate with potatoes, corn, and two large meaty objects.

"What are these?" he asks.

"Cojones, señor."

"What are cojones?"

"Cojones," the waiter explains, "are the testicles of the bull who lost at the arena this afternoon."

At first the man is disgusted but, being the adventurous type, he decides to try this local delicacy. To his amazement, the dish is quite delicious. In fact, it is so good that he decides to come back the next night and order it again. After dinner the man informs the waiter that these were even better than the pair he had had the previous night— but the portion was much smaller.

"Señor," the waiter explains, "the bull does not lose every time."

A man walks into a bar with a monkey on his shoulder, orders a drink and sits down. The monkey jumps off his shoulder, runs down the bar to the olive bowl, swallows one whole, then jumps on the pool table and swallows the cue ball whole.

The bartender cries out to the man, "Oh my God, did you see what your monkey just did?"

"What, what?" says the man.

"He just swallowed the cue ball whole!"

"Well, I'm not surprised," said the man. "He eats everything in sight."

Two weeks later the man and his monkey return to the bar. The man orders his drink and the monkey jumps off his shoulder, runs to the cherry bowl, grabs one, shoves it up his butt then pulls it out and swallows it whole. Once again the bartender cries out, "Oh my God, did you see what your monkey just did?"

"What? What did he do this time?" asks the man.

"He just shoved a cherry up his butt, then took it out and swallowed it whole. That was disgusting!"

"Well, I'm not surprised. He still eats everything in sight, but ever since that cue ball incident, he checks everything first."

W hat do you get when you cross an owl and a rooster?

A cock that stays up all night.

A man suspects that his wife is cheating on him but he can't prove it since they work opposite shifts. He decides to get a talking parrot and hide it in the bedroom closet while he is at work, to spy on his wife.

He goes to the pet store and the clerk says, "We only have one parrot that can talk, but he is sort of handicapped. The bird was born with no legs, so he holds himself up on his perch by wrapping his long dick around it.

The man agrees to buy the parrot anyway.

He goes home and puts the parrot in the bedroom closet, instructing it to watch every move his wife makes. Leaving the closet door partially open so that the parrot can see everything, he leaves for work.

The man's wife has already left for work when he arrives home the next morning. He immediately asks the parrot, "What did you see?"

"You're right, your wife is cheating on you!" the parrot says. "About a half hour after you left, she came into the bedroom with another man!

They took off all of their clothes and got in bed! Then that guy started kissing your wife and sucking on her tits!"

"Then what happened?"

"Then the guy put his head between her legs and started licking her pussy!"

"Then what?"

"I don't know," says the parrot. "My dick got hard and I fell off the perch!"

A tour bus in Egypt stops in the middle of a town square. The tourists all get out and start shopping at the little stands surrounding the square. One tourist, worried that he might miss the bus, turns to a local who is squatting next to his camel and asks, "What time is it, sir?"

The local reaches out and softly cups the camel's genitals in his hand, and raises them up and then back down. "It's two o'clock," he says.

The tourist can't believe what he saw.

He runs back to the bus and sure enough, it is two o'clock. He tells a few of his friends about the man. "I swear, he can tell the time by the weight of the camel's genitals!"

One of the doubting tourists decides to see this miracle for himself. He walks back to the local and asks him the time—and the same thing happens! After weighing the camel's genitals in his hand, the man reports that it is 2:05 p.m.

The tourist runs back to tell the story. Finally, the bus driver gets curious. He walks over and speaks to the local in his native language, asking him how he could tell the time in that unusual way.

"Sit down here and grab the camel's genitals," says the man. "Now, lift them up in the air. Now, look underneath them to the other side of the courtyard, where that clock is hanging on the wall."

$\bullet\quad\bullet\quad\bullet\quad\bullet$

In New York it's just one thing after another. We finally get the murder rate to go down and then the mosquitoes start killing us.

—GREG GIRALDO, A NIGHT OF COMEDY, 1999

$\bullet\quad\bullet\quad\bullet\quad\bullet$

Neighbor 1: Hi there, neighbor, it sure is a nice day to be moving in.

New Neighbor: Yes, it is, and people around here seem extremely friendly.

Neighbor 1: So what is it you do for a living?

New Neighbor: I am a professor at the university. I teach deductive reasoning.

Neighbor 1: Deductive reasoning? What is that?

New Neighbor: Let me give you an example. I see you have a doghouse out back. By that I deduce that you have a dog.

Neighbor 1: That's right.

New Neighbor: The fact that you have a dog leads me to deduce that you have a family.

Neighbor 1: Right again.

New Neighbor: Since you have a family I deduce that you have a wife.

Neighbor 1: Correct.

New Neighbor: And since you have a wife, I can deduce that you are heterosexual.

Neighbor 1: Yup.

New Neighbor: That is deductive reasoning.

Neighbor 1: Cool.

Later that same day…

Neighbor 1: Hey, I was talking to that new guy who moved in next door.

Neighbor 2: Is he a nice guy?

Neighbor 1: Yes, and he has an interesting job.

Neighbor 2: Oh, yeah? What does he do?

Neighbor 1: He is a professor of deductive reasoning at the university.

Neighbor 2: Deductive reasoning? What is that?

Neighbor 1: Let me give you an example. Do you have a doghouse?

Neighbor 2: No.

Neighbor 1: Fag.

An old maid needs to go to the pet cemetery with the remains of her cat, but she doesn't know how to drive. As she boards the bus, she whispers to the driver, "I have a dead pussy."

The driver points to the woman in the seat behind him and says, "Sit with my wife. You two have a lot in common."

What does a horny frog say?

"Rub-it."

A zebra has lived her entire life in a zoo and she is getting on a bit, so the zookeeper decides that, as a treat, she can spend her final years in bliss on a farm. When she arrives, the zebra is thrilled to see beautiful wide-open space, green grass, hills, trees—and lots of strange animals.

She sees a big fat weird-looking brown thing and runs up to it all excited. "Hi! I'm a zebra, what are you?"

"I'm a cow."

"Right, and what do you do?"

"I make milk for the farmer."

The zebra then sees this funny looking little white thing and runs over to it. "Hi, I'm a zebra, what are you?"

"I'm a chicken."

"Oh, right, what do you do?"

"I make eggs for the farmer."

Then the zebra sees this very handsome beast that looks almost exactly like her but without the stripes. She runs over to it and says, "Hi, I'm a zebra, what are you?"

"I am a stallion."

"Wow," says the zebra. "What do you do?"

"Take off your pajamas, sweetie, and I'll show you."

Little Jimmy got a parrot for Christmas. The bird was fully grown, with a very bad attitude and a worse vocabulary. Every other word out of its beak was an expletive; those that weren't expletives were, to say the least, rude. Jimmy tried to change the bird's habits by constantly saying sweet, polite words, playing soft music, anything he could think of. Nothing worked.

He yelled at the bird and the bird got worse. He shook the bird and the bird got madder and even more revolting. Finally, in a moment of desperation, Jimmy put the parrot in the freezer. For a few moments he heard the bird swearing, squawking, kicking, and screaming and then, suddenly, there was absolute quiet.

Jimmy was frightened that he might have actually hurt the bird, and quickly opened the freezer door. The parrot calmly stepped out onto Jimmy's extended arm and said, "I'm sorry that I offended you with my language and my actions, and I ask your forgiveness. I will endeavor to correct my behavior."

Jimmy was astounded at the change in the bird's attitude and was about to ask what had changed him, when the parrot said, "May I ask what the chicken did?"

T hree mice are sitting in a bar late at night, in a pretty rough neighborhood, trying to impress one another about how tough they are. The first mouse slams back a shot of scotch, pounds the shot glass to the bar, turns to the other mice, and says, "When I see a mousetrap, I get on it, lie on my back, and set it off with my foot. When the bar comes down, I catch it in my teeth and then bench-press it a hundred times."

The second mouse orders up two shots of tequila. He grabs one in each paw, slams back the shots, and pounds the glasses to the bar. He turns to the other mice and says, "Yeah, well when I see rat poison, I collect as much of it as I can and take it home. In the morning, I grind it up into a powder and put it in my coffee so I get a good buzz going for the rest of the day."

At that point the first two mice turn to the third, wondering how he can possibly top this. The third mouse lets out a long sigh and says, "I don't have time for this bullshit. I gotta go home and fuck the cat."

Why does the Easter Bunny hide his eggs?

Because he doesn't want anyone to know he is having sex with the chicken.

A koala bear escapes from the zoo. He hasn't had sex in a long time, so he hails a cab and asks the driver to take him to the red-light district. He picks up a hooker and tells the cabbie to drop them at a cheap hotel.

When they get to the room the koala goes down on the hooker and really goes at it. This goes on for hours. Finally, the little bear gets up, wipes his snout, and starts for the door.

The hooker says, "Hey there, I'm a prostitute," and holds out her hand. "Yeah, I'm a koala, see ya later."

"I don't think you understand, you little furball. You play, you pay."

"For the last time, I'm a koala!"

She sighs and pulls out a dictionary, flips through it and says, "Prostitute: one who does sexual favors FOR MONEY!"

The koala snatches the dictionary, flips back a few pages, and says, "Koala: a small marsupial that eats bushes and leaves!"

● ● ● ●

I quit smoking. I tried to wean myself off cigarettes, but that was really hard on my dog's nipples.

—GREGG ROGELL, FRIARS FROLICS IN HONOR OF PAT COOPER, 1998

● ● ● ●

What's green, slimy, and smells like Miss Piggy?

Kermit's finger.

Why can't Miss Piggy count to seventy?

Because she gets a frog in her throat at sixty-nine.

I want to become an egg in my next life. That way I'll get laid every morning, get eaten every day, and get hard in three minutes.

A preacher visiting his flock in the country happens to see a pig walking around on three legs. The preacher stops the farmer and says, "My son, what's happened to your poor pig?"

"Well," says the farmer, "this pig is very special to my family and me. Just two months ago, I was working underneath my tractor when the jack fell and the tractor was crushing me. I yelled and my pig rushed to my rescue, dug me out, and pulled me away from the tractor."

"That's very commendable," says the preacher, "but—"

"That's not all, preacher. Last week, my house caught fire and my pig pulled my two young daughters to safety. The little fella even received a hero's gold ribbon from the mayor."

"That's marvelous," says the preacher, "but that still doesn't explain the missing leg."

"Like I said preacher, this pig is very special to my family and, well, we just can't bring ourselves to eat it all at once."

If you think your life is bad, how would you like to be an egg? You only get laid once. You only get eaten once. It takes four minutes to get hard but only two minutes to get soft. You share your box with eleven other guys. But worst of all, the only chick that ever sat on your face was your mother. So cheer up, your life ain't that bad!

There once was an old man and all he had in the world was his donkey. One day, he won the lottery and got fifty thousand dollars. He didn't know what to do with all that money, so he decided to spend a night in a five-star hotel. He asked for the finest room and started going up the stairs with the donkey.

The manager immediately intervened, asking him where he thought he was going.

"Anywhere I go, she goes," he said.

"I'm sorry, sir, but you can't take that donkey upstairs. Leave her down here with us and we'll take good care of her."

So the man went up to his room alone. It was a beautiful room—everything was made of gold, there was a table full of food, and a huge television. He didn't want to hurt anything so he carefully removed his raggedy clothes and slept on the floor.

The next morning he went down to the desk. The manager asked him how he'd enjoyed his stay.

"It was just great! What do I owe you?" the man asked.

"Well... first of all, one thousand dollars for the food."

"But I never touched the food."

"It was right there, so you should have. Two thousand dollars for the TV."

"But I didn't even know how to turn the damn thing on!"

"It was there, though, so you should have asked. Five thousand for the bed."

"But I slept on the floor! I didn't use the bed."

"It was there, so you should have. Your total is eight thousand dollars."

"Okay. But . . . you owe me ten thousand dollars for screwing my donkey," said the man.

"But sir, I didn't screw your donkey."

"It was there, so you should have!"

Everybody I know who has a dog calls him Rover or Spot. I call mine Sex. Now, Sex has been very embarrassing to me. When I went to City Hall to renew the dog's license, I told the clerk that I would like a license for Sex. He said, "I would like to have one, too!" Then I said, "But she is a dog!" He said he didn't care what she looked like. I said, "You don't understand, I have had Sex since I was nine years old." He replied, "You must have been quite a strong boy."

When I decided to get married, I told the minister that I would like to have Sex at the wedding. He told me to wait until after the wedding was over. I said, "But Sex has played a big part in my life and my whole world revolves around Sex." He said he didn't want to hear about my personal life and would not marry us in his church. I told him everyone would enjoy having Sex at the wedding. The next day we were married by the justice of the peace. My family was barred from the church from then on.

When my wife and I went on our honeymoon, I took the dog with me. When we checked into the motel, I told the clerk that I wanted a room for my wife and me, and a special room for Sex. He said that every room in the motel is a place for sex. I said, "You don't understand, Sex keeps me awake at night." The clerk said, "Me, too!"

One day, I entered Sex in a contest. But before the competition began, the dog ran away. Another contestant asked me why I was looking around. I told him that I wanted to have Sex in the contest. He said that was definitely against the rules. "You don't understand," I said. "I hoped to have Sex on TV." He called me a show-off.

When my wife and I separated, we went to court to fight for custody of the dog. I said, "Your Honor, I had Sex before I was married but Sex left me after I was married." The Judge said, "Me, too!"

Last night, Sex ran off again. I spent hours looking all over for her. A cop came over and asked me what I was doing in the alley at four o'clock in the morning. I said, "I'm looking for Sex." My case comes up next Thursday.

Well, now I've been thrown in jail, been divorced, and had more damn troubles with that dog than I ever foresaw. Why, just the other day when I went for my first session with the psychiatrist, she asked me, "What seems to be the trouble?" I replied, "Sex has been my best friend all my life but now it has left me forever. I can't live any longer, I'm so lonely." The doctor said, "Look mister, you should understand that sex isn't man's best friend. Go get yourself a dog."

W here is an elephant's sex organ?

In his feet—if he steps on you, consider yourself fucked.

A man is driving his eighteen-wheeler down the road when he sees a hitchhiker. He stops and picks up the man. While they are driving along, the trucker says, "Hey man, you wanna see something pretty cool?"

"Sure," says the hitchhiker.

The trucker gets a monkey from the back of the truck, smacks the monkey in the head, and the monkey gives him a blow job. Then the trucker asks the hitchhiker if he'd like a piece of the action.

"Sure," says the hitchhiker, "but just don't smack me so hard."

A FEW DIRTY WORDS FROM JUDY GOLD

My family was very polite and reserved, although sometimes my mother would lose her temper in public. My parents always read and we were always making very dry jokes. We could really joke about anything and, of course, that became the Band-Aid that helped us to communicate.

I definitely had racy material when I started, but I built up to much edgier, over-the-line stuff when I felt more comfortable on stage. I remember a joke I told when I first started. I had a black eye because I was swimming laps at the Y and the person sharing my lane hit me by accident. It was at the time of the Robert Chambers/Jennifer Levin murder. So when I got on stage, I acknowledged my black eye by saying, "Oh, rough sex in the park." That was edgy for me then. Now I feel that I've earned the right to say whatever I want—as long as it's funny.

When I became a mother I began talking about being gay because there were so many funny scenarios that went along with being one of two moms. This is something I hadn't addressed before. Some might think it's edgy, I think it's just funny. My material comes from truth and life experiences. It's the way that I see things, so it always works for me. If I'm working a country club or at a corporate gig, I definitely tone down the language, but the content is always there. When I'm in a club, anything goes. The thing is, when a comic goes to a private party or corporate gig, it is always much more difficult than when they come to you. It's as if you're their personal court jester and it can be quite a frustrating situation.

My material comes from my life. It's the true situations and conversations that I find hilarious. I tell lots of stories about my elderly mother, my children, and my experiences being a mother, a daughter, and an ex-partner. I never change gears, but I always acknowledge what is happening, especially if they're not laughing. I'll ask the audience how they can possibly think something is not funny when it clearly is. I am totally in the moment. I'm right there with them, and believe me, it has gotten ugly at times.

I think most audiences want you to succeed. There are so many factors that affect whether or not an audience is responding—from temperature to bad service to sound to the fact that they might be uncomfortable with their dates. I do everything I can to get a laugh.

I am a firm believer in free speech. As long as it's funny, it's okay with me. However, I think we as performers have a responsibility to not be overtly racist, anti-Semitic, homophobic, etc. It's just not funny. There are no boundaries in this medium, but there are different contexts and ways to get one's point across. Listen, stand-up comedy is subversive. It wouldn't be funny if it wasn't.

Roasts are a safe environment to let loose, plus it is such an honor to have someone actually take the time to write a joke about you. I don't think of "edgy" and "blue" as the same thing at all. I listen to the joke, to the point, to the total content. Blue for shock value equals NOT FUNNY. Edgy because it's who you are equals FUNNY. It is definitely more difficult right now to do risqué political material because of the right-wing agenda to curb our free speech and censor us. I've had personal experiences with this issue and it's maddening. They want less government in our pocketbooks but not in our homes, schools, etc. We are so divided that I now avoid working in certain areas of the country because I don't want the Jewish lesbian mom comic getting beaten up on the way to her car. That being said, it actually, in a way, makes it much more fun to do risqué political material.

My being pregnant during the filming of *The Aristocrats* [a documentary film about the oldest dirtiest joke] added a whole new dimension. I gave birth a couple of weeks later. I remember after we filmed it, I called [producer] Paul Provenza and told him to take me out of it, that I was a mother and I couldn't have anyone see me speaking like that. I think it was a hormonal thing, although my children will never see that film. I must say it was definitely an honor to be included with such a bunch of amazing performers.

I am who I am. I use a certain vernacular. That is how I communicate. I'm not going to change. I do think that generally women do not get away with more because of their gender. I think that comedy is a very masculine art form. It's quite powerful and some people are uncomfortable seeing women being "edgy." That's their problem. It is a matter of listening, and I think there are men AND women out there that don't want to listen to "girls."

● ● ● ●

My mom told me nobody will want to buy the cow if you give away the milk for free. And I didn't give away any milk, not one free drop. But no one has bought the fucking cow. And now the milk's not as fresh as it used to be and every man I meet is lactose intolerant.

—Debbie Pearlman, Friars New Faces of Comedy, 2002

● ● ● ●

One day a rabbit managed to burrow under a chain-link fence and break free from the laboratory where he had been born and brought up. As he scurried away from the compound, he felt grass under his little feet and saw the dawn breaking for the first time in his life. "Wow, this is great," he thought. It wasn't long before he came to a hedge and, after squeezing under it, he saw a wonderful sight: lots of other bunny rabbits, all free and nibbling at the lush grass.

"Hey," he called. "I'm a rabbit from the laboratory and I've just escaped. Are you wild rabbits?"

"Yes. Come and join us," they cried.

The rabbit hopped over to them and started eating the grass. It tasted so good. "What else do you wild rabbits do?" he asked.

"Well," one of them said. "You see that field there? It's got carrots growing in it. We dig them up and eat them."

The newly freed bunny was ecstatic. He spent the next hour eating the most succulent carrots. They were wonderful. Later, he asked them, "What else do you do?"

"You see that field there? It's got lettuce growing in it. We eat the lettuce as well."

The lettuce tasted just as delicious, and the bunny returned a while later completely full. "Is there anything else you guys do?" he asked.

One of the rabbits came close to him and spoke softly. "There's one other thing you must try. You see those rabbits there," he said, pointing to the far corner of the field. "They're girls. We fuck them. Go and try it."

The rabbit spent the rest of the morning screwing his little heart out and then staggered back over to the guys. "That was fantastic," he panted.

"So, are you going to live with us then?" one of them asked.

"I'm sorry, I had a great time but I can't."

The wild rabbits all stared at him, a bit surprised. "Why? We thought you liked it here."

"I do," he replied. "But I have to get back to the laboratory. I'm dying for a cigarette."

A circus owner runs an ad for a lion tamer and two people show up. One is a good-looking guy in his mid twenties and the other is a gorgeous blond woman about the same age. The circus owner tells them, "I'm not going to sugarcoat it. This is one ferocious lion. He ate my last tamer, so you guys better be good or you're history. Here's your equipment: chair, whip, and a gun. Who wants to try out first?"

"I'll go first," says the girl. She walks past the chair, the whip, and the gun and steps right into the lion's cage. The lion starts to snarl and pant and begins to charge her. About halfway there, she throws open her coat, revealing her beautiful naked body. The lion stops dead in his tracks, sheepishly crawls up to her, and starts licking her ankles. He continues to lick her calves, kisses them, and rests his head at her feet.

The circus owner's mouth is on the floor. He says, "I've never seen a display like that in my life." He then turns to the young man and asks, "Can you top that?"

"No problem," says the man. "Just get that lion out of the way."

Why did the man call his legless dog "Cigarette?"

Because every so often he'd take him for a drag.

A horse and a chicken are playing in a meadow. The horse falls into a mud hole and is sinking fast. He calls to the chicken to go and get the farmer to help pull him out to safety. The chicken runs to the farm but the farmer can't be found, so he drives the farmer's Mercedes back to the mud hole and ties some rope around the bumper. He then throws the other end of the rope to the horse and drives the car forward, saving him from sinking!

A few days later the chicken and the horse are playing in the meadow again and the chicken falls into the same mud hole. The chicken yells to the horse to go and get the farmer to save him.

The horse says, "There's no time for that! I think I can stand over the hole!" So he stretches over the width of the hole and says, "Grab for my cock and pull yourself up."

The chicken does as he's told and pulls himself to safety.

The moral of the story? If you are hung like a horse, you don't need a Mercedes to pick up chicks.

One sunny day, a bunny rabbit named Peter was walking along the water's edge when he saw an island. Straining his eyes, Peter spied what looked like hundreds of thousands of carrot leaves. "Boy," he thought, "if I could just get over to that island, I'd be the happiest bunny in the world."

Now, bunnies hate water, but all those delicious carrots proved a huge temptation to Peter, so he decided to try to get out to the island. Summoning all his courage, he took three running hops and PLOP! landed right on the island. What he had seen from shore were indeed carrot leaves, and he began to munch happily away. "I am the happiest bunny in the world," thought Peter as he hopped happily along eating carrots.

About half an hour later, a cat was walking along the shore and saw the rabbit hopping around happily on the island. Her eyes not being as good as the rabbit's (for she did not eat carrots), she had no idea that it was all those carrots that were making the bunny so happy. "Boy," she thought, "look how happy that bunny is. If I could just get over to that island, I'd be the happiest cat in the world."

Cats hate water even more than bunnies do, but this cat was determined to be as happy as Peter was. Getting up all her courage, she crouched, sprang, and SPLASH! landed in the water and drowned.

The moral of the story? Behind every satisfied Peter there is a wet pussy.

●　●　●　●

You got all the young, hot stars here tonight—like Vanilla Ice. Vanilla Ice, what the fuck happened to you? You disappeared faster than my cock in a St. Bernard.

—Triumph the Insult Dog, Rob Reiner Roast, 2000

●　●　●　●

It was my father's birthday and I wanted to buy him a bird dog, so I went to the pet store. The owner of the pet store had a bird dog, but it cost a thousand dollars. I couldn't believe a bird dog cost a thousand dollars. The owner of the pet store said it was a special dog: this dog could tell you just how many birds are in the bush. "I'll prove it to you," he said.

So he got the dog and we went out back. The owner let the dog loose and the dog went up to a bush and started shaking his head. The dog shook his head five times. The owner said, "There are five birds in the bush." He went up to the bush and shook it, and out flew five birds.

"I still don't believe it," I said.

So the owner said he'd show me again. Again, he let the dog loose and the dog went up to a bush and shook his head three times. The owner shook the bush and three birds flew out.

Well, I was almost ready to believe him, but I still thought it might be a trick. So the owner took me farther into the woods and set the dog loose again.

The dog started running around a bush wildly, humping, and madly shaking a wooden stick he had found nearby. I didn't know what the hell was going on, so I said, "What the hell is the dog doing running around the bush and humping and shaking the shit out of that stick?"

"He's trying to tell you that there are more fucking birds in that bush than you can shake a stick at."

A farmer is giving his wife last-minute instructions before heading to town to do chores: "A guy will be along this afternoon to inseminate one of the cows. I've hung a nail by the right stall so you'll know which one I want him to impregnate." Satisfied that even his mentally challenged wife could understand the instructions, the farmer leaves for town.

That afternoon, the inseminator arrives and the wife dutifully takes him out to the barn and directly to the stall with the nail. "This is the cow right here," she tells him.

"What's the nail for?"

"I guess it's to hang up your pants."

A lady says to a priest, "Father, I have a problem. I have these two talking female parrots, but they only know how to say one thing."

"What do they say?" the priest asks

"They only know how to say, 'Hi, we are prostitutes. Do you want to have some fun?'"

"That's terrible! But I have a solution to your problem. Bring your two talking female parrots over to my house and I will put them with my two male talking parrots. I have taught my birds to pray and read the Bible. My parrots will teach your parrots to stop saying that terrible phrase and your parrots will learn to pray and worship."

"Thank you, Father, that's very helpful."

The next day, the lady brings her parrots to the priest's house. The two male birds are holding rosary beads and praying in their cage. The lady puts her females in with them and the birds immediately say, "Hi, we are prostitutes! Do you want to have some fun?"

One male parrot looks over to the other one and screams, "Frank! Put the Bibles away, our prayers have been answered!"

A professor at the University of Texas is giving a lecture on the supernatural. To get a feel for his audience, he asks, "How many people here believe in ghosts?"

About ninety students raise their hands.

"Well, that's a good start. Out of those of you who believe in ghosts, do any of you think you've seen a ghost?"

About forty students raise their hands.

"That's really good. I'm really glad you take this seriously. Has anyone here ever talked to a ghost?"

About fifteen students raise their hands.

"Has anyone here ever touched a ghost?"

Three students raise their hands.

"That's fantastic. Now let me ask you one question more. Have any of you ever made love to a ghost?"

Way in the back, Bubba raises his hand. The professor takes off his glasses and says, "Son, all the years I've been giving this lecture, no one has ever claimed to have made love to a ghost. You've got to come up here and tell us about your experience."

The big redneck student nods and grins, and begins to make his way up to the podium. When he reaches the front of the room, the professor says, "So, Bubba, tell us what it's like to have sex with a ghost."

"Awww...Hell! From way back there I thought you said 'goats!'"

W hat do you get when you cross a rooster with a telephone pole?

A twelve-foot cock that wants to reach out and touch someone.

W hat do you get when you cross a donkey with an onion?

A piece of ass that brings tears to your eyes.

A little girl is walking through the park when she sees three dogs lying by the path. Being an animal lover, she approaches the dogs and proceeds to pet one of them on the head. She says to the dog, "How are you? Are you happy? I wish you could tell me your name."

The dog suddenly speaks up. "My name is Moe and I had a great day going in and out of puddles."

The girl is amazed. "You can talk?! Do your friends talk too?"

The second dog then speaks up. "My name is Larry and I had a great day going in and out of puddles."

The girl is delighted. She approaches the third dog and says, "Now let me guess, your name is Curly and you had a great day going in and out of puddles?"

"No," the third dog says. "My name is Puddles and I had a lousy day."

● ● ● ●

Bill Clinton is the horniest guy ever. They say that back in Arkansas the farm animals weren't even safe around him. When he showed up, chicks and geese and ducks better scurry.

—DICK CAPRI, FRIARS FROLICS IN HONOR OF PAT COOPER, 1998

● ● ● ●

A father stork and baby stork are sitting in their nest. The baby stork is crying and crying and father stork is trying to calm him. "Don't worry, son. Your mother will come back. She's just out bringing people babies and making them happy."

The next night, it's the father's turn to do the job. Mother and child are sitting in the nest and the baby stork is crying and crying. The mother stork says, "Son, don't cry. Your father will be back soon. He's just out bringing joy to new mommies and daddies."

A few days later, the stork parents are desperate: their son is absent from the nest all night! Shortly before dawn, the little chick returns and the parents ask him where he's been all night.

"Nowhere," says the storklet. "Just out scaring the shit out of college students!"

T wo pals go moose hunting every winter without success. Finally, they come up with a foolproof plan. They get a very authentic female moose costume and learn the mating call of a female moose. They plan to impersonate a female, lure the bull moose, then jump out of the costume and shoot him.

They set themselves up on the edge of a clearing, don their costume, and begin sending out the moose love call. Before long, their call is answered as a bull comes crashing out of the forest and into the clearing. When the bull is within range, the guy in front says, "Okay, let's get out and get him."

After a moment that seemed like an eternity, the guy in the back shouts, "The zipper is stuck! What are we going to do?"

"Well, I'm going to start nibbling grass, but you'd better brace yourself."

A man owns a bar out in the middle of nowhere. Not too many people come in, so he is trying to think of a good gimmick to attract customers. It so happens that he is watching a circus parade on TV and, as the elephants go by, he remembers reading somewhere that elephants don't laugh. Brainstorm!

He goes down to the circus and buys an old bull elephant that was ready for retirement. Back at the bar he puts out a large jar with a sign reading: "Make the elephant laugh, $5.00 a shot. Winner gets $5,000."

A lot of people think they can make the elephant laugh—but no one can—and soon the jar is almost full. Then one night a man walks in and says, "I hear you will give anyone who can make the elephant laugh $5,000."

"Yeah, he's out back."

After about five minutes, everyone in the bar can hear deep, thundering laughter coming from behind the bar. They all race back to see what's going on. The elephant is LAUGHING!!! The bar owner can't believe his eyes. But, a deal is a deal, after all, and he pays the stranger.

A few weeks pass and the elephant is still laughing. The bar owner can't stand it any more—so he puts a sign on the bar reading: "Make the elephant cry, $5.00 a shot. Winner gets $5,000." Again, a lot of people try but they can't get the elephant to stop laughing. Finally, the same stranger walks in. Upon seeing the sign, he inquires as to whether anybody has had any luck in stopping the elephant from laughing. Since no one has, he goes back behind the bar to see the elephant.

In less than a minute a wail of grief cascades over the bar. All of the patrons run out to see what's up. The elephant has huge tears running down big elephant cheeks. Once again, the bar owner must pay the man. But before the stranger can leave, the barkeep grabs him by the sleeve and says, "Listen, mister. I gotta know. How'd you get that elephant to laugh in the first place? And then how'd you get him to cry?"

"Easy," said the man. "When I first went back there I told the elephant that my dick was bigger than his. And now I just proved it."

A bear and a bunny are out in the forest taking a shit. The bear leans over to the bunny and says, "Do you ever have the problem of shit sticking to your fur?"

"No, not really," says the bunny.

So the bear grabs the bunny and wipes his ass.

T wo leprechauns have a bet and to settle it they go to a convent. Mother Superior answers the door, and says, "Oh my goodness! Leprechauns!"

"Take it easy, sister," says the first leprechaun. "I only wanna ask you a question. Are there any nuns in your convent that are my size?"

"No, little man, there are no nuns in my convent that are your size."

"All right then. Are there any nuns in all of Ireland that are my size?"

"No, little man, there are no nuns in all of Ireland that are your size."

"All right then. One more question: are there any nuns in all of the world that are my size?"

"No, little man, I am quite sure there are no nuns in all of the world that are your size!"

The second leprechaun starts laughing uncontrollably, but through the laughter, he manages to say, "You see, I told you that you fucked a penguin!"

T he Forest Service has issued a bear warning for the summer. They're urging everyone to protect themselves by wearing bells and carrying pepper spray. Campers should be alert for signs of fresh bear activity, and they should be familiar with the difference between black bear dung and grizzly bear dung: Black bear dung is rather small and round. Sometimes you can see fruit seeds and/or squirrel fur in it. Grizzly bear dung has bells in it and smells like pepper spray!

A foursome was on the last hole when one golfer drove off the tee and hooked into a cow pasture. He advised his friends to play through and he would meet them at the clubhouse. They followed the plan and waited for their friend.

After a considerable time he appeared disheveled, bloody, and badly beaten up. They all wanted to know what happened. He explained that he went over to the cow pasture but could not find his ball. He noticed a cow wringing her tail in obvious pain. He went over and lifted her tail and saw a golf ball solidly embedded. It was a yellow ball, though, so he knew it was not his.

A woman came out of the bushes, apparently also searching for her lost golf ball. The helpful golfer lifted the cow's tail and asked, "Does this look like yours?" That was the last thing he could remember.

● ● ● ●

I like being right here, next to Rob Reiner. For once, no one will blame me for farting.

—TRIUMPH THE INSULT DOG, ROB REINER ROAST, 2000

● ● ● ●

A computer programmer happens across a frog in the road. The frog pipes up, "I'm really a beautiful princess and if you kiss me, I'll stay with you for a week."

The programmer shrugs his shoulders and puts the frog in his pocket.

A few minutes later, the frog says, "Okay, okay, if you kiss me, I'll give you great sex for a week."

The programmer nods and keeps walking.

A few minutes later the frog says, "Turn me back into a princess and I'll give you great sex for a whole year!"

The programmer smiles and walks on.

Finally, the frog says, "What's wrong with you? I've promised you great sex for a year from a beautiful princess and you won't even kiss a frog?"

"I'm a programmer," he replies. "I don't have time for sex, but a talking frog is pretty neat."

T here once was a bear hunter who was getting frustrated at having no luck in finding his quarry. Suddenly, he felt a tap on his shoulder. It was a huge grizzly bear. The hunter was shocked when the bear spoke to him. "You are hunting me, I'll bet," said the bear. "You may choose your punishment. Either I will maul you to death or fuck you up the ass!"

The hunter didn't want to die, so he consented to the latter suggestion. The bear left satisfied and the hunter returned to his cabin.

The next day, the hunter decided to kill the bear for revenge—but sadly, the grizzly found him first. Once again, the hunter felt a tap on his shoulder and the bear offered him the same choice. The hunter shrugged, dropped his pants, bent over, and took what the beast had to offer.

The third day, the hunter was really irate and decided he would torture that bear and then kill him! Once more, though, the bear was the better hunter. When the man felt the familiar tap on his shoulder, his heart sank. He waited for the bear to offer him that dreadful choice. But this time the bear just said, "You're not really in this for the hunting anymore, are you?"

A swarm of bees was heading south for the winter and one wanted to make a pit stop at an ESSO station. The rest of the swarm refused to wait, so the bee zoomed on alone.

The moral of the story? There is an ESSO bee in every crowd.

The circus was offering a thousand-dollar prize to the first person that could make the elephant nod his head. Dozens of people tried and failed. Finally, a little old man walked over to the elephant, grabbed his balls, and squeezed as hard as he could. The elephant roared in pain and tossed his head up and down. The old man collected his prize money and departed.

The next year, a similar contest was held using the same elephant, but this time the winner had to make the elephant shake its head from side to side. Again dozens tried and failed. Finally, the little old man who had won the contest the year before appeared. He walked up to the elephant. "Remember me?" he asked.

The elephant nodded.

"Want me to do what I did to you last year?"

The elephant shook his head back and forth violently. Once again, the old man walked off with the prize money.

An elephant was having an awful time in the jungle because a horsefly kept biting her near her tail and there was nothing she could do about it. She kept swinging her trunk, but he was far out of reach. She tried blowing dust at him but that did no good either.

A little male sparrow observed this and suddenly flew down and snipped the horsefly in half with his beak.

"Oh, thank you!" said the elephant. "That is such relief."

"My pleasure, ma'am," said the sparrow.

"Listen, Mr. Sparrow, if there's anything I can ever do for you, don't hesitate to ask."

"Well, ma'am—" he said.

"What is it?" said the elephant. "You needn't be shy with me."

"Well...The truth is that, all my life, I've wondered how it would feel to fuck an elephant."

"Go right ahead," said the elephant. "Be my guest!"

The sparrow flew around behind the elephant, landed on her pussy, and began to fuck away.

Up above them, a monkey in a tree watched and began to get very excited. He started to masturbate. This shook a coconut loose and it fell from the tree, hitting the elephant smack on the head.

"Ouch!" said the elephant.

At which point, the sparrow looked up and said, "What's the matter, babe? Am I hurting you?"

CHAPTER 5

Men in This Corner— Women in That Corner

Now come out fighting.

E veryone thought God created man before woman. That is not true. In fact, he created woman first, but with three boobs.

God: So now that you are here, how do you feel about yourself?

Eve: Well, to be honest, I feel all right, however I don't think I need this center boob.

God: We can correct that. There, now how do you feel?

Eve: I feel great! But . . . excuse me, God?

God: Yes?

Eve: Now what do I do with this useless boob?

—POOF—Man was created.

Why is eating pussy better than driving in the fog?

At least when you eat pussy you can see the asshole in front of you.

What's another name for a zipper?

A penis flytrap.

• • • •

My mom sent me a self-help book called "How to Marry a Rich Man." Chapter 1 was "Bald Can Be Beautiful." Chapter 2 was "Height Is Highly Overrated." And my favorite, Chapter 3: "Not Everyone Likes Anal Sex but Then Again Not Everyone Gets to Drive a Porsche."

—Cory Kahaney, Friars Frolics in Honor of Pat Cooper, 1998

• • • •

As an airplane is about to crash, a female passenger jumps up frantically and announces, "If I'm going to die, I want to die feeling like a woman." She removes all of her clothing and asks, "Is there someone on this plane who is man enough to make me feel like a woman?"

A man stands up, takes off his shirt, and says, "Here, iron this!"

What's the definition of eternity?

The time between when you come and she leaves.

Mr. Smith, the president of a large corporation, calls his vice president into his office and says, "Dave, we're making some cutbacks, so either Jack or Barbara will have to be laid off."

"Well," says Dave, "Barbara is my best worker, but Jack has a wife and three kids. I don't know whom to fire."

The next morning, Dave waits for his employees to arrive. Barbara is the first to come in. Dave says, "Barbara, I've got a problem. I've got to lay you or Jack off—and I don't know what to do."

"You'd better jack off. I've got a headache."

A woman puts an ad in the newspaper: "Looking for man with these qualifications: won't beat me up or run away from me and is great in bed."

She gets lots of replies, but one seems perfect. He shows up at her door and says, "Hi, I'm Bob. I have no arms so I won't beat you up and no legs so I won't run away."

"Yeah . . . but what about the 'great in bed' part?"

"I knocked on the door, didn't I?"

• • • •

I bang black guys, that's my thing. It ain't by choice, I just haven't lost enough weight to get a white guy to fuck me. I have banged so many black guys my neighbors think my apartment is a stop on the Underground Railroad.

—LISA LAMPANELLI, CHEVY CHASE ROAST, 2002

• • • •

A young woman is so depressed and desperate that she decides to end her life by throwing herself into the ocean. She goes down to the docks where a handsome young sailor notices her tears and feels sorry for her.

"Look," he says, "you've got a lot to live for. I'm off to Europe in the morning, and if you like, I can stow you away on my ship. I'll take good care of you and bring you food every day." Moving closer, he slips his arm around her shoulder and adds, "I'll keep you happy, and you'll keep me happy."

The girl nods yes. After all, what does she have to lose? That night, the sailor brings her aboard and hides her in a lifeboat. From then on, every night he brings her some sandwiches and a piece of fruit and they make passionate love until dawn.

Three weeks pass and then, during a routine search, she is discovered by the captain. "What are you doing here?" he demands.

"I have an arrangement with one of the sailors. He's taking me to Europe, and he's screwing me."

"He sure is, lady. This is the Staten Island Ferry."

W hat's the best part of having a homeless girlfriend?

After you screw her, you can drop her off wherever you want.

A guy is driving his girlfriend home when she decides she wants to go to her friend's house instead. Her friend lives far out of the way, so in return for the favor, she offers to get naked. The guy agrees and the girl takes off all her clothes.

The boyfriend is so busy looking at her that he smashes the car into a tree and gets stuck between the steering wheel and the seat. "You'll have to go get help!" he tells her.

"But I can't. I don't have any clothes on—and I can't reach them."

"Take my shoe and cover your snatch with it, and go for help!"

She reluctantly agrees and runs off to the nearest gas station. She finds the clerk and says, "Help, my boyfriend is stuck! Can you help us?"

"I'm sorry, ma'am . . . but I think he's too far in."

A cowboy traveling across the desert comes across a lovely woman, naked and battered, her limbs tied to four stakes in the ground.

"Thank God, you've come!" she cries.

"If you don't mind my askin', ma'am, how did this happen?" asks the cowboy, climbing down off his horse.

"I was on my way to San Francisco when a whole tribe of Indians attacked our wagon train. They stole our food, kidnapped our children, torched our wagons, and left me here to die."

"Ma'am," says the cowboy as he unbuckles his belt, "today just ain't your day."

• • • •

Today's modern women think that sucking and fucking are cities in China.

—Norm Crosby, Danny Aiello Roast, 1997

• • • •

The Seven Most Important Men in a Woman's Life:

1. The Doctor, who tells her, "Take off all your clothes."

2. The Dentist, who tells her, "Open wide."

3. The Milkman, who asks her, "Do you want it in the front or the back?"

4. The Hairdresser, who asks her, "Do you want it teased or blown?"

5. The Interior Designer, who assures her, "Once it's inside, you'll LOVE it!"

6. The Banker, who warns her, "If you take it out too soon, you'll lose interest!"

7. The Hunter, who always goes deep into the bush, always shoots twice, always eats what he shoots, but keeps telling her, "Keep quiet and lie still!"

How do you know when a male porn star is at the gas station?

Right before the pump turns off, he pulls out the nozzle and sprays it all over the car.

The madam opens the brothel door to find a dignified, well-dressed, good-looking man in his late forties. "May I help you?" she asks.

"I want to see Valerie," the man replies.

"Sir, Valerie is one of our most expensive ladies. Perhaps you would prefer someone else?"

"No. I must see Valerie."

So Valerie is summoned and she tells the man that she charges a thousand dollars a visit.

Without hesitation, the man pulls out ten one-hundred dollar bills and hands them to her, and they go upstairs. After an hour, the man leaves.

The next night, the man appears again, demanding to see Valerie.

Valerie is surprised. She tells him that no client has ever come back two nights in a row, because of her high price. She warns him that there are no discounts—the price will still be a thousand dollars.

Again the man calmly pays the fee and they go upstairs. After an hour, he leaves.

The next night, there he is again, and again he pays Valerie and they go upstairs. Valerie's curiosity is getting the better of her. "No one has ever been with me three nights in a row. Where are you from?" she asks.

"South Carolina."

"Really? I have family in South Carolina."

"I know. Your father died, and I am your sister's attorney. She asked me to give you your three thousand dollar inheritance."

Do you know what Rodeo Sex is? It's when you mount your woman from behind, start out nice and slow, take her hair and pull her head back slightly, and whisper in her ear, "Your sister was better than you"—and then try to hold on for eight seconds!

Why do blondes have bruised belly buttons?

Because they have blond boyfriends.

• • • •

The blacks love a big ass. That way they have something to hide behind when the cops start shooting.

—LISA LAMPANELLI, FRIARS CLUB COMEDY MARATHON FOR POLICE AND FIREFIGHTERS, 2001

• • • •

One day a young woman is walking home when a man grabs her, drags her into a back alley, and starts molesting her. "Help! Help me, someone," she cries. "I'm being robbed!"

You ain't being robbed, lady," interrupts the man, "you're being fucked."

"Well, if this is being fucked," she says, "I'm being robbed."

One day, the sheriff notices Billy Bob walking around town with nothing on but his gun belt and his boots. "Billy Bob," he says, "what the hell are you doing walking around town like that?"

"Sheriff, it's a long story!"

"Well . . . I ain't in no hurry."

"Okay, then. Me and Mary Lou was down on the farm and we started a-cuddlin'. Mary Lou said we should go in the barn, so we did. We started a-kissin' and a-cuddlin' and things got pretty hot and heavy— but then Mary-Lou said we should go up on the hill—so we did. Up on the hill we started a-kissin' and a-cuddlin' and then Mary Lou took off all her clothes. She said that I should do the same—so I took off everything except my gun belt and my boots. Then Mary Lou lay down on the ground and opened her legs and said, "Okay Billy Bob, go to town."

How does a blonde turn on the light after sex?

She opens the car door.

• • • •

Richard Belzer and I have been friends for years but we didn't get off to such a rousing start. The first time I met him, out of nowhere, he said, "Whore." I was so appalled I got up off my knees and I marched out of that stall with my dignity intact.

—SUSIE ESSMAN, RICHARD BELZER ROAST, 2001

• • • •

A woman walks into a store and purchases the following:

1 small box of detergent

1 bar of soap

3 individual servings of yogurt

2 oranges

1 stick of women's deodorant

She then goes to the checkout line.

Cashier: Oh, you must be single.

Woman: You can tell that by what I bought?

Cashier: No, you're fucking ugly!

A young doctor moved to town and proceeded to set up his practice. He had a new sign painted proclaiming his specialties: Homosexuals & Hemorrhoids."

The town fathers were upset by the sign and demanded that he change it.

The young physician was eager to please, so he put up a new sign: "Queers & Rears."

As you can imagine, the town fathers were really fuming about that one, and they demanded that the doctor come up with a decent sign, one that would not offend the townspeople.

"Aha!" said the doctor. Soon the sign over his office proclaimed: "Odds & Ends."

M an: Haven't I seen you someplace before?
Woman: Yes, that's why I don't go there anymore.

Man: Is this seat empty?
Woman: Yes, and this one will be if you sit down.

Man: Your place or mine?
Woman: Both. You go to yours, and I'll go to mine.

Man: So, what do you do for a living?
Woman: I'm a female impersonator.

Man: What's your sign?
Woman: Do not enter.

Man: How do you like your eggs in the morning?
Woman: Unfertilized.

Man: Your body is like a temple.
Woman: Sorry, there are no services today.

Man: I would go to the ends of the earth for you.
Woman: But would you stay there?

Man: If I could see you naked, I'd die happy.
Woman: If I saw you naked, I'd probably die laughing.

T hree nuns are talking. The first one says, "I was cleaning Father's room the other day and do you know what I found? A bunch of pornographic magazines."

"What did you do?" the second nun asks.

"Well, of course I threw them in the trash."

"Well, I can top that," says the second nun. "I was in Father's room putting away his laundry and I found a bunch of condoms!"

"Oh my!" gasps the first nun. "What did you do?"

"I poked holes in all of them!"

At which point, the third nun faints.

W hat's the speed limit for sex?

Sixty-eight. Because at sixty-nine you have to turn around.

● ● ● ●

I had the honor of meeting all of Hef's seven girlfriends before, and it was a little weird because they've all been in *Playboy* and as I was meeting them I realized that I had come on all their faces.

—ARTIE LANGE, HUGH HEFNER ROAST, 2001

● ● ● ●

A guy has been asking the prettiest girl in town for a date and finally she agrees to go out with him. He takes her to a nice restaurant and buys her a fancy dinner with expensive wine. On the way home, he finds a secluded spot and pulls over to the side of the road. They start necking and he's getting pretty excited. He starts to reach under her skirt and she stops him, saying she's a virgin and wants to stay that way.

"Well, okay," he says, "how about a blow job?"

"Yuck!" she screams. "I'm not putting that thing in my mouth!"

"Well then ... how about a hand job?"

"I've never done that. What do I have to do?"

"Well, remember when you were a kid and you used to shake up a Coke bottle and spray your brother with it?"

She nods.

"Well, it's just like that."

So, he pulls out his dick and she grabs hold of it and starts shaking it. A few seconds later, his head snaps back against the headrest, his eyes roll up in his head, wax blows out of his ears, and he screams in pain.

"What's wrong?" she cries out.

"Take your thumb off the end!!!"

According to archaeologists, for millions of years Neanderthal man was not fully erect. That's pretty easy to understand considering how ugly Neanderthal women were.

● ● ● ●

Richard started on *Homicide* and then took the same character, Detective Munch, to *Law and Order: Special Victims Unit.* Coincidentally, "Detective Munch" is also Ellen DeGeneres's party name.

—PAUL SHAFFER, RICHARD BELZER ROAST, 2001

● ● ● ●

A guy is riding the bus when it pulls up to the most beautiful woman he has ever seen, and she gets on. The only problem is that she is a nun. He finds that he just has to approach her anyway. "Sister, you are the most beautiful woman I've ever seen and I must have sex with you," he says.

"I'm sorry, but I've given my body to God," she replies. In a few more stops she gets off the bus.

At that point, the bus driver turns around to the guy and says, "Hey buddy, I know a way you can get her in the sack." The bus driver tells the guy that the nun goes to confessional every day at three in the afternoon, and then he whispers something in his ear. The guy breaks into a smile, knowing he's going to get some.

The next day at three, the guy is in the confession booth dressed as a priest. When the nun enters her side of the confessional he says, "Sister, God has told me I must have sex with you."

"Well, if God has said it, we must do it," she replies. "However, because of my strong commitment to God, I will only take it up the ass."

The guy has no problem with this and proceeds to have the best sex of his life. After it is over he turns on the light and says, "Surprise! I'm the guy on the bus."

With that the nun turns around and says, "Surprise! I'm the bus driver."

• • • •

Freddie wanted to get President Clinton impeached. Why should he be the only man in history to ever get a blow job from a Jewish girl?

—JOY BEHAR, FREDDIE ROMAN ROAST, 1999

• • • •

W hat's the difference between a whore and a bitch?

Whores fuck everyone at the party. Bitches fuck everyone at the party except YOU.

A couple is having sex when the man notices that with each movement of his pelvis, his partner's toes curl up.

Later that night, they are going at it again, this time in the shower, and he notices that her toes remain still. Curious, he asks, "Why is it that when we do it in bed, your toes curl up, but when we do it in the shower, they don't?"

"Silly," she replies. "I take my pantyhose off in the shower!"

What do a clitoris, an anniversary, and a toilet have in common? Men always miss them.

An exhibitionist is taking a trip on an airplane. When the man gets to the top of the stairs where the stewardess is examining the tickets, he opens his coat and exposes himself.

Says the stewardess, "I'm sorry, sir, you have to show your ticket here, not your stub."

Mr. Feeney hired a new secretary who was young, sweet, and polite. One day while taking dictation, she noticed his fly was open. While leaving the room, she courteously said, "Oh sir, did you know that your barracks door was open?"

He didn't understand her remark, but later on happened to look down and saw that his zipper was open. He decided to have some fun with his new employee. Calling her in, he asked, "By the way, Miss Jones, when you saw my barracks door open this morning, did you also see a soldier standing at attention?"

The witty secretary replied, "Why, no sir, all I saw was a little disabled veteran, sitting on two duffel bags!"

• • • •

Richard Belzer was once known for his wonderful Mick Jagger impersonation. I say "wonderful" because he was skinny, ugly, and he once blew a guy who looked like David Bowie.

—PAUL SHAFFER, RICHARD BELZER ROAST, 2001

• • • •

A guy is walking past a bus stop and says to a woman, "Can I smell your pussy?"

"Fuck off! No, you can't smell my pussy!" the woman yells back at him.

"Oh," he replies, looking confused. "It must be your feet, then."

What is the difference between "Oooh!" and "Aaah!"?

About three inches.

Why can't women read maps?

Because only the male mind can comprehend the concept that one inch equals a mile.

Three girls all have boyfriends with the same name. In order to keep themselves from getting confused when they talk about them, the girls decided to give their boyfriends nicknames. The first girl says, "I think I'll call my man 7-up."

"Why do you want to call your man that?" the second girl asks.

"Because he's seven inches long and he's always up."

The second girl says, "I'm going to call my man Mountain Dew."

"Why do you want to call your man that?" asks the third girl.

"Because he likes to mount me and to do me."

Finally, the third girl says, "I'd like to call my man Jack Daniels."

"Why do you want to call your man Jack Daniels?" the first girl asks. "That's hard liquor."

"Exactly."

There are five people on a small plane, four guys and one girl. Suddenly, the engine stalls and they crash. Miraculously, all five of them survive the crash but are stranded on a small, deserted island. The four guys realize that they will need to have their natural urges satisfied, so they make up a schedule. Each guy will get a week to screw the woman as often as he wants, and then it is the next guy's turn—and so on. When they present this plan to the woman she agrees immediately, being something of a nymphomaniac.

This arrangement works out very well for years, but then, sadly, the woman dies. The first month goes by and it is terrible; the second month is even worse; the third month is just about unbearable. When the fourth month rolls around, the guys just can't handle it anymore—so they bury her.

• • • •

Joy Behar did for ABC daytime television what Monica Lewinsky did for cigars.

—STEVEN SCOTT, FREDDIE ROMAN ROAST, 1999

• • • •

Three guys go on a trip to Saudi Arabia and one day they stumble into a harem tent filled with more than a hundred beautiful women. They start getting friendly with these exotic beauties, when suddenly the sheik comes in.

"I am the master of all these women. No one can touch them but me. You three men must pay for what you have done today. You will be punished in a way that corresponds to your profession." With that, the sheik turns to the first man and asks him what he does for a living.

"I'm a cop," he says.

"Then we will shoot your penis off!" says the sheik. He then turns to the second man and asks him what he does for a living.

"I'm a fireman," says the man.

"Then we will burn your penis off!" says the sheik. Finally, he asks the last man, "And you, what do you do for a living?"

With a sly grin, the man says, "I'm a lollipop salesman!"

What is it called when a man talks dirty to a woman?

Sexual harassment.

What is it called when a woman talks dirty to a man?

$3.99 a minute.

A FEW DIRTY WORDS
FROM LISA LAMPANELLI

We were raised Catholic. My mother always hated it when we cursed but when I think back, I remember that all she DID was curse. She'd be like, "You son of a bitch of a bastard!" about EVERYTHING! She had such a dirty mouth, but she kept it at home, so everybody thought she was always so upstanding and Catholic. But, she'd never say "fuck" and she would NEVER say "cunt." She always just stuck with the basics. She would say "shit" and everything like that, so one day I got sick of it. I said, "Mom, you gotta learn the f-word." Of course, she was like, "I can't, I can't." So, I taught her how to give the finger—I thought that was a nice contribution since she taught me so much. But she gave it backwards all the time, so she was always giving the finger to herself.

I took a class in Connecticut on comedy and the guy had great exercises to help us find material. He said to write a list of fifty things you love and fifty things you hate. At the time I was losing weight but I hated Weight Watchers 'cause these bitches would come in and they'd be like, "Oh, I found the greatest recipe. You take a rice cake and you put a sliver of apple and you put some cinnamon on it and you would swear to Jesus Christ on the cross that it was apple pie." So I wrote a joke about that, and I was supposed to say at my first performance ever, "Apple friggin' pie? Are you kidding me?"— you know, some innocent punch line. Well, I don't know what happened during the show, but I just went off instead. I said, "Apple friggin' pie? Why don't you just eat ME instead?" It got a huge laugh.

I said "friggin' pie" instead of "fuckin' pie" because I just think it's funny anyway. If I did that joke today, I still would say "friggin'"— it's much funnier. There are times when curses are funnier but sometimes it's funnier to say, "Look at this friggin' guy." It has more attitude.

My theory has always been, I talk this way in real life so I talk this way onstage. I would never edit myself, unless it's during my Friars Club admissions interview so I can get in past the Jews. Then it's like, whatever. If I don't talk onstage how I talk offstage, I'll seem disingenuous to the audience. It'll seem like I'm holding back.

When I do broadcast TV, I have to find really good substitutes for curses if I want to sell the joke. I had a joke on *Premium Blend* once about banging the blacks. The joke is: "I may never buy a new car again but every night I get an Escalade in the old box." Now, you can't say Escalade, because it's a proper noun, and you can't say "box" when it means snatch, so I had to come up with all these words that were just as funny. I ended up saying, "I may never buy a new car again but every night I get an SUV in the old hoo-hah." That was so much funnier than "box." Now I say "hoo-hah" all the time because it's funnier. Sometimes dirty is funny, sometimes the little cleaned-up version is funnier. You just never know.

I cannot believe my life consists of, "Wow, what word is better than twat?" Or, "How many times did I say 'cunt' onstage tonight. Did I lose count? Did I over-cunt them?" Hey, that's a verb I just made up–"over-cunt." I'm claiming that verb, "I over-cunted tonight."

I hate when comics put other comics down for doing stuff. Who are you, the freaking judge and jury? The critic of comedy? You're Richard Pryor? The minute you're Richard Pryor, tell me what to do onstage. That's why Bill Cosby is no good anymore. He has to criticize Howard Stern; he has to criticize Ozzy Osbourne. Hey, you banged a chick and got her pregnant. Don't even start, Mr. Jell-O Pudding Pop. It makes me very annoyed.

There's never a line in comedy for me. I'll never go, "Oh my God, I've gone too far." There never is "too far" because with comedy, it's not possible to go too far. If you're good at it, you can't go far enough.

I do a joke that says that white women should suck black dick as payback–you know, reparations–for slavery. Because it's a heavy subject, instead of saying, "I suck the black dick," I think it's much cuter when I say, "Let me tell you something, when I used to suck a white one . . . " and I kind of whisper it into the audience, " . . . I didn't like it. It wasn't so nice. It looks sort of veiny and gristly. Sort of like a bratwurst with a mushroom on the end." And then, instead of saying, "When I was sucking the black cock," I say, "With the blacks, I think I deluded myself into thinking it would taste like a big freaking chocolate éclair. It doesn't, it's the same shit." I don't know why, but it comes off cuter without using the graphic words.

It didn't even dawn on me to be scared when I started telling racial jokes. I got such a kick out of it, I figured the audience would like it. Because, honestly, if you've got a good heart and you don't mean any of the ridiculous things you say, if the audience doesn't get it, that's THEIR problem. That's on them. This beautiful black woman came up to me once with this gorgeous black guy and she was like, "Oh, I love that you make fun of stereotypes. Oh my God, it's so outlandish what you say. If anyone believes it, they're retarded." I was like, "Wow! Thank you." I always thought, "Well, I don't mean it, and it's funny." And it's always whitey who has to look at the blacks to make sure they're getting it. I'm like, "Would you stop it? The blacks are laughing. I see teeth and eyes. Shut up already." So when I occasionally get a hate letter, I'm so sad. I act all tough but I really get upset. I think, "Oh my God, they didn't get it. Oh shit."

But you can only do racial jokes if there's a ton of blacks who love you—or none at all—because you don't want to do it if it's gonna make one guy uncomfortable. Sometimes I'll even go, "Black guy, listen, you're really cool, can I do this next joke? If you say no, I don't want to offend you because you've been so nice." And he'll say, "Go for it, baby." And then I'll be like, "Okay, guys, if you don't like this joke, don't blame me. Blame the darkie. He told me I could tell it." Or if I sense a guy's uncomfortable with the gay stuff, I get off him real quick because he paid money. Your job isn't to make them miserable. Your job is to make them laugh. They're paying a lot of money at Caroline's, so you better freaking deliver.

Every time I'd fuck with the audience, I'd be like, Oh my God, this is great. Then I went for coaching at the Comic Strip, and this guy told me, "Oh, listen man, I know you like to do audience work but nobody makes a living that way." Well, what about Don Rickles? "Oh, that's an exception." What about Mike Sweeney? "That's an exception." There's always a fucking exception. Well, guess what? So am I. I had to look past that dude's own limits and realize that something's telling me to do this.

Sometimes in the audience I'll get these twats—these soccer mom-types-of-bitches—who don't know who I am. They figure, "Oh, it's a woman comic, let's go see her. She's gonna talk about dating and shopping." Well, that's the last thing you're gonna hear from me. So they'll come in and think, "Oh my God, she's the reason we have school shootings!"

There are some sensitive issues that I have—the N-word is pretty sensitive, and the AIDS and the rape. But sometimes if I see that there's some sensitive women, I'll just be like, "Rape is nothing to joke about but you bitches have gotta stop overreacting. It ain't a rape if the guy is good-looking."

Cancer, I joke about because I bought the bracelet. Once you get the bracelet of the disease, by the way, you can make fun of it. If you give a dollar to AIDS research, the joke is on, baby. I make a joke where I shake the gay guy's hand and thank him for being such a gentleman, and say, "Great, now I have the AIDS, too . . . that's not true, I already had it. You don't lose as much weight as you'd think . . . Oh shut-up. You fat bitches all know if you could get it and be cured in a month, you'd get it and drop a quick eighty. Everyone wants to be skinny." But then I show them I have the bracelet, so I can make fun of it. I show all the bracelets and say, "This is my tit cancer, my nut cancer. I'm waiting for my cunt cancer one—that's coming tomorrow. It has hair on it." That bracelet thing is out of control. There's a bracelet for everything. I even bought the MS bracelet just because it's orange and I needed it to match an outfit. I draw my own lines but I'll never change how I am. I'll never go, "Oh my God, I better not insult anyone." Or, "I better not do dirty."

All those old cunts at the Friars Club, those Jew broads, they love me. I'm always shocked because they just get it. They see your heart. They know I'm a nice person. If I get bitter, on or off stage, I'll quit. I'd rather work at Kinko's or do something not related if I'm not gonna be loveable. I don't make any money by being all intellectual and all that shit. I'm not Dennis Miller.

Bill rents an apartment in Chicago and goes immediately to the lobby to put his name on the group mailbox. While he's standing there, an attractive young lady comes out of the apartment next to the mailboxes, wearing a robe. Bill smiles at her and they begin to chat.

As they talk her robe slips open, and it's quite obvious that she has nothing on underneath it. Poor Bill breaks into a sweat trying to maintain eye contact. After a few minutes, she places her hand on his arm and says, "Let's go into my apartment. I hear someone coming."

Bill follows her inside, and once the door is closed she leans against the wall, allowing her robe to fall off completely. As she reveals her beautiful nude body she purrs, "What would you say is my best feature?"

Flustered, Bill manages to squeak out, "Oh, your best feature has to be your ears!"

She's astounded! "Why my ears? Looks at these breasts! They're full, they don't sag, and they're one hundred percent natural! My ass is taut and round and completely without cellulite! My waist is slim and inviting. My skin is silky and begs to be touched. Why in the world would you say my EARS are my best feature?"

"Be-be-because," he stammers, "when we were in the hallway you said you heard someone coming... That was me!"

A NASCAR driver picks up a girl after a race and takes her home to bed. A few hours later he falls into a satisfied sleep, only to be rudely awakened by a smack in the face.

"What's the matter? Didn't I satisfy you?" he asks.

"It's not that. It's what happened after you fell asleep that got you into trouble," replies the angry woman. "In your sleep, you felt my tits and mumbled, 'What perfect headlights.' Then you felt my thighs and murmured, 'what a smooth finish.'"

"What's wrong with that?" asks the driver.

"Nothing—but then you felt my pussy and yelled, 'Who the hell left the garage door open?'"

● ● ● ●

The Friars Club is the best. They judge everyone on talent. Not looks, not color. Except for Beverly D'Angelo. They let her in because she's got big tits. What a rack. I'm not even a dyke and I want to put my face in there and see the sound it makes. Chevy, she was your beautiful wife in those Vacation movies. What sparks flew between those two! I haven't seen chemistry like that since Rosie O'Donnell poked Tom Cruise with her strap-on.

—LISA LAMPANELLI, CHEVY CHASE ROAST, 2002

● ● ● ●

A tall woman meets a midget at a party. The midget is barely three feet tall but they are attracted to each other. After a few drinks they go back to the woman's apartment. "I can't imagine what it will be like making love to a midget," says the woman.

"Just take off your clothes, lie back on the bed, spread your legs apart, and close your eyes," says the midget.

The woman does as she is told and soon she feels the biggest thing she's ever experienced inside her. Within a few minutes the woman has climaxed eight times.

"Ooohhhh, stop, I can't take it anymore!" she screams in ecstasy.

"If you think that was good," says the midget with a smirk, "Just wait till I get BOTH legs in there!"

A guy is on his first date with a notoriously loose girl. He parks the car and starts kissing and fondling her, and, as befits her reputation, she is quite responsive. The petting continues, and soon he puts his hand inside her panties. She seems to be enjoying it, but suddenly she pushes him away, screaming, "Ouch! That ring is hurting me!"

"That's not a ring. That's my watch!"

• • • •

I once said to George Burns, "How is your sex life, George?" And he said, "It's like shooting pool with a rope."

—ALAN KING, RICHARD BELZER ROAST, 2001

• • • •

J ack arrives at work one Monday morning with two black eyes. His colleagues are understandably curious. "Hey, Jack, what happened to you?" one of them asks.

"It's the damndest thing! I was at church yesterday and this fat lady stood up in front of me. You know how a dress can get stuck in the crack of the butt of a fat lady? It looked funny. I figured she wouldn't like that, so I just reached over and pulled it out with a little tug. Next thing I know, she spins around and socks me one!"

"Jeez, you got TWO black eyes in one blow?"

"Nah, after she turned back around, I figured she was angry that I pulled the dress out of her crack, so I tried to poke it back in."

Why did God create Adam before he created Eve?

Because he didn't want anyone telling him how to make Adam.

Two women are having lunch together and discussing the merits of cosmetic surgery. The first woman says, "I'll be honest with you, I'm getting a boob job."

"Oh, that's nothing," says the second. "I'm thinking of having my asshole bleached!"

"Whoa," says the first. "I just can't picture your husband as a blonde!"

● ● ● ●

If you love Richard Belzer and have a soft spot in your heart for him, we're about to change all that. Chances are you won't be hearing what a great guy he is—unless Paul Shaffer tells you how good he is in bed.

—FREDDIE ROMAN, RICHARD BELZER ROAST, 2001

● ● ● ●

Aman is sitting on a train across from a busty blonde wearing a tiny miniskirt. Despite his best efforts, he is unable to stop staring at the tops of her thighs. To his delight, she isn't wearing any underwear and nothing is left to his imagination. The blonde senses him staring and inquires, "Are you looking at my pussy?"

"Yes, I'm sorry," replies the man, and promises to avert his eyes.

"It's quite all right," replies the woman. "It's very talented. Watch this: I'll make it blow a kiss at you."

Sure enough, her pussy blows him a kiss.

Intrigued, to say the least, the man inquires as to what else this miraculous organ can do.

"I can make it wink," says the woman.

The man stares in amazement as the pussy winks at him.

"Come and sit next to me," suggests the blonde, patting the seat. When the man moves over, she asks, "Would you like to stick a couple of fingers in?"

"Good grief!" the man exclaims. "Can it whistle, too?"

One dismal, rainy night, a taxi driver spots an arm waving from the shadows of an alley halfway down the block. Even before he rolls to a stop at the curb, a figure leaps into the cab and slams the door. Checking his rearview mirror as he pulls away, the driver is startled to see a dripping wet, naked woman sitting in the back seat. "Where to?" he stammers.

"Union Station," answers the woman.

"You got it," he says, taking another long look in the mirror.

The woman catches him in the act and asks, "Just what the hell are you looking at, driver?"

"Well, ma'am, I notice that you're not wearing any clothes, and I was just wondering how you'll pay your fare."

At that the woman spreads her legs wide open and says, "Does this answer your question?"

Still looking in the mirror, the cabbie asks, "Got anything smaller?"

A man is standing at the gates of Heaven. To his right is an attractive woman and to his left is a ladder. The woman says, "Come with me through the gate and spend eternity with me, or climb the ladder to success."

The man, who had always been eager to get ahead in life, chooses to climb the ladder. When he gets to the top, the man finds an even more beautiful woman standing in front of another gate. Next to her is another ladder.

The woman says, "Come with me through the gate and all your fantasies will be realized in perpetuity, or climb the ladder to success."

This time, the man is tempted by the lovely woman but his ambitions take over and he climbs the ladder. He again encounters a woman, and this time she is the most breathtaking creature he has ever seen.

She says, "Come with me and I will satisfy your deepest desires forever, or climb the ladder to success."

Oh . . . what to do? He'd love to stay and gratify his carnal desires—but he is just so driven by greed and ambition that once again he decides to climb the ladder.

He comes to another gate—but this time there is no woman waiting for him. Instead, a chubby and rather unkempt, elderly man with a scruffy white beard approaches him.

"Are you God?" the man asks.

"No, I'm Sess."

What do you do if your girlfriend starts smoking?

Slow down and use some lubricant.

● ● ● ●

I was in the car with my girlfriend and she said, "Kiss me where it smells." So I drove her to New Jersey.

—GILBERT GOTTFRIED, RICHARD BELZER ROAST, 2001

● ● ● ●

A couple is on holiday in Pakistan. They are touring around the marketplace looking at the goods when they pass a small sandal shop. From inside they hear a local gentleman say, "You, out there. Foreigners! Come in. Come into my humble shop."

So the couple walk in and the shopkeeper says, "I have some special sandals I think you will be interested in. They have a special power. They make you wild at sex, like a great desert camel."

Well, the wife is really interested in buying the sandals but her husband feels he really doesn't need them, being the sex god he is.

The husband asks the man, "How can sandals improve my abilities?"

"Just try dem on, Saheeb. The sandals will prove themselves to you."

After much badgering from his wife, the man agrees to try them on. As soon as he slips the sandals onto his feet, he gets a wild look in his eyes—something his wife hasn't seen in many years—raw sexual power!

In a blink of an eye, the husband grabs the Pakistani man, bends him violently over a table, yanks down the man's pants and then his own, and grabs firm hold of the other man's thighs.

The Pakistani screams, "WAIT! YOU HAVE DEM ON DE WRONG FEET!"

One day God is walking through the Garden of Eden and sees Adam standing by the fountain of life with his head under the water. God says, "Adam, what are you doing?"

"Lord, I'm gargling."

"I can see that, Adam, but why are you doing it?"

"Well, Lord, Eve and I just got through having oral sex and I am trying to get the taste out of my mouth. You don't mind do you?"

God thinks for a moment and says, "I guess not, Adam, but it's going to take forever to get the smell out of the fish."

A guy and his date are parked on a back road some distance from town. They are messing around when the girl stops the boy abruptly. "I really should have mentioned this earlier, but I'm actually a hooker and I charge twenty dollars for sex."

The boy reluctantly pays her, and they carry on. After the obligatory cigarette, the boy sits in the driver's seat, staring out the window.

"Why aren't we going anywhere?" asks the girl.

"Well, I really should have mentioned this earlier, but I'm actually a taxi driver, and the fare back to town is twenty-five dollars."

• • • •

Have you heard about the new super-sensitive condom? After you fuck her, it stays and talks to her.

—JACKIE MARTLING, FRIARS CLUB COMEDY MARATHON FOR POLICE AND FIREFIGHTERS, 2001

• • • •

Why is being in the military like a blow job?

The closer you get to discharge, the better you feel.

A couple of women are playing golf one sunny Saturday morning. The first of the twosome tees off and watches in horror as her ball heads directly toward a foursome of men playing the next hole. The ball hits one of the men and he immediately clasps his hands over his groin, falls to the ground, and rolls around in evident agony.

The woman rushes down to the man and begins apologizing profusely. "Please allow me to help. I'm a physical therapist and I know I could relieve your pain if you'd allow me," she told him earnestly.

"Ummph, oooh, nnooo, I'll be all right. I'll be fine in a few minutes," he replies breathlessly, as he remains doubled over in pain.

The woman persists in trying to help and he finally agrees.

She gently takes his hands away from his groin and lays them to his sides. She loosens his pants and she puts her hands inside. She begins to massage him, asking, "How does that feel?"

"It feels great—but my thumb still hurts like hell."

After sex:

A hooker says, "Well, sweetheart, did you get your money's worth?"

A mistress says, "Darling, did you enjoy that as much as I did?"

A wife says, "Beige…beige…I think I'll paint the ceiling beige."

Women, you are the stronger gender. As a man, I'll never know what it's like to have anything leave my body that will eventually go to college.

—JOEY CALLAHAN, FRIARS NEW FACES OF COMEDY, 2002

A young man wants to purchase a gift for his new sweetheart's birthday, and as they have not been dating very long, after careful consideration, he decides a pair of gloves will strike the right note: romantic, but not too personal. Accompanied by his girlfriend's younger sister, he goes to the store and buys a pair of white gloves. The sister purchases a pair of panties for herself.

While wrapping up the order, the clerk mixes up the items and the sister takes home the gloves while the boyfriend's package contains the panties. Without checking the contents, the young man sends it to his sweetheart with the following note:

"I chose these because I noticed that you are not in the habit of wearing any when we go out in the evening. If it had not been for your sister, I would have chosen the long ones with the buttons, but she wears short ones that are easier to remove.

"These are a delicate shade, but the lady I bought them from showed me the pair she had been wearing for the past three weeks and they were hardly soiled. I had her try yours on for me and she looked lovely in them.

"I wish I was there to put them on for you the first time, as no doubt other hands will come in contact with them before I have a chance to see you again.

"When you take them off, remember to blow in them before putting them away as they will naturally be a little damp from wearing.

"Just think how many times I will kiss them during the coming year. I hope you will wear them for me on Friday night. All my love.

"P.S. I'm told that the latest style is to wear them folded down with a little fur showing."

A guy approaches the window of a movie theater with a chicken under his arm, and asks for two tickets. The girl behind the ticket counter wants to know who is going in with him.

"Well, my pet chicken, of course!"

"Mister, I'm sorry but you can't take a chicken into the theater!"

Annoyed, he goes around the corner, stuffs the chicken into his trousers, and returns. He buys one ticket and goes in.

Inside the theater, the chicken starts to get hot and begins to squirm, so the man unzips his fly so the chicken can stick its head out, get some air, and watch the movie.

Sitting next to the chicken man are Agnes and Myrtle. Agnes elbows Myrtle and whispers, "Myrtle, this man next to me just unzipped his pants!"

"Oh, don't worry about it," replies Myrtle. "If you've seen one, you've seen them all."

"I know...but this one's eating my POPCORN!"

A man goes to a shrink and says, "Doctor, my wife is unfaithful to me. Every evening she goes to Larry's bar and picks up men. In fact, she sleeps with anybody who asks her! I'm going crazy. What do you think I should do?"

"Relax," says the doctor. "Take a deep breath and calm down. That's better. Breathe deeply. Now. Tell me, exactly where is Larry's bar?"

• • • •

A guy has lost all interest in sex so his wife goes to a sex shop and buys a pair of crotchless panties. She goes home and waits for him on the bed wearing nothing except the panties. When he gets home she says, "I'm up here." He walks into the bedroom and she says, "Do you see anything you like?" He says, "Why would I want that? Look what it did to your panties."

—JACKIE MARTLING, FRIARS CLUB COMEDY MARATHON FOR POLICE AND FIREFIGHTERS, 2001

• • • •

Why do men become smarter during sex?

A: Because they are plugged into a genius.

Q: Why don't women blink during foreplay?
A: They don't have time.

Q: Why does it take one million sperm to fertilize one egg?
A: They won't stop for directions.

Q: Why did God put men on earth?
A: Because a vibrator can't mow the lawn.

Q: Why don't women have men's brains?
A: Because they don't have penises to put them in.

A woman is having a passionate affair with an inspector from a pest-control company. One afternoon they are carrying on in the bedroom together when her husband arrives home unexpectedly.

"Quick," says the woman to her lover, "hide!" She bundles him into the closet stark naked. The husband is suspicious and after a search of the bedroom, he discovers the man in the closet.

"Who are you?" he asks him.

"I'm an inspector from Bugs-B-Gone," says the exterminator.

"Well, what the hell are you doing in my wife's closet?"

"I'm investigating a complaint about an infestation of moths."

"And where, may I ask, are your clothes?"

The man looked down at himself and said, "Those little bastards!"

• • • •

Danny Aiello and I slept together many years ago. I was straight when I slept with Danny, but his dick was so small that I got used to it. He wore a push-up bra and panties and I got turned on and could never be with another man again.

—SANDRA BERNHARD, DANNY AIELLO ROAST, 1997

• • • •

A famous pilot is having dinner with a brunette and when they finish, they head to a hotel. He calls room service and asks for a bottle of red wine. When it arrives, he opens the bottle and puts some of the wine on the brunette's lips and then starts kissing her. She asks what he's doing and he replies, "When I have red meat, I must have red wine."

"Oooohh," she says.

A little while later the pilot calls room service again and orders some white wine. It arrives moments later and he proceeds to splash it on the brunette's breasts and then starts kissing them. She asks what the white wine is for and he replies, "When I have white meat, I must have white wine."

"Oooohh," she says.

Eventually, he works his way down to her cunt, pulls out a can of lighter fluid and a match, sprinkles it on her muff, and lights it on fire.

"Aaahhhhhhh! Why the fuck did you do that!?!" she yells.

"When I go down, I want to go down in flames."

B ruce is driving over a bridge one day when he sees his girlfriend, Sheila, about to throw herself off. Bruce slams on the brakes and yells, "Sheila, what the hell do you think you're doing?"

Sheila turns around with a tear in her eye and says, "Good-bye, Bruce. You got me pregnant and now I'm gonna kill myself."

Bruce gets a lump in his throat when he hears this. Tears spring to his eyes. "Damn! Sheila, not only are you a great fuck, but you're a real sport, too." With that he drives off.

* * * *

Susie Essman can be seen starring Off Broadway in the *Vagina Monologues*, playing the smell.

—PAUL SHAFFER, RICHARD BELZER ROAST, 2001

* * * *

G od was just about done creating the universe, but he had two extra things left in his bag of creations, so he decided to split them between Adam and Eve. He told the couple that one of the things he had left was the ability to stand up while urinating. "It's a very handy thing," God told the couple.

Adam jumped up and yelled, "Oh, give that to me! I'd love to be able to do that! It seems the sort of thing a man should do. Oh please, oh please, oh please, let me have that ability. It'd be so great! When I'm working in the garden or naming the animals, I can just stand there and let it fly. It'd be so cool. I could write my name in the sand. Oh please, God, let it be me who you give that gift to, let me stand and pee, oh please!"

Eve just smiled and told God that if Adam really wanted that so badly, he should have it. It seemed to be the sort of thing that would make him happy, and she really wouldn't mind if Adam were the one given this ability. So Adam was given this wonderful gift. He celebrated by wetting down the bark on the tree nearest him, laughing with delight all the while.

"Now let's see," God said, looking back into his bag, "what's left here? Oh yes, multiple orgasms..."

T hree guys are discussing women. "I like to watch a woman's tits best," the first guy says.

The second responds, "I like to look at a woman's ass. What about you?" he asks the third guy.

"Me? I prefer to see the top of her head."

B ubba is fixing a door and he finds that he needs a new hinge, so he sends Mary Louise to the hardware store. At the store Mary Louise sees a beautiful teapot on the top shelf while she is waiting for Joe Bob to finish waiting on a customer. When Joe Bob is finished, Mary Louise asks, "How much for the teapot?"

"That's silver and it costs a hundred dollars," he replies.

"My goodness, that sure is a lotta money!" She then proceeds to describe the hinge that Bubba had sent her to buy, and Joe Bob goes to the backroom to find one. From the backroom Joe Bob yells, "Mary Louise, you wanna screw for that hinge?"

"No," she replies. "But I will for the teapot."

A woman was shaking out a rug on the balcony of her seventeenth-floor condominium when a sudden gust of wind blew her over the railing. "Damn, that was stupid," she thought as she fell. "What a way to die."

As she passed the fourteenth floor, a man standing at his railing caught her in his arms. While she looked at him in disbelieving gratitude, he asked, "Do you suck?"

"No!" she shrieked, aghast. So, he dropped her. As she passed the twelfth floor, another man reached out and caught her. "Do you screw?" he asked.

"Of course not!" she exclaimed before she could stop herself. He dropped her, too. The poor woman prayed to God for one more chance. As luck would have it, she was caught a third time, by a man on the eighth floor. "I suck! I screw!" she screamed in panic.

"Slut!" he said, and dropped her.

A FEW DIRTY WORDS ABOUT
THE ARISTOCRATS

The Aristocrats is revered as one of the oldest dirty jokes in entertainment history. Long considered an "inside joke" told by comics for comics, it has been an enormous source of amusement backstage at comedy clubs and at roundtable discussions among members of the profession.

Rarely does a stand-up comic tell this bizarre and very shaggy story onstage, but behind closed doors they have all taken a crack at it, each comedian placing his own stamp on it with personal embellishments, flourishes, and demented improvisations. The Aristocrats has become a kind of acid test of talent, wit, and unflinching nerve. Who can out-cringe whom? It's the final showdown.

In 2005, smart alecks and entertainers extraordinaire Penn Jillette and Paul Provenza threw back the curtain on the dirtiest joke of all time in an eponymous documentary featuring no fewer than one hundred comedians telling the joke and talking about it. The film's tagline, "No nudity, no violence, unspeakable obscenity," says it all. Despite its banishment from the AMC chain of movie theaters (apparently it lacks the requisite amount of gunplay and sexual innuendo for their tastes), it enjoyed surprising mainstream success, premiering at the Sundance Film Festival and going on to run in many theaters around the country (okay, maybe not in Peoria), to phenomenal reviews. A couple of film critics even put it in their Top Ten lists at the end of the year.

Bear in mind that, like all stand-up humor, the joke as written (or improvised) is only half the fun—the delivery is the other half. You'll just have to trust us that, upon hearing a particularly rousing rendition of The Aristocrats, people have been know to fall on the floor, clutch their sides, and go apopleptic with laughter. That's a sure sign that the teller has crafted and choreographed the joke to perfection.

In 2001, just weeks after 9/11, the Friars convened to Roast Hugh Hefner. Here is the version of The Aristocrats told on that occasion by Gilbert Gottfried. Hey—we needed a laugh.

A talent agent is sitting in his office and a family walks in, two kids and their little dog, and the talent agent says, "What kind of an act are you?" And all of them start taking their clothes off. The father starts fucking his wife, the wife starts jerking off the son, the son starts going down on the sister, the sister starts fingering the dog's asshole. Then the son starts blowing his father. . . *Want me to start from the beginning? If you missed anything, I'll repeat it. The Amazing Kreskin is going right now, "What is he saying?"*. . .

Then the daughter starts licking out the father's asshole, then the father shits on the floor. The mother shits on the floor. The dog pisses and shits on the floor. They all jump down into their shit and piss and cum and they start fucking and sucking each other. And then they take a bow.

And the talent agent says . . . *I'll wait till you're ready. They might have to clean this up for TV. Right now Hugh Hefner's going, "Why can't they write jokes the way we write the magazine? Two curvaceous nymphs and their amorous male suitor." That's funny from like 1702. Where was I? Oh, yes.* . . . The son is licking out his father's asshole. Then they shit and piss and cum all over the floor and they fuck and suck each other and they take a bow.

And the talent agent says, "Well, that's an interesting act." Which is kind of an understatement. He says, "What do you call yourselves?"

And they say, . . . "The Aristocrats!"

PAUL PROVENZA ON THE ARISTOCRATS

Penn Jillette and I always laugh at different versions of the Aristocrats that we've heard over the years. We always talk about Gilbert Gottfried, about Bob Saget, and about all these different people that we've heard tell the joke and what they did with it. For years we've been saying it would be really interesting to put a string of, like, ten or twenty versions together and just see what it looks like. We started with five or six people and they all met at the Improv one night and we did it in the bathroom and in the parking lot. That first night was proof that the concept was really vivid. We were like, fuck, man, we've got to do this. We started calling some other people, even people that we didn't think would be interested but who we respected and admired. They all sort of got it and came on board and before we knew it, it turned into something huge.

We've been able to reasonably trace the joke to at least the middle of the nineteenth century and there's a suggestion that at the time it was written it may have actually been a political statement, a comment on the actual aristocracy. A lot of the old-timers in the movie, like Larry Storch and Chuck McCann, actually heard it as the Sophisticates, which sort of places it in that 1920s café society era. "Sophisticates" kind of changes it from a political thing to more of a cultural, social thing. As Eddie Gorodetsky says, "sophisticates" is a self-imposed sort of impression, where aristocracy is real, it's genuine. So there's a lot of fascinating little minutia in the history of the joke.

It has gotten dirtier over the years. It definitely seems to have taken a little turn in the sixties and seventies. It got this vibe of being somewhat anti-establishment; it's just the nature of it. At that time comedy in general took that turn, with *National Lampoon* leading to the early days of *Saturday Night Live*, a lot of recorded comedy, Cheech and Chong getting really, really, really gross and vulgar.

One of my favorite moments in the movie is when the guys at *The Onion* say, "What if the guy took the shit that was on the stage and rubbed it on his face and did a minstrel act?" That's the perfect crossover, the mentality of scatology and shitting on the stage and rubbing it all over. But then you get this other layer of political correctness.

We shot Gilbert about three weeks before 9/11, and then the Friars Club Hugh Hefner Roast was about three weeks after 9/11. So we had spent time with Gilbert working on the joke, talking about it, and it was sort of percolating, it was a little further forward in the back of his mind than it might have been. It just was the perfect confluence of something inside of him, that moment, who he is, all that stuff just came together to give it this sort of resonance that nobody could have anticipated. If we hadn't been dwelling on the Aristocrats, it's a big question whether he would have come up with it at the Roast. Unwittingly, we actually ended up outside of ourselves creating a huge arc with the movie and a huge defining moment in the story of this joke—though we had no intention of anything like that.

In the film, I made the choice of putting the *South Park* clip containing the first 9/11 reference prior to the Friars Roast because I wanted the 9/11 reference to have the impact of coming out of nowhere, pushing the edges. Then a few minutes later we start telling the story about the Roast and how the Friars, Comedy Central, and Hugh Hefner raised half a million dollars for a 9/11-related charity. I thought to myself, how wonderful to have the 9/11 reference do what it does to people's heads, have people sit back and say, "Wow, that's really offensive, you've really crossed the line," and then a few minutes later have to ask themselves, "Well, what the fuck did I do for 9/11? These guys raised half a million dollars." That spoke volumes to me, it just brought up so many interesting conflicts.

Another interesting conflict in the film that I love watching is when Andy Richter and Doug Stanhope tell it to kids. These kids can't understand a fucking word. It's like telling it to your dog—but the knee-jerk reaction that people have is so interesting. Of course we're bulletproof, nobody can say that's horrible, because the kids can't understand a fucking word. So saying, "Oh, that's wrong," is not even rational and people get to work through that. It's so clearly pushing buttons but really there's nothing going on there. Why is it any more edgy that there's an infant in the room when you're telling this joke? What makes it different is the audience, what you're bringing to the table, your own thing. Why is this any more offensive than anything that has preceded it? Because of something in our heads. I mean those kids could be footstools.

Joketelling is really very much in the oral tradition of storytelling and I think that the great jokes deserve the kind of respect that a great haiku or a great O'Henry short story gets. There is the human condition, there's craft, technique. And then, for a joke like this, there's the storytelling tradition, how it changes, and the many different interpretations. Different people bring different things to bear on it. Jokes don't really get that kind of respect, they're just sort of thought of as disposable—but they really encapsulate things. People don't talk about a joke the way they would talk about a poem, but I think they're equally valid as literary entities.

PENN JILLETTE ON THE ARISTOCRATS

If you pitch this film to anybody, "Ok we're going to have three Academy Award winners out of a hundred comics and they're all going to tell the same joke," you couldn't get a penny.

I just made this rule to myself I think out of laziness, really, but also because I wanted this to be different, nobody was given a sales pitch, nobody. I called up Drew Carey and I said, "Hey Drew, this is Penn. You know in jazz you hear people play the same song but in comedy you never hear the same joke?" and without thinking he said, "I'm in, I'm in. When do you want to shoot?" Then he goes, "What's the joke?" I say The Aristocrats; he went, "Fucking brilliant. Let's set it up, when are you in town?" That was the entire conversation.

I called Saget, he said, "You fucker! This is my idea. I didn't get it yet but it's my idea. I was going to have this idea, it's so much more me than you. Sure." I called up Carlin and Carlin went, "Aw, you are not smart enough to have this idea. Someone else should have gotten this idea. You're not smart enough but we're stuck with you. Ok, I'm behind it, just don't fuck it up, man."

We would come in with a camera and people would say, "Oh, what did Gilbert do, what is going on?" You see a little bit of that in the movie with Paul Reiser. He didn't see Gilbert but Reiser had just heard me say, "Gilbert said he fisted a twelve-year old girl with a fist like Popeye." And you see Reiser, in one of my favorite moments of the movie go, "Oh, a fist like Popeye. I had the fist and the twelve-year old, but I just didn't have the imaging. I just didn't know the bill I was on." It just shows Paul Reiser giving so much respect to Gilbert and I just love that.

These professionals, they know this joke, they know how to take it and run with it and I just find this phenomenal. It's in their genes, that comic gene, I just find that fascinating.

My feeling on this movie is there's a hundred people in the back-room here, we're telling filthy, dirty, ugly jokes and laughing our asses off. You're invited but please don't come if you're going to be offended. If you've ever been offended by a joke why don't you go see *Lord of the Rings,* which is my way of saying, go fuck your-self. Go see something else. My sister, who is twenty-three years older than me and I love dearly, I was brought up with her kind of as an aunt, if you can imagine, she's seventy-three years old and your classic schoolmarm-looking, New England woman who has seen everything her little brother does. I told her she isn't invited to this, just because she wouldn't like it.

This movie, *The Aristocrats,* says really powerful stuff about free-dom of speech. It says you don't fight for freedom of speech, you take liberties and liberties don't mean anything unless you take them. You've got to just say, "Oh, I'll say whatever the fuck I want," then you're free. We do live in a free country where we can say whatever we want.

What I love about The Aristocrats is there is no sense. It's not blue states and red states. Everybody tells dirty jokes. George W. Bush tells dirty jokes. If you took an aerial photo of a barbecue on the

4th of July with NASCAR people and all what's called "true hate the red states"—which incidentally I live in and I'm not a liberal—you could take a grease pencil and circle the group of eight people standing around the motorcycle, men and women, and say, "You know, those people are telling dirty jokes." There's nothing more American than that: a group of people splitting off and telling a dirty joke.

The guy, who in front of everybody that doesn't want to hear it at the picnic table says something inappropriate, he's a dick, right? But the person who says, "I got a few good ones for you, Tom, come over here," and you gather around and do that. That's all we're trying to do with this movie. We're not trying to put it during halftime of the Super Bowl. We're not trying to shock anybody, it's just, "Hey, come here."

GILBERT GOTTFRIED ON THE ARISTOCRATS

The Aristocrats has everything going on, but I guess it gets lost in the sauce, if that's a good way of saying that. If it's just a joke where the punch line has to do with pedophilia or incest, audiences tend to get to feel like they shouldn't react.

The whole show I did at the Hefner Roast was a big hit. When I made an Empire State Building joke, though, it seemed like it was the worst thing that an American could have said. Like after any event, when it's fresh in people's minds, everyone becomes very moralistic about everything. I just figured I hadn't heard any out-and-out bad taste jokes about the World Trade Center yet, so I figured I wanted to jump in and be the earliest.

It's funny with bad taste jokes, whenever something happens it seems like within ten minutes there's at least five jokes that come out. So I wanted to be the first. It was at a weird time period where people weren't sure if they were supposed to laugh or smile about anything. Then, of course, there was that kind of silliness with the awards shows going on, and they decided to keep the awards shows, but basically the actresses wouldn't be showing their tits out of respect to those who perished in the World Trade Center. It was like they were all dressing down. I thought, yeah, I'm sure all of the firemen who died in the World Trade Center are somewhere going, "Oh thank God, they're wearing that dress. Thank God Pam Anderson is wearing a turtleneck."

In the film, *The Aristocrats,* they make it sound like there's something about the joke being this deep, dark show business secret. Like someone will be killed if it's told. No, it's an old dick joke. It's weird because you either like it or you don't and if you try to explain it to someone without acting it out, they'll just look at you because it's almost like a non-joke joke. When I did it for my DVD, *Gilbert Gottfried Dirty Jokes,* I did a really extended version and someone said, "How come it took him so long to get to the punch line?" That's someone who obviously never heard the joke, never saw the movie, someone who doesn't quite get what it's about.

CHAPTER 6

Kids Say the Darndest Things

And the dirtiest...

A little boy and his grandfather are raking leaves in the yard when the boy sees an earthworm trying to get back into its hole. He says, "Grandpa, I bet I can put that worm back in that hole."

"I'll bet you five dollars you can't," says Gramps. "It's too wiggly and limp to put back in that little hole."

The boy runs into the house and comes back out with a can of hair spray. He sprays the worm until it is straight and stiff as a board, and proceeds to put it right back into the hole. Grandpa hands the little boy five dollars, grabs the hair spray, and runs into the house. Thirty minutes later, the old man comes out and hands the boy another five dollars.

"Grandpa, you already paid me," says the boy.

"I know. This is from your Grandma."

• • • •

A dad goes into his son's room and says, "Son, you keep doing that, you'll go blind." He says, "I'm over here, Dad!"

A little boy says, "Dad, can I have fifty dollars for a blow job?" He says, "I don't know, are you any good?"

—Gilbert Gottfried, Richard Belzer Roast, 2001

• • • •

Matt is sitting in the back of math class, clearly daydreaming, when the teacher calls his name.

"Yeah, teach?" he replies.

"If there are three ducks on a fence and you shoot one of them with a shotgun, how many are left?"

"Well... none. Because, if I shoot one of them with a shotgun, the loud noise is gonna make the others fly off."

"No, Matt, there will be two left if you shoot one with a shotgun, but I like the way you think."

"Well, teach, I've got a question for you. Three women come out of an ice-cream parlor. One is biting her ice-cream cone, one is licking it, and one is sucking on it. Which one is married?"

The teacher, a little taken aback by the question, answers, "Well, uh, gee Matt, I guess the one that's sucking on the ice cream."

"No teach, the one that has the wedding ring on her finger—but I like the way you think!"

Two little boys are standing at the urinal to pee. One says, "Your thing doesn't have any skin on it!"

"I've been circumcised," the other replies.

"What's that mean?"

"It means they cut the skin off the end."

"How old were you when it was cut off?"

"My mom said I was two days old."

"Did it hurt?"

"You bet it hurt! I didn't walk for a year."

• • • •

So this Mafia don says to his right-hand man, "Anthony, go into the bathroom and jerk off and when you're done bring it out here, I want to see it."

The henchman says, "I don't understand…"

"Just do it."

So he goes into bathroom, jerks off, and brings it out for the don to see.

"That's good, now do it again."

So he goes back in, does it again, and the don says, "Good, now do it again."

So he goes in again and he's in there for twenty minutes, comes back out with just a drop, and the don says,

"Good, now drive my daughter back to Brooklyn."

—Tony Darrow, Sopranos Night, 2005

• • • •

One day the teacher walks into her classroom and notices that someone has written the word PENIS in tiny letters on the blackboard. She scans the class looking for a guilty face. Finding none, she erases the obscenity and begins class. The next day, the word PENIS is written on the board again, this time in bigger letters stretching about halfway across the board. Again, the teacher looks around in vain for the culprit, erases the graffito and proceeds with the day's lesson.

Every morning for nearly a week the trend continues, and each day the word appears in larger letters. Each day she rubs them out vigorously. At the end of the week, the teacher walks in expecting to be greeted yet again by the offending word. Instead, she finds this: "The more you rub it, the bigger it gets."

● ● ● ●

My mom can't wait for me to get remarried. All the weddings we go to, she says, "Next time, maybe you?" So now I take her to all the funerals I can, and say, "Next time, maybe you?"

—LISA LAMPANELLI, FRIARS CLUB COMEDY MARATHON FOR POLICE AND FIREFIGHTERS, 2001

● ● ● ●

Frankie lives on a farm. One morning he is outside playing when his mom calls him in for breakfast. On his way to the kitchen door, he kicks a cow, a pig, and a chicken. When he gets to the table all that is in front of him is a dry bowl of cereal.

"What's the deal?" he asks.

"You kicked the cow, so no milk for you; you kicked the pig, so no bacon for you; and you kicked the chicken, so no eggs for you."

Just then, his father walks into the kitchen and accidentally kicks the cat. The boy says, "You gonna tell him—or do you want me to?"

A delivery man knocks on a door and it is opened by a young boy. The man asks the boy, "Where is your mother?"

"She's in the backyard, screwing the goat."

"Son, it's not nice to make up stories like that!"

"Come on in and I'll show you."

So the man follows the little boy to the back of the house and looks out the window into the backyard. There, he sees a woman screwing a goat. Disgusted, he turns to the boy and says, "That is gross! Doesn't that bother you?"

"Naaaaaaaaah!"

W hat did the blonde say to her unwed, pregnant daughter?

"Look on the bright side, maybe it's not yours."

• • • •

When I was a kid I was afraid of the boogeyman. My four-year-old nephew sleeps with the light on because he is afraid of Islamic jihad.

It's so nerve-racking being a parent because you are just constantly worrying . . . what if they aren't mine?

It's kind of an unwritten rule that if your kids are under the age of four or five you can bring them into an opposite-sex bathroom. I actually had someone roll their eyes at me when I brought my three-year-old into the ladies' room.

—Brian Kiley, A Night of Comedy, 1999

• • • •

A boy and girl have been out on a date. As they pull into the girl's driveway, she invites him to come over for dinner the next night to meet her parents. He agrees, and the girl promises that after dinner they will make love. The boy is pretty excited, as it will be his very first time having sex—so on his way home, he decides to stop by the pharmacy and buy some condoms.

The next night at dinner, the girl's mother asks the boy to say grace before dinner. He obliges with great enthusiasm, going on and on about repentance, forgiveness, mercy, and salvation.

"I didn't know you were such a religious person," says the girl.

"I didn't know your dad was a pharmacist."

One summer, a bachelor farmer hires a college student to help around the farm.

Says the farmer, "Son, since you have done such a fine job here this summer, I am going to throw a party for you. You better be able to handle a few beers because there will be lotsa drinkin' going on."

"Hey, I'm a college man—I can hold my liquor, believe you me. I should do just fine."

"There is also going to be a lot of fightin', so I hope you can handle yourself with your fists."

"I have been working hard all summer and I think I'm in pretty good shape to defend myself."

"Okey-dokey, but did I mention that there will be lotsa sex?"

"Thank God! I have been out here all summer without a date and I have been dying for some action. Say... what should I wear to this party?"

"I don't care. Its just gonna be me and you."

The kindergarten class had a homework assignment: find out about something exciting and relate it to the class. When the time came, the kids rose and gave their reports one at a time, talking about such things as baseball, firefighting, and the circus. The teacher was reluctant to call upon little Johnny, as she never knew what might come out of his mouth—but eventually his turn came.

Johnny walked to the front of the class, and with a piece of chalk made a small white dot on the blackboard, then sat back down.

The teacher couldn't figure out what the little boy had on his mind, so she asked him what the dot was supposed to mean.

"It's a period," reported Johnny.

"Well, I can see that," said the teacher patiently, "but what is so exciting about a period?"

"Damned if I know but this morning my sister said she missed one. Then Daddy had a heart attack, Mommy fainted, and the man next door shot himself."

●　●　●　●

I was never politically correct. Even in elementary school the teacher used to say "sit Indian style," so I'd get a bottle of whiskey and lay at the curb.

When I was married I had a stepson, which was great because that way I didn't have to hit my kids.

When I was a kid, I had big teeth. The local pervert tried to lure me into the car with carrots.

—RICH VOS, FRESH FUNNY FACES, 1999

●　●　●　●

A young woman who worked as a prostitute was very careful to keep this a secret from her grandmother. One day, the police raided a brothel and rounded up the working girls, including the young woman. The prostitutes were instructed to line up single-file on the sidewalk. Well, who should be walking through the neighborhood just then but little old Grandma.

The young woman was frantic—and sure enough, Grandma noticed her and asked curiously, "What are you lining up for, dear?"

Thinking quickly, the young woman told her that some people were passing out free oranges and that she was lining up for some. Mmm, sounds lovely," said Grandma. "I think I'll get some myself." And with that, she made her way to the back of the line. A police officer was working his way down the line, questioning each girl. When he got to Grandma, he was bewildered. "But you're so old, how do you do it?"

"Oh, it's quite easy, sonny, I just remove my dentures and suck 'em dry!"

A young man excitedly tells his mother he's fallen in love and is going to get married. "Just for fun, Ma, I'm going to bring over three women, and you try and guess which one I'm going to marry."

The mother agrees. The next day, he brings three beautiful women into the house and sits them down on the couch, where they chat with Mom for a while. The young man finally says, "Okay, Ma. Guess which one I am going to marry."

Without a moment's hesitation she replies, "The redhead in the middle."

"That's amazing, Ma. You're right. How did you know?"

"Cuz that's the one I don't like."

A FEW DIRTY WORDS FROM
JACKIE "THE JOKEMAN" MARTLING

My mother was a character; she was very funny. As a little kid I would have my zipper open and instead of saying, "Jackie pull your zipper up," she'd say, "Look, it's Ever-Ready Eddie." That was her sense of humor; she was a fucking riot. My father was a very quiet guy but occasionally he'd do something funny. He came in drunk one night and I was at the kitchen table with some friends, having dinner with my mother, brothers, and sister, and my mother said, "Where were you?" He said, "Oh, I hit a lady's cat with my car down by the stores." We were like, Yeah? He said, "Yeah, and I killed it. I felt bad. The lady came out and I didn't know what to do, so I told her, 'I feel bad, lady. I'll give you a hundred dollars for the cat.' She said, 'A hundred dollars? It was a pedigreed cat, I want five hundred dollars.' I said, 'Oh, come on, it was just a cat, I'll give you a hundred dollars.' She said, 'Five hundred dollars.' Then a cop came and gave me a ticket." My mother said, "A ticket for what?" And my father said, "For discussing the price of pussy on a public highway!" We fucking went nuts but this was not usually my father. This was not his character. He must have heard it a day before, and we screamed and screamed.

I never set out to be a comic; I didn't think it was an option. I thought there were people who were just chosen by the hand of someone. I started learning the guitar in ninth grade to try and get laid like everybody else. The old joke is that 99 percent of musicians are in it to get laid and the other 1 percent is lying.

When I first started playing with a band in the early seventies, people would come up to tell me a joke, because we told jokes between songs. I'd say, "I'll start counting down from ten and by the time I get to one, if I don't know the punch line to the joke, I'll buy you a drink." I never bought anybody a drink because I always recognized that the three nuns in a canoe was the same joke as the three pilgrims and a bobcat. So when I decided to just tell jokes onstage I was equipped already. I knew a bazillion jokes, and I wanted to stay onstage because I certainly wasn't going to get a job. I stayed up there telling dirty jokes.

My goal is to make you laugh as hard as I can make you laugh because, the harder you laugh, the more fun it is for me, and the more fun it is for you. You learn pretty quickly that a dick joke is going to get a lot bigger laugh than a nondick joke. That is human nature. It's where you're not supposed to go. I used to watch Carson and he would break his balls for eight minutes talking about the state of the country, talking about international politics, talking about the economy, and getting laughs. Toward the end of his monologue, he would make an obscure penis reference, and the house would come down. It's fucking human nature, it's that simple.

I wasn't out to get on Leno, I wasn't out to get on Carson. The other guys were doing seven minutes of fantastic, homegrown materi-al, things like, "My apartment is too small . . . my girlfriend treats me like hell," to get on TV. I was the guy who was producing shows and then closing them with forty-five minutes of dirty jokes to get people in there and make some money.

I used to run Governor's Comedy Shop and when we first started, once in a while, people would go, "Oh man, Jackie, there are some older people out there tonight." By older people they meant like forty-year-old people. I said, "You don't understand, that's my gang. If I've got an eighteen-year-old kid out there on a first date, he's not going to laugh nearly as hard at a marriage joke or a blow job joke. He's trying to get blown; he's not going to laugh. The forty-year-old guy that's been married for twelve years, that can't get his wife to suck his dick, he's going to howl at this shit. And older people, seventy-year-old people, what do you think? That they went through their lives without shitting and pissing, fucking and blowing? Everybody loves this stuff."

When I first started I went to a bachelor party, it was maybe fif-teen guys. I was telling jokes and insulting them, which is what they wanted me to do. I was looking at the clock on the back wall because, as my principal Mrs. Fox used to say, "Project. Look at the clock on the back wall." This one idiot thought I was looking at him when I said the insults. He actually came over and grabbed me by the scruff of the neck and said, "What'd you say to me, man?" "I didn't say anything to YOU," I said, "I was talking to the group." I thought to myself, "Holy shit, this is not going to be an easy job," but in twenty-six years, that's the only time something like that ever happened.

I remember working at a club somewhere in Ohio and they brought in this kid in a wheelchair. His mother came up and said, "Will you do some wheelchair jokes and some cripple jokes, because he really gets a kick out of it." I said, "I would love to, but I can't. I don't give a fuck about him, I would tell cripple jokes all day long to make him laugh, and he'd have a great time, but it would make everybody else uncomfortable."

Don't get me wrong though, I'll tell all kinds of jokes, I'll tell a Chinese joke, and I'll see a black guy laughing, and I'll say, "You might as well laugh now, because I'll get to you later." One thing that happened to me years ago is word got back to some guy that had a Polish newsletter in Jersey, and he wrote to me and said, "I hear you're doing Polish jokes, and we shut down Joan Rivers and we'll take care of you, blah blah blah . . ." My response was, "Listen, I don't know if you've ever seen my act, but it's fun. We're having a great time. I pick on everybody. Why don't you send some of your people down before you get all bent out of shape?" At the time, I was doing Rascal's Comedy Hour and they came down and I made sure I had Polish jokes in my monologue. They came up afterward and said, "You're the funniest guy we've ever seen. We have no problem with this." I really believe it's harmless.

I don't say "cunt" on stage and it's not because I have a problem with the word. But it sends everyone out to lunch a little bit. I don't tell Jesus jokes for the most part, because the audience goes away. There's a great joke, "What's the difference between Jesus and a picture of Jesus? It only takes one nail to hang up a picture of Jesus." This is creative, it's funny, but I when I would tell that joke, I'd lose the audience for a joke or two because they'd be uncomfortable. If it's going to throw off my audience, I'm not going to do it just to be a bully. I have some stuff at the end of my act that can get especially crazy and I usually say to the audience, "Listen, I have a couple more that are pretty bad. What should we do? Should we keep going?" In twenty-six years, they've never said no.

I'm making a living having fun and we're here to laugh. Using religious and racial and ethnic stuff, it's just a great shortcut. Maybe it's shitty but it's fun and it's not like you're creating it. Is it perpetuating a stereotype? Yeah, I guess, but everybody really needs to lighten the fuck up. There are bigger problems than me in the world—I'm Jackie the Joke Man, not Jackie the Hitler Man!

A FEW DIRTY JOKES FROM JACKIE THE JOKEMAN

The teacher says to her class, "On Monday you're going to have a five-hour exam."

Mario, the class wise guy, says, "Five hours? What if I'm exhausted from sex?"

"Then write with your other hand."

A gynecologist has a midlife crisis and decides to become a mechanic. She goes to night school and studies very hard. She's pretty nervous while taking the final exam, but thinks she did all right. When she goes to check the scores, she sees 150 PERCENT next to her name. Afraid that it's a mistake, she goes to see the professor. She says, "How did I get 150 percent on the final?"

"You took the engine apart piece by piece perfectly. I gave you 50 percent for doing that. And you put it back together perfectly. In fact, the engine runs better and quieter than it did before you took it apart. So I gave you 50 percent for that."

She says, "So how'd you get to 150 percent?"

He says, "I gave you extra credit for doing it all through the muffler."

Dirty Johnny is playing with his train set in the living room. He says, "Okay: All you cocksuckers getting on, get off. And move your asses, we're in a hurry."

The maid overhears him and says, "Such language! Go to your room!"

Johnny obeys, and she closes the door on him. After two hours she opens the door and says, "I'll let you play with your trains if you promise to not use any more foul language."

She goes back to the kitchen. Johnny goes back to his trains and says, "Ladies and gentlemen, please take your seats. You're kindly advised to quickly place your luggage on the rack, because we'll be on our way very soon. And if any of you cocksuckers has a complaint that we're late, take it to the bitch in the kitchen."

Mrs. Ludwig: "How's your sex life?"

Mrs. Schultz: "Infrequent."

Mrs. Ludwig: "Is that one word or two?"

A guy is out one night with his girlfriend and they're driving eighty miles an hour in his new sports car. She leans over to him, opens his fly, and reaches in. Suddenly a deer jumps in front of the car. He turns the wheel and finally comes to a rest. When the police get to the scene, they guy is still buckled in and alive.

The cop says, "Your girlfriend was thrown from the car and killed. You sure are lucky."

"Lucky? Go look in her hand!"

Here's a great template for any time you want to get up and get a huge laugh with a not too horribly off-color story and nail a guest of honor or a friend or whoever. To assure the howls, use your best Munchkin voice when you're doing the midgets' dialogue, put your target's name in the obvious place, and make sure you bark out the punch line nice and slow and crystal clear, even though you're talking in Munchkin:

Three midgets meet in front of the world headquarters of the Guinness Book of World Records.

The first midget says, "I'm gonna go in and get into the *Guinness Book of World Records* for having the world's smallest hands," and he goes in. He comes out a few minutes later and says, "I did it. I'm now in the *Guinness Book of World Records* for having the world's smallest hands."

The second midget says, "I'm gonna go in and get into the *Guinness Book of World Records* for having the world's smallest feet," and he goes in. He comes out a few minutes later and says, "I did it. I'm now in the *Guinness Book of World Records* for having the world's smallest feet."

The third midget says, "I'm gonna go in and get into the *Guinness Book of World Records* for having the world's smallest penis." He comes out a few minutes later, and he's in tears. The first midget says, "What happened?"

The third midget says, "I only got into the *Guinness Book of World Records* for having the world's SECOND–smallest penis . . . Who the fuck is [Barry Dougherty]?"

W hat did Cinderella do when she got to the ball?

Gagged.

• • • •

I heard that the Smothers Brothers came from an alternative home. Tom, Mommy liked you best, but Dad really liked Dick.

—Susie Essman, Smothers Brothers Roast, 2003

• • • •

T he class composition assignment was to write about something unusual that had happened during the past week. Little Irving got up to read his: "Papa fell in the well last week . . ." he began.

"Good heavens!" shrieked his teacher. "Is he all right now?"

"He must be," said little Irving. "He stopped yelling for help yesterday."

T hree black roosters are sitting on a fence. A little boy asks his mother how many feet those three roosters have.

"Six," she replies.

"Well, how many eyes do the three roosters have?"

"Six."

"Okay, but how many beaks do the three roosters have?"

"Three, honey."

"Uh huh . . . So, see that white cat sitting over there by the roosters? How many hairs are on that white cat's head?"

"I don't really know the answer to that one, sweetie."

"Mom! How come you know so much about black cocks and nothing about white pussy?"

O n the first day of college, the dean addresses the students and goes over some of the rules: "The female dormitory will be out of bounds for all male students, and the male dormitory to the female students. Anybody caught breaking this rule will be fined twenty dollars the first time." He continues, "Anybody caught breaking this rule the second time will be fined sixty dollars. Being caught a third time will cost you a fine of a hundred and eighty dollars. Are there any questions?" At this point, a male student in the crowd raises his hand.

"Yes?" asks the dean.

"How much for a season pass?"

A virgin is going out on her first date, and she tells her grandmother about it. Says the wise old grandmother, "Sit right down here and let me tell you about young boys. He is going to try to kiss you; you are going to like that, but don't let him do it. He is going to try to feel your breast; you are going to like that, but don't let him do it. He is going to try to put his hand between your legs; you are going to like that, but don't let him do it. And most important, he is going to try to get on top of you and have his way with you. You are going to like that but, for heaven's sake, don't let him do it! It will disgrace the family!"

Keeping all of that in mind, the young girl goes on her date. The next day she tells her grandmother that the evening had gone just as the older woman had predicted. "Don't worry, grandma," she says, "I didn't let him disgrace the family. When he tried to climb on top of me I flipped him over, got on top of him, and disgraced HIS family!"

● ● ● ●

I remember, as a kid going to Hebrew school, how disappointed I was when I found out that Adam was a schmuck. God gave him a woman and an apple—and he ate the apple!

—Norm Crosby, Chevy Chase Roast, 1990

● ● ● ●

A guy meets a girl at a disco and she invites him back to her house for the night. Her parents are out of town, so she figures it is the perfect opportunity. They get home and go into her bedroom, where the guy notices that every surface is covered with stuffed toys. There are hundreds of them, fluffy animals and dolls everywhere: on top of the wardrobe, on the bookshelves, covering the windowsills, all over the floor, and of course covering the bed. Somehow, they manage to find space to have sex and afterward he turns to her and says, "So, how was I?"

"Well, you can take anything from the bottom shelf."

Little Joey was very curious, and one day he decided to sneak into a strip club to see what it was like. He waited until the bouncer's back was turn and scurried quietly to the front of the club, where he watched the strippers dance. When they had removed nearly all of their clothing he bolted out the door and ran down the street as fast as he could. He was running so fast he smacked right into a man and fell back on his bottom.

"What's wrong young man?" said the adult. "You look like you just saw a ghost!"

"My mommy and daddy told me that if I ever watched anybody undress, I'd turn to stone. Well I was watching two ladies and all of a sudden I felt something hard!"

A teacher addresses her third grade class: "Today, everyone, we will be telling stories that have a moral to them." She explains what a moral to a story is, and asks for volunteers. Little Suzie raises her hand.

Suzie: "I live on a farm and we have a chicken that laid twelve eggs. We got very excited to have twelve more chickens, but only six of them hatched."

Teacher: "That's a good story; now, what is the moral?"

Suzie: "Don't count your chickens before they are hatched."

Teacher: "Very good Suzie. Anyone else?"

Ralphie: "Yes, teacher. I was carrying some eggs in my bicycle basket one day and I crashed my bike and all the eggs broke."

Teacher: "Now, what might be the moral there, Ralphie?"

Ralphie: "Don't put all your eggs in one basket."

Teacher: "Very good! Anyone else?"

Johnny: "Yes teacher. My Aunt Karen is in the army and when she was in the Gulf War, she parachuted down with only a gun, twenty bullets, a knife, and a six-pack of beer. On her way down, she drank the six-pack. When she landed, she shot twenty Iraqis and then killed ten more with her knife."

Teacher: "Why, that's very dramatic, Johnny. What is the moral of your story?"

Little Johnny: "Don't fuck with Aunt Karen when she's drunk."

• • • •

All the Stillers are here and they're all in show business—like the Judds—only ugly.

Jerry really is their father. Could you imagine that mouth screaming at you at a Little League game? I tell ya what, Ben, if I had a father like that, I'd be gay, too.

Jerry, was it weird growing up in your son's shadow?

—JIMMY KIMMEL, JERRY STILLER ROAST, 1999

• • • •

What do your parents' car and testicles have in common?

Hit either one of them and you're grounded.

The teacher is starting a new lesson on multisyllable words. She decides to ask a few of the children to come up with examples of words with more than one syllable. She first calls on Jane.

After some thought, Jane proudly comes up with "Monday."

"Very good, Jane. That has two syllables, Mon-day. Does anyone know another word?"

Johnny yells out from the back of the room, "I do! I do!"

Wary of Johnny's rather sophisticated sense of humor, the teacher calls on Mike instead.

"Saturday," says Mike.

"That is correct, Mike. Saturday has three syllables."

Hoping to outdo everyone, Johnny says, "I know a FOUR-syllable word. Pick me! Pick me!"

Taking her chances, the teacher reluctantly says, "Okay, Johnny, what is your four-syllable word?"

"Mas-tur-ba-tion."

Trying to retain her composure, the teacher says, "Wow, Johnny. Four syllables! That certainly is a mouthful."

"No, Ma'am, you're thinking of 'blow job.' That's only TWO syllables."

A young Amish girl is going on her first date and her mother is helping her get ready. She puts on gloves, because it is cold out that night and the Amish still ride in buggies. Asks her mother, "Why are you wearing gloves? It isn't ladylike to wear gloves."

"It's supposed to be cold tonight. What do I do with my hands if they get cold?"

"Just stick your hands between your knees, and they will get warm."

Reluctantly, the girl agrees.

Her date picks her up and they go on their way. On the way home the girl's hands get cold so, following her mother's orders, she sticks them between her knees.

Her date looks over and says, "Why on earth do you have your hands between your legs?"

"My mother told me that if my hands got cold, I should stick them between my legs."

"Well, my dick is frozen solid; do you care if I stick it between your legs to get it warm?"

"Hmmm . . . well, I guess I don't see any harm in it."

After returning home from her date the girl asks her mother, "What do you know about dicks?"

"Why?" asks the concerned mother. "What do YOU know about dicks?"

"All I know is that when they thaw out they make an awful mess!"

• • • •

From a very early age, my father brought me to Friars Roasts. The first time I saw Red Buttons and Jack Benny and Milton Berle was at a Roast. The first time I saw my dad kill in front of big celebrities was at a Roast. The first time I heard the word cunt . . . look, I'm tearing up.

—ALAN KIRSCHENBAUM (FREDDIE ROMAN'S SON), FREDDIE ROMAN ROAST, 1997

• • • •

A Sunday school teacher is concerned that his little preschool students might be a confused about Jesus. He asks his class, "Where is Jesus today?"

Steven raises his hand and says, "He's in heaven."

Mary answers, "He's in my heart."

Little Johnny, waving his hand furiously, blurts out, "I know! I know! He's in our bathroom!"

The teacher blinks a few times. "Why, Johnny, do you think that Jesus is in your bathroom?"

"Well, every morning, my father gets up, bangs on the bathroom door, and yells, 'Jesus Christ, are you still in there?!'"

What happened to the pope when he went to Mount Olive?

Popeye almost killed him!

• • • •

What's the difference between a Jewish mother, an Irish mother, and a pit bull?
　A pit bull will eventually let go.

—JOEY CALLAHAN, FRIARS NEW FACES OF COMEDY, 2002

• • • •

A woman takes her three grown sons to the doctor for physicals for the first time in their lives. The doctor examines the boys and tells the woman that they are healthy but she needs to give them iron supplements. She goes home and wonders how she can carry out the doctor's orders. She decides to go to the hardware store and buy iron ball bearings, which she mixes into their food.

Several days later, the youngest son tells her that he is pissing BBs. She tells him that it is normal because she has been putting them in his food. Later, the middle son comes to her and says that he is crapping BBs. Again, she says that it is perfectly understandable and nothing to worry about.

That evening the eldest son comes in very upset. He says, "Ma, you won't believe what happened."

"I know, son. You're passing BBs."

"No! I was out behind the barn jacking off and I shot the dog!"

How did Pinocchio find out he was made of wood?

He was masturbating and his hand caught on fire.

Little Johnny is sitting in class one day when he needs to go to the bathroom. "Miss Jones," he cries, "I need to take a piss!!"

"Now, Johnny, that is NOT the proper word to use in this situation. The polite word is 'urinate.' Please use the word 'urinate' in a sentence correctly, and I will allow you to go."

Little Johnny thinks for a bit, then says, "You're an eight, but if you had bigger tits, you'd be a ten."

Why did Raggedy Ann get thrown out of the toy box?

Because she kept sitting on Pinocchio's face moaning, "Lie to me!"

Three boys receive their grades from their female sex education instructor. One receives a D+, the second a D-, and the third an F. "One day we should get her for this," says the first boy.

"I agree. We'll grab her..." says the second.

"Yeah," says the third. "And then we'll kick her in the nuts!"

● ● ● ●

My mama was so fat she had to iron her pants in the drive-way. My mama was so ugly she walked by the bathroom and the toilet just flushed itself. My mama was so fat the left side of her ass had a different area code. My mama was so fat she had a real horse on her polo shirt.

—GEORGE WALLACE, JERRY STILLER ROAST, 1999

● ● ● ●

T wo young guys are picked up by the cops for smoking dope. The following Friday they appear before the judge. The judge says, "You seem like nice young men, and I'd like to give you a second chance rather than jail time. I want you to go out this weekend and try to show others the evils of drug use and get them to give up drugs forever. I'll see you back in court Monday."

Monday, the two guys are in court, and the judge says to the first one, "How did you do over the weekend?"

"Well, your honor, I persuaded seventeen people to give up drugs forever."

"Seventeen people? That's wonderful. What did you tell them?"

"I used a diagram, your honor. I drew two circles like this . . . O o . . . and told them the big circle is your brain before drugs and the small circle is your brain after drugs."

"That's admirable," says the judge. "You are free on probation." Turning to the second boy, he says, "And you, how did you do?"

"Well, your honor, I persuaded a hundred and fifty-six people to give up drugs forever."

"A hundred and fifty-six people! That's amazing! How did you manage to do that?"

"Well, I used a similar approach," he says, also drawing a large and small circle. "I said this is your asshole before prison . . ."

Dear Santa,

You must be surprised that I'm writing you today, the 26th of December. Well, I would very much like to clear up certain things that have occurred since the beginning of the month! You may recall that I wrote you a letter asking for a bicycle, an electric train set, a pair of rollerblades, and a football uniform. I reminded you that I had worked very hard studying the whole year! Not only was I the first in my class, but I had the best grades in the whole school. The truth is, there was no one in my entire neighborhood that behaved better than I did. I did good deeds for my parents, my brothers, my friends, and my neighbors. I even helped elderly strangers cross the street. There was virtually nothing I wouldn't do for humanity!

WHAT BALLS YOU HAVE LEAVING ME A FUCKING YO-YO, A STUPID-ASS WHISTLE, AND A PAIR OF SOCKS! WHAT THE FUCK WERE YOU THINKING, YOU FAT SON OF A BITCH? YOU'VE TAKEN ME FOR A SUCKER THE WHOLE FUCKING YEAR, TO COME OUT WITH SOME SHIT LIKE THIS UNDER THE DAMN TREE. AS IF YOU HADN'T FUCKED ME ENOUGH, YOU GAVE THAT LITTLE SHITHEAD ACROSS THE STREET SO MANY FUCKING TOYS THAT HE CAN'T EVEN WALK INTO HIS DAMN HOUSE! PLEASE DON'T LET ME SEE YOU TRYING TO FIT YOUR BIG FAT ASS DOWN MY CHIMNEY NEXT YEAR! I'LL FUCK YOU UP! I'LL THROW ROCKS AT THOSE STUPID-ASS REINDEER OF YOURS AND SCARE THEM THE FUCK AWAY, SO YOU'LL HAVE TO WALK YOUR BIG FAT ASS BACK TO THE NORTH POLE, JUST LIKE I HAVE TO DO SINCE YOU DIDN'T GET ME THAT FUCKING BIKE, YOU PUNK BITCH! YOU KNOW WHAT SANTA, FUCK YOU!!! NEXT YEAR YOU'LL FIND OUT HOW BAD I CAN REALLY FUCKING BE . . . YOU'VE BEEN SLEEPING ON A MOTHERFUCKER FAR TOO LONG! SO WATCH YOUR BACK NEXT YEAR, YOU FAT BITCH!

Sincerely,

Johnny

My girlfriend would have been here, but she had to finish her homework. You know your girlfriend is young when you haven't seen her in a couple of weeks and she's actually gotten taller.

—Dom Irrera, Smothers Brothers Roast, 2003

Mrs. Cohen, Mrs. Levy, and Mrs. Lefkowitz are discussing their sons. Mrs. Cohen says, "Now, my Sheldon, what a man! A world-famous lawyer he is, with big-shot clients, a mansion in Beverly Hills, a summer home in Hawaii. He has a beautiful wife and everything a man could want in the world."

Mrs. Levy says, "That's nice. Lemme tell you about my son Jonathan. He is a doctor, a world-famous researcher. He travels across the world on conferences, talks, lectures. He was nominated for a Nobel Prize in medicine. What a man!"

Mrs. Lefkowitz says, "My Herschel, he's an engineer. Now, he makes maybe $35,000 a year, and he's not famous. But his pee-pee is so long, you can line up ten pigeons in a row on it."

The ladies sip their tea for a while. Then, Mrs. Cohen says, "Actually, I got a confession to make. Sheldon's an up-and-coming lawyer in Los Angeles, but he doesn't have a mansion or a summer home. He's a bright young man with a good future."

Mrs. Levy says: "Well, I got a confession too. Jonathan is a good doctor, and he's got his share of scholarships, but a Nobel Prize-winner, he isn't."

They all look expectantly at Mrs. Lefkowitz. "Well, all right, I'll come clean, too. The last bird's gotta stand on one leg."

A baby emerges from the womb and he is a beautiful little bundle of joy. He has all his parts, he's pink and round—but there's one thing strange about him. He never stops laughing. Doctors and nurses gather round to examine him trying to figure out what would possess a newborn to laugh that way. The jolly baby just keeps on laughing, his tiny fists curled into a ball and tears rolling from his eyes. Finally, one of the doctors unfolds his tiny fingers one at a time to check if his hands are all right. In the palm of his tiny hand he is holding . . . a birth control pill!

● ● ● ●

My generation is all about where we were when Kennedy was shot. I was in the third grade. My teacher, Mrs. Lamb, came and said, "Kids, go home; your parents have something they need to tell you." I went home and said, "Dad, Mrs. Lamb was crying and said there's something you need to tell me." He said, "Son, she's a liar and a whore, I never touched her!"

—Ross Bennett, Salute to Jackie Green, 2003

● ● ● ●

Little Johnny is sitting in Beginning Sex Ed class one day when the teacher draws a picture of a penis on the board. "Does anyone know what this is?" she asks.

"Sure, my daddy has two of them!" says Johnny.

"Two of them?" the teacher says, quite amused.

"Yeah. He has a little one that he uses to pee with and a big one that he uses to brush mommy's teeth!"

Mr. White is a biology professor at a posh suburban girl's school. One day during class he says, "Miss Smith, would you name the organ in the human body which, under the appropriate conditions, expands to six times its normal size? And please define the conditions."

"Mr. White," the student gasps, "I don't think that is a proper question to ask me. I assure you that my parents will hear of this." With that, she sits down red faced.

Unperturbed, Mr. White asks Miss Jones the same question.

With complete composure she replies, "Why, of course, it is the pupil of the eye, which expands in dim light."

"Correct," says the teacher. "Now, Miss Smith, I have three things to say to you: one, you have not studied your lessons. Two, you have a dirty mind. And three, you will someday be faced with a dreadful disappointment."

A young lady comes home from a date looking depressed. "Mom," she says. "Anthony proposed to me an hour ago."

"Then why do you look so sad?"

"Because he also told me he is an atheist. Mom, he doesn't even believe there's a hell."

"Marry him anyway. Between the two of us, we'll show him how wrong he is."

A twenty-year-old girl says to her mother, "Mom, I think I'm pregnant." Her mom runs to the store, gets the pregnancy kit, she tries it out, and the kid's pregnant. The mother asks, "What rat did this to you?"

Twenty minutes later a dapper guy, distinguished, gray hair, in a Ferrari comes to the house. He says to the parents, "I cannot marry your daughter because I have my own family problems, but I'll make you a deal. If it's a boy, I'll give him fifteen million dollars and a factory. If it's a girl, I'll give her a beach house, a condo, and two million dollars. If it's twins, each will get a factory and one million dollars. If she miscarries, what do you want me to do?"

The father puts his arm around his shoulder and says, "Well, you could fuck her again."

—DICK CAPRI, SALUTE TO JACKIE GREEN, 2003

● ● ● ●

A little boy gets up to go to the bathroom in the middle of the night. As he passes his parents' bedroom he peeks in through the keyhole. He watches for a moment, then continues on down the hallway, muttering to himself, "Boy, and she gets mad at me for sucking my thumb!"

A young guy walks his girlfriend home after a date. When they reach her front door he leans up against the house with one hand and says to her, "How about a blow job?"

"What! Are you crazy?"

"Don't worry, it will be quick."

"No! Someone might see us."

"It's just a little blow job," he insists, "and I know you like it."

"No! I said no!"

"Baby... don't be like that."

Suddenly, the girl's younger sister shows up at the door in her night-gown, with her hair a mess, rubbing her eyes. She says to her sister, "Dad says either you blow him, I blow him, or he'll come downstairs and blow the guy himself—but for God's sake tell your boyfriend to take his hand off the intercom."

● ● ● ●

Donald Trump, restyle your fucking hair. What do you say to a barber to get that kind of haircut? "I fucked your daughter"?

Don't you laugh at a hair joke, Don King. Your hair looks like Freddie Roman's nutsack.

—LISA LAMPANELLI, DON KING ROAST, 2005

● ● ● ●

Annoyed by the professor of anatomy who likes to tell "naughty" stories during class, a group of female students decides that the next time he starts to tell one, they will all rise and leave the room in protest. The professor gets wind of their scheme, so he bides his time. A few weeks later, about halfway through a lecture, he leans in toward the class and says, "They say there is quite a shortage of prostitutes in France."

The girls look at one another, rise as one, and start for the door.

"Young ladies," says the professor with a broad smile, "the next plane doesn't leave till tomorrow afternoon."

What do you get when you cross Raggedy Ann and the Pillsbury Doughboy?

A red-headed bitch with a yeast infection.

● ● ● ●

Ice T is one of rap's founding fathers. Finally a black man who admits to being a father.

—SUSIE ESSMAN, RICHARD BELZER ROAST, 2001

● ● ● ●

A mother is walking down the hall when she hears a humming sound coming from her daughter's bedroom. When she opens the door she finds her daughter naked on the bed, with a vibrator. "What are you doing?" she exclaims.

"I'm thirty-five and still living at home with my parents and this is the closest I'll ever get to a husband!"

Later that week, the father is in the kitchen and hears a humming sound coming from the basement. When he goes downstairs, he finds his daughter naked on a sofa with her vibrator. "What are you doing?" he shrieks.

"I'm thirty-five and still living at home with my parents and this is the closest I'll ever get to a husband."

A couple of days later the mother hears the humming sound again, this time coming from the den. She goes in and finds her husband watching television with the vibrator buzzing away beside him. "What are you doing?" she asks.

"Watching the game with my son-in-law."

A man gets home early from work and hears strange noises coming from the bedroom. He rushes upstairs to find his wife naked on the bed, sweating and panting. "What's up?" he asks.

"I'm having a heart attack," cries the woman.

He rushes downstairs to grab the phone, but as he's dialing 911, his young son says, "Daddy! Daddy! Uncle Ted's hiding in your closet and he's got no clothes on!"

The guy slams the phone down and storms upstairs into the bedroom, past his screaming wife, and rips open the wardrobe door. Sure enough, there is his brother, totally naked, cowering on the closet floor.

"You bastard!!!" says the husband. "My wife is having a heart attack, and all you can do is run around the house naked, scaring the kids?"

● ● ● ●

These female Siamese twins were members of the Friars. It's true. They were honorary members and the great George Jessel was the abbot back then. And he told me that he fucked one of the Siamese twins. And Jessel, in his inimitable style, said that he didn't see the girls for three years and then one day he was walking down Michigan Boulevard and there they were. They came up to him and said, "Mr. Jessel, you may not remember us . . ."

—ALAN KING, SMOTHERS BROTHERS ROAST, 2003

● ● ● ●

T he dean of women at an exclusive girls' school is lecturing her students on sexual morality. "We live in very difficult times for young people. In moments of temptation, ask yourself just one question: Is an hour of pleasure worth a lifetime of shame?"

A young woman in the back of the room rises and say, "Excuse me, but how do you make it last an hour?"

A boy walks into his dad's bedroom one day only to catch him sitting on the side of his bed, sliding on a condom. His father, in attempt to hide his full erection, bends over as if to look under the bed. The boy asks curiously, "What ya doin', Dad?"

His father quickly says, "I thought I saw a rat go underneath the bed," to which his son replies, "What ya gonna do, fuck him?"

● ● ● ●

The sad part about the Catholic priests is what they did to all those boys. There's a part of me that's so insecure and neurotic. I was an altar boy. I look back and say, "What about me, Father? I wasn't sexy enough for you? You twisted old bastard."

—DOM IRRERA, SMOTHERS BROTHERS ROAST, 2003

● ● ● ●

A fter discovering her young daughter playing doctor with the neighbor's boy, the angry mother grabs the boy by the ear and drags him to his house to confront his mother.

Says the neighbor, "It's only natural for young boys and girls to explore their sexuality by playing doctor."

"Sexuality my ass!" the mother yells. "He took out her appendix!"

W hat do you call kids born in whorehouses?

Brothel sprouts.

T hree eight-year-old boys, one British, one American, and one French, meet at a Caribbean resort. They are strolling past a row of cabanas when they happened to look in an open window and spot a couple making love.

"I say, what are they doing?" asks the British lad.

"They're making love," says the American boy.

Adds the young French boy, "Yes—and badly."

•   •   •   •

My kids were conceived on Easter Sunday. Don't tell my mom. I was supposed to be in church. But you know what? I was saying, "Oh, God!" the entire time.

—KERRI LOUISE, SUNSHINE COMMITTEE VARIETY SHOW, 2005

•   •   •   •

A woman has been away for two days visiting a sick friend in another city. When she returns, her little boy greets her by saying, "Mommy, guess what! Yesterday I was playing in the closet in your bedroom and Daddy came into the room with the lady next door. They got undressed and got into your bed and then Daddy got on top of her..."

Sonny's mother holds up her hand. "Not another word. Wait till your father comes home and then I want you to repeat that, just as you are telling me now."

The father comes home and as he walks into the house, his wife says, "I'm leaving you. I'm packing now and I'm leaving you."

"But why?" asks the startled father.

"Go ahead, Sonny. Tell me again just what you told me before."

"Well," Sonny says, "I was playing in your bedroom closet and Daddy came upstairs with the lady next door and they got undressed and got into bed and Daddy got on top of her and then they did just what you did with Uncle John when Daddy was away last summer."

● ● ● ●

Woody Allen has Billy really frightened, because Woody is getting so much publicity at the same time that Billy's movie is coming out, and Billy is a really competitive guy. He's having a press conference next week to announce that he's been fucking Macaulay Caulkin.

—GARRY SHANDLING, BILLY CRYSTAL ROAST, 1992

● ● ● ●

A FEW DIRTY WORDS FROM SAMM LEVINE

The very first time I ever actually performed stand-up I was eleven years old. It was pathetic. For at least the first six months to a year that I was doing it, I was barely doing any of my own jokes because I had no faith in the material, and I was right because it was terrible; I was doing mostly Richard Jeni jokes. Then I started writing my own material and performing at friends' bar and bat mitzvahs and it was a good mix of the cleanest Richard Jeni stuff intercut with me telling jokes about my parents and my father being a dentist.

At the time I got laughs, don't ask me how. I think I got laughs when I was younger because people were much more entertained by the idea of such a young, short guy telling jokes. I got into serious trouble as a young kid doing dirty jokes. I must have been thirteen years old; we had the Levine family reunion. The first night we went out and had a very nice dinner and we rented out this lounge room at the hotel that we could all hang out in, and it was lots of fun. Everyone knew that I had been doing stand-up at friends' parties and stuff like that. The first night they all asked me if I would get up and I said, sure, I'd be happy to oblige. I got up there and did all my wonderful clean jokes and we all had a high ol' time. The next night it was the same thing, we had a really nice dinner and we rented out the lounge again and somebody said, "Samm, do some more stand-up."

So I got up and did all the rest of the jokes I had in my repertoire at the time. Now, at this reunion I was the second or third youngest person there, it was a room almost entirely of people in their forties and fifties, with the exception of two cousins of mine that I'd never met. The boy was maybe ten years old; the girl was four-teen. Their mother had not laughed through any of my bits, even the clean ones. I could almost see the look in her eyes, like, "You know, my kids can do stuff, too. It's just a shame Janie didn't bring her cello so we could show the entire family how talented Janie is. Or Bobby here, we don't have a baseball diamond where Bobby could knock one out of the park for you." Just this fucking arrogant look on her face that really bugged me.

So somebody said, "Do more, do more!" and I'm looking around the room because the only jokes that I haven't told yet are the dirty ones. I said, "Well, look guys, I'd love to do more comedy but it's gonna get a little blue." They all laughed at that, saying, "Oh, what do you mean?" And I said, "It's a little off-color." And they said, "Well, it's not like racist jokes, is it?" and I told them no. They said, "Well, then that's okay, tell whatever jokes you want." I said, "Well, all right!" How often do you get an invitation like that? So I launched right in: "You know, a defining moment in a young man's life has to be his first blow job, am I right?"

Without missing a beat this woman pops up in her seat with her two kids next to her and says, "Okay! That's enough for us!" like she'd been waiting for a joke that had the word 'crap' in it just so she could say that. I've never seen a chain reaction of "Oh no! Oh but! He's a young man, he doesn't know what he's talking about! Oh no, I'm sorry we don't mean to offend!" I would not apologize. I remember my brother stood up and pulled me out of the spot-light, if you will.

Everyone had to leave the room and we're all kind of walking around the hotel and, as I was walking back to my room with my brother, I see the father walking with his ten-year-old son. The only sentence I actually heard him say to his son was, "Some people just don't have values like us." I thought, That's a low fuckin' blow sir, I don't have values because I told a joke for adults?

There's a company called Clean Comedians and I looked over the contract that you sign and it says you can't use certain words, like crap, damn, hell; and if you do, they don't have to pay you for a gig. I was at one of those gigs with a buddy of mine and he did his set; he got an okay reaction and people were congratulating him, saying, "Oh, you were great. You were fantastic," but then you could hear people say, "I wish you could have been dirtier." And my friend said, "Me, too!" Clean Comedians usually get called on to do corporate gigs and family picnics. To their credit, though, they do rather well, but it's just the idea that a comedian is under contract to be clean.

If you're doing a "nooner" in Queens, as Tom Hanks tends to do in the movie *Punchline*, in a hospital—that's a real thing, I'm sorry to say—I think it would be wrong to go in there and tell jokes about death. But as far as going too far, it all depends on the room. For a room like my buddy was playing, for a vitamin company, he probably could have gotten away with a lot more, although I don't think he could have told jokes about fucking his father. I think there are limits but the limits are set not by the comedian but by the room. That's the mark of a great comedian, knowing those limits within the first two minutes of your act.

It is easier to tell racier types of jokes for a live audience in a show that is not being recorded. People know that they're not going to see or hear what they want to see on television and radio any-more, so more people are going to comedy clubs, more people are going to shows where they can see comedians. I think the alternative comedy movement is bigger now than it ever has been because people want to laugh, they want to hear the taboo stuff, and it's easier now for comedians to get away with that. There's not a club owner in the country who's going to turn away a comedian he knows is blue. That's why I think when you're playing live audiences and comedy clubs and small rooms you're gonna hear filthy stuff you didn't hear fifteen years ago.

● ● ● ●

Bill Maher is here. The host of *Politically Incorrect*. A man Jonathan Katz calls "the thinking man's pedophile."

—AL FRANKEN, RICHARD BELZER ROAST, 2001

● ● ● ●

Four men get together at a reunion. Three of them have sons and they start bragging about them, while the fourth guy leaves to take a leak. The first man says his son is doing so well, he now owns a factory for manufacturing furniture. "Why, just the other day he gave his best friend furniture for his new house."

The second man says his son is doing just as well. He is a manager at an exclusive car dealership. "Why, just the other day he gave his best friend a Ferrari."

The third man says his son was thriving, too. He is a manager at a bank. "Why, just the other day he gave his best friend money to buy a house."

The fourth man comes back from the bathroom, and the other three tell him that they've been discussing their very successful sons. He just shakes his head and says his son is gay and hasn't amounted to much—but he must be doing something right, because in the past few weeks he's been given a house, furniture, and a Ferrari by his three boyfriends!

The dentist is called away from the dinner table to take an urgent phone call. It is Mr. Tuckerman, explaining that young Junior has gotten himself into quite a fix. "See, he was kissing his girlfriend Corinne, and when my wife and I came back from the movies we found them stuck together."

"I'll come right over, Mr. Tuckerman," says the dentist calmly, "and don't worry about a thing. I have to unlock teenagers' braces all the time."

"Yes, but from an IUD?"

Judge: Look here Mickey Mouse, I cannot grant you a divorce from Minnie.

Mickey (stunned): Why not?

Judge: I have reviewed all the information you gave the court, but I can't find any evidence at all to support the grounds that she is crazy.

Mickey (exasperated): Your honor! I didn't say she was crazy! I said she was fucking Goofy!

Little Eddie attends a horse auction with his father. He watches as his father moves from horse to horse, running his hands up and down the horses' legs, rump, and chest. After a few minutes, Eddie asks, "Dad, why are you doing that?"

"Because when I'm buying horses, I first have to make sure that they are healthy and in good shape."

Eddie, looking worried, says, "Dad, I think the milkman wants to buy Mom."

A married woman is having an affair. Whenever her lover comes over, she puts her young son in the closet. One day the woman hears a car in the driveway and puts her lover in the closet as well. Inside the closet, the little boy says, "It's dark in here, isn't it?"

"Yes, it is," the man replies.

"You wanna buy a baseball?"

"No, thanks."

"I think you do want to buy a baseball," the little extortionist continues.

"OK. How much?" the man replies, after considering the position he is in.

"Twenty-five dollars."

"TWENTY-FIVE DOLLARS?!" But after a minute the man realizes he'd better comply, based on his precarious position.

The following week, the lover is visiting the woman again when she hears a car in the driveway and, again, places the man in the closet with her little boy. "It's dark in here, isn't it?" the boy starts off.

"Yes, it is," replies the man.

"Wanna buy a baseball glove?"

"Okay, how much?"

"Fifty dollars," the boy replies, and the transaction is completed.

The next weekend, the little boy's father says, "Hey, son. Go get your ball and glove and we'll play some catch."

"I can't. I sold them," replies the little boy.

"How much did you get for them?" asks the father, expecting to hear the profit in terms of lizards or candy.

"Seventy-five dollars," the little boy says.

"SEVENTY-FIVE DOLLARS? That's thievery! I'm taking you to church right now. You must confess your sin and ask for forgiveness," the father says, as he hauls the child away. At church the little boy goes into the confessional, draws the curtain, sits down, and says, "It's dark in here, isn't it?"

"Don't you start that shit in here," the priest says.

B less me, Father, for I have sinned. I have been with a loose woman."

"Is that you, little Johnny Parisi?" asks the priest.

"Yes, Father."

"And who was the woman you were with?"

"I can't tell you, Father. I don't want to ruin her reputation."

"Well, Johnny, I'm sure to find out her name sooner or later, so you may as well tell me now. Was it Tina Minetti?"

"I cannot say."

"Was it Teresa Volpe?"

"I'll never tell."

"Was it Nina Capeli?"

"I'm sorry but I can't give her up."

"Was it Cathy Piriano?"

"My lips are sealed, Father."

"Was it Rosa D'Angelo, then?"

"Please, Father, stop asking me."

The priest sighs in frustration. "You're very tight-lipped, Johnny Parisi, and I admire that. But you've sinned and have to atone. You cannot attend church services for four months. Now you go—and behave yourself from now on."

Johnny walks back to his pew and his friend Nino slides over and whispers, "What'd you get?"

"Four months' vacation and five good leads!"

● ● ● ●

The Smothers Brothers were big, big stars back in the sixties. They fucked every folk singer who was around in those days. Burl Ives. Peter, Paul, and Mary. I'm not sure about Mary. And Dickie tried to get a blow job from Karen Carpenter, but you know her, she won't eat anything.

Tommy claims that he once got oral sex from Mamma Cass. Then she had to eat a ham sandwich to get the taste out.

Tommy is the horny one. His hormones are still raging. Last week he was in a jerk-off contest. He came in first, third, and ninth.

—DICK CAPRI, SMOTHERS BROTHERS ROAST, 2003

● ● ● ●

One day, Janey becomes puzzled about her origins. "How did I get here, Mommy?" she asks.

"Why, God sent you, honey."

"And did God send you too, Mommy?"

"Yes, sweetheart, he did."

"And Daddy, and Grandma, and Grandpa, and their moms and dads, too?"

"Yes, baby, all of them, too."

The child shakes her head in disbelief. "Then you're telling me there's been no sex in this family for over two hundred years? No wonder everyone is so grouchy!"

● ● ● ●

I had the worst Passover. I had a yeast infection and the family couldn't come over.

—JUDY GOLD, BAD GIRLS OF COMEDY, 1998

● ● ● ●

A teenager is left to baby-sit his little brother. As his parents leave the house, his dad says, "Now, don't you bring your girlfriend over, or you're in big trouble, young man."

The teen reassures them, but as soon as they pull out of the driveway he puts his little brother to bed and calls up his girlfriend. She comes over and they start going at it in the bedroom.

She says, "Okay, 'lettuce' means harder and 'tomato' means faster."

So they're having sex, shouting, "Lettuce, tomato! Lettuce, tomato!" The little brother chooses this moment to come into the bedroom and say that he can't sleep. When he sees them he asks, "What are you doing?"

Thinking quickly, the older brother says, "Oh, we're making a sand-wich." They continue to bang away, shouting, "Lettuce, tomato! Lettuce, tomato!"

Suddenly, the little brother puts his hand to his cheek and says, "Yuck, you got mayonnaise on my face!"

●　●　●　●

I'm a fat broad. My whole family is big. My sister is five hundred pounds. You know what that fat bitch calls her-self? "Heavy." Heavy? I'm like, FURNITURE is heavy. You are one fat bitch.

—LISA LAMPANELLI, FRIARS CLUB COMEDY MARATHON FOR POLICE AND FIREFIGHTERS, 2001

●　●　●　●

A man walks into a drugstore with his young son. They hap-pen to walk by the condom display, and the boy asks, "What are these, Dad?"

"Those are called condoms, son. Men use them to have safe sex."

"Oh, I see. I've heard of that in health class at school." He looks over the display and picks up a package of three and asks, "Why are there three in this package?"

"Those are for high school boys. One for Friday, one for Saturday, and one for Sunday."

"Cool!" He notices a six-pack and asks, "Then who are these for?"

Those are for college men. Two for Friday, two for Saturday, and two for Sunday."

"Wow! Then who uses these?" he asks, picking up a twelve-pack.

With a sigh, the dad replies, "Those are for married men. One for January, one for February, one for March..."

Three sisters are engaged but their parents can't afford three elaborate weddings, so they all decide to get married on the same day. Since they can't afford to go on honeymoons, either, they all decide to stay home with their new hubbies. On the triple wedding night, the mother can't sleep, so she gets up.

When she goes past her oldest daughter's room, she hears screaming. When she passes her middle daughter's room, she hears laughing. As she walks past her youngest daughter's room, she doesn't hear anything at all.

The next morning when the men have gone off to work, the mother asks her oldest daughter, "Why were you screaming last night?"

"Mom, you always told me if something hurt I should scream."

She turns to her second daughter. "Why were you laughing so much last night?"

"Mom, you always said that if something tickled me I should laugh."

Finally, the mother looks over at her youngest daughter. "Why was it so quiet in your room last night?"

"Mom, you've always told me I shouldn't talk with my mouth full."

● ● ● ●

I'm the youngest in my family and I was always getting beaten up by the two oldest. Mom and Dad.

I had a GI Joe—it had no penis. The GI stood for "groin incomplete." Are you aware of that? Action figure, my butt. No penis equals no action. I should know; I'm Irish.

—TOM COTTER, FRESH FUNNY FACES, 1999

● ● ● ●

A city boy wants to marry a country girl. She insists that he ask her father for her hand in marriage, so off he goes to their farm to seek his approval. "I want to marry your daughter," he says to the man.

"Well, my boy, you will have to prove to me that you are a man worthy of my daughter."

"I'll do anything for my love."

"You see that cow out in the pasture? Well, go screw it."

A little puzzled, the boy says, "Okay, anything for my love." He makes love to the cow. "Now can I marry your daughter?"

"Not so fast. See that goat over yonder? Well, go screw it."

Again, the boy does the deed and returns, saying, "Now can I marry your daughter?"

"There's one more thing. See that pig in the sty? Well, go screw it."

Once again, the lovesick boy obliges and returns.

Finally, the father says the words the boy has been dying to hear: "Now you can marry my daughter."

"SCREW YOUR DAUGHTER! HOW MUCH YOU WANT FOR THAT PIG?"

S itting at home one night with his wife, a man is casually tossing peanuts into the air and catching them in his mouth. As the couple takes in the latest episode of their favorite TV program, the man loses concentration for a split second and a peanut goes into his ear. He tries to get it out but succeeds only in forcing it in deeper.

After a few hours of fruitless rooting, the couple decides to go to the emergency room, but on their way out the door they meet their daughter coming in with her boyfriend. The boyfriend takes control of the situation; he tells them he's studying medicine and that they're not to worry about a thing. He then sticks two fingers up the man's nose and asks him to blow, and low and behold, the nut shoots from the ear and out across the room.

As the youngsters go into the kitchen to get drinks, the man and his wife sit down to discuss their luck. "So," the wife says, "what do you think he'll become after he finishes school? A GP or a surgeon?"

"Well," says the man, rubbing his nose, "by the smell of his fingers, he damn well better become our son-in-law."

●　●　●　●

I myself like black women. I once almost married a black woman. I took her to the cemetery where my parents are buried. I wanted to see if dead people actually rolled over in their graves.

—DICK CAPRI, DON KING ROAST, 2005

●　●　●　●

The Mother Superior in a convent school is chatting with her young charges, and she asks them what they want to be when they grow up. A twelve-year-old says, "I want to be a prostitute." The Mother Superior faints dead away on the spot.

When they revive her, she raises her head from the ground and gasps, "What...did...you...say...?" The young girl shrugs. "I said I want to be a prostitute."

"A prostitute!" the Mother Superior says, "Oh, praise sweet Jesus! I thought you said you wanted to be a Protestant."

The science teacher stands in the front of the class and says, "Children, if you could have one raw material in the world, what would it be?" Little Stevie raises his hand and says, "I would want gold, because gold is worth a lot of money and I could buy a Corvette."

The teacher nods, and then calls on little Susie, who says, "I would want platinum because platinum is worth more than gold and I could buy a Porsche."

The teacher smiles, and then calls on Little Johnny. Johnny stands up and says, "I would want silicone."

"Silicone? Why silicone?"

"Because my mom has two bags of the stuff and you should see all the sports cars outside our house!"

At school, a boy hears the older kids talking about "pussy," and "their bitch." Confused by these terms, he goes to his mother. "Mom," the boy asks. "What's a pussy?"

The mother, thinking quickly, finds the family dictionary and opens it up to a picture of a cat. "Son, that is a pussy," she says.

He then asks "What's a bitch?"

The mother opens to a picture of a dog and says, "Son, this is a bitch."

The kid walks away, still confused, and sees his father watching television. He says, "Dad, what's a pussy?" The father doesn't want to miss the baseball game so he quickly whips out his *Penthouse* magazine to the centerfold, grabs a marker, and draws a circle around the vagina and says, "Son, this is a pussy!"

The son, now starting to understand what the older boys are talking about asks, "Then, what is a bitch?"

The dad replies, "That's everything outside the circle!"

Two parents take their son on vacation and go to a nude beach. The father goes for a walk along the sand while the son plays in the water. Soon, the boy runs to his mother and says, "Mommy, I saw some ladies with boobies a lot bigger than yours!"

"The bigger they are, the dumber they are!" replies Mom.

With that, the little boy runs back into the water and continues to play. Several minutes later, though, he is back, saying, "Mommy, I saw some men with pee-pees a lot bigger than Daddy's!"

"The bigger they are, the dumber they are!" she replies again.

Satisfied, the boy goes back to play—but it's not long before he returns to his mother. "Mommy, I just saw Daddy talking to the dumbest lady on the beach—and the more he talked, the dumber he got!"

• • • •

This agent called in to the William Morris Agency and spoke to his boss. He said, "I'm not coming in today; I'm sick." The boss said, "How sick are you?" The agent said, "I'm lying in bed right now and I'm fucking my sister. Is that sick enough?"

—NORM CROSBY, DANNY AIELLO ROAST, 1997

• • • •

A farmer is driving along the road with a load of horse manure. A little boy, playing in front of his house, sees him and calls, "PEEyew! Whatcha got in your truck, mister?"

"Fertilizer," the farmer replies.

"What are you going to do with it?"

"Put it on my strawberries."

"You ought to live here! We put sugar and cream on ours."

Little Johnny comes home from school to find the family's pet rooster dead in the front yard. Rigor mortis has set in and it is flat on its back with its legs in the air. When his Dad comes home Johnny says, "Dad our rooster's dead and his legs are sticking straight up in the air. Why are his legs sticking up like that?"

Thinking quickly, his father says, "Son, that's so God can reach down from the clouds and lift the rooster straight up to heaven."

"Gee Dad, that's great," says little Johnny. A few days later, when Dad comes home from work, Johnny rushes out to meet him, yelling, "Dad, Dad, we almost lost Mom today!"

"What do you mean?" says Dad.

"Well . . . I got home from school early, and went up to your bedroom and there was Mom flat on her back with her legs in the air screaming, 'Jesus, I'm coming, I'm coming.' If it hadn't been for Uncle George holding her down, we'd have lost her for sure!"

● ● ● ●

When I was a kid, safe sex meant not getting your foot caught in the glove compartment.

—Vic Arnell, Salute to Soupy Sales, 2002

● ● ● ●

The priest at Sunday mass notices that Michael took a ten-dollar bill and two one-dollar bills from the collection plate, instead of putting something in. He thinks to himself, "I'd better keep an eye on Michael."

The next week he notices the same thing. So he waits outside the church when mass is over and, as Michael comes out, accosts him and says, "Michael, my lad, tell me, why did you take out a ten-dollar bill and two one-dollar bills two weeks in a row, instead of putting money into the collection plate?"

"Father," Michael replies, "I'm embarrassed, but I did it because I needed a blow job."

The priest is surprised but maintains his composure. "Listen, my son. You have sinned against the church and that is very serious. I'll be watching you from now on."

When he goes back to the rectory, the priest calls Mother Agatha at the convent. He says, "Mother, you've been such a good friend to me and I know that I can confide in you. I have a question. What is a blow job?"

Replies the nun, "Oh, about twelve dollars."

● ● ● ●

I have a six-year-old daughter. She woke up the other day and said, "Daddy I had a dream that Barbie slept with me."

I said, "You too? Was she bad?"

"No, Daddy, Barbie isn't bad."

"Well, she was in Daddy's dream."

—JOEY CALLAHAN, FRIARS NEW FACES OF COMEDY, 2002

● ● ● ●

A man is invited to meet his fiancée's mother for the very first time and is understandably nervous. Unfortunately, he is also a little gassy. He is sitting in the living room, right next to the dog and directly across from his future mother-in-law, when suddenly a small fart escapes from him. "Rover!" the woman yells.

"Whew," the man thinks, "she's blaming the dog!" Emboldened, he leans to his side and farts a little more.

"Rover!" the woman yells again.

"Ha!" the man thinks. "I've got it made now!" He leans a little further and unleashes a gigantic fart.

"Rover!" the woman screams. "Get over here before that pervert shits on you!"

A salesman stops at a farmhouse one evening to ask for room and board for the night. The farmer tells him he has no spare room. "I could let you sleep with my daughter," he says, "if you promise not to bother her."

The salesman agrees.

After a hearty supper, the stranger is taken to the room. He undresses in the dark, slips into bed, and feels the farmer's daughter at his side. Well... he can't resist: he gently turns her over to face him and begins caressing her. As she doesn't resist, he soon has his way with her. She never lets out a single sound of protest, so the salesman can only assume that she is pleased with his attentions.

The next morning he asks for his bill.

"It'll be just two dollars, since you had to share the bed with my daughter," says the farmer.

"Your daughter was very cold," the salesman says.

"Yes, I know," says the farmer. "We're going to bury her today."

• • • •

I've known Chevy Chase a long time. I knew his family.
His dad told me an interesting story about Chevy. When
Chevy was a little boy, he used to masturbate a lot. One
day his father caught him and said, "You keep doing that
and one day you're going to star in *Fletch Lives*."

—RICHARD BELZER, CHEVY CHASE ROAST, 2002

• • • •

A young man invites his parents to meet his fiancée over
cocktails at the Waldorf Hotel in New York. After his family has
departed, the girl wants to know what kind of impression she's made.

"I'm sorry to tell you this, dear," the young man says. "But while you
were in the ladies' room, my mother told me that she considered you
rather uncouth."

"Did you tell them I graduated from finishing school and from
Bennington?"

"Yes."

"Did you tell them my family enjoys the highest social standing in
Southampton?"

"I certainly did, dear."

"Then what the fuck is all this uncouth shit about?"

An inexperienced young blond man is about to get married.
He asks his father what he should do to his wife on their wedding
night.

"Well," attempting delicacy, "you must take the thing you used to play with more than anything else when you were a teenager and put it where your wife wee-wees."

"Really, Dad?"

"Believe me, son, you'll love it."

So on his wedding night, the young man takes his baseball and throws it into the toilet.

W hen it is time for milk and cookies at nursery school, Joey refuses to line up with the rest of the class. "What's the matter, Joey?" the teacher asks. "Don't you want any cookies today?"

"Fuck the milk and cookies," Joey answers.

Shocked, the teacher figures that it is a plea for attention and the best way to handle the incident is to ignore it.

The next day, when it comes time for milk and cookies, Joey again holds back. The teacher asks the same question and gets the same reply: "Fuck the milk and cookies." This time, she calls Joey's mother and asks her to intervene.

The mother comes to class the next day and hides in the closet in time to observe milk-and-cookie time. The teacher asks Joey if he wants his snack, and once again he replies, "Fuck the milk and cookies."

With that, the teacher opens the closet door and asks Joey's mother what she thinks of that!

"Shit," she says. "If the little bastard doesn't want any, then fuck him! Don't give him any!"

• • • •

I must tell you, Susie Essman came here tonight under duress because she spent last night at the hospital awaiting the birth of her next boyfriend.

—FREDDIE ROMAN, BAD GIRLS OF COMEDY, 1998

• • • •

"**D**addy, what are those two dogs doing to each other?"

"Uhh . . . one's sick and the other one's pushing him to the hospital!"

A Jewish mother walks her son to the school bus stop on his first day of kindergarten. "Behave, my *bubbaleh*," she says. "Take good care of yourself and think about your mother, *tataleh*! And come right back home on the bus, *scheine kindeleh*. Your mommy loves you a lot, my *ketsaleh*!"

At the end of the school day the bus comes back and she runs to her son and hugs him. "So what did my *pupaleh* learn on his first day of school?"

"I learned my name is Jerry!"

Four Catholic friends are having tea. The first woman tells her friends, "My son is a priest. When he walks into a room, everyone calls him 'Father.'"

The second woman chirps, "My son is a bishop. Whenever he walks into a room, people call him, 'Your Grace.'"

The third Catholic friend can't wait to chime in. "My son is a cardinal. When he walks into a room, people say, 'Your Eminence.'"

The fourth Catholic mother sips her tea in silence for a while. When she can't withstand the expectant stares of her friends any longer, she says, "My son is a gorgeous, six foot two, hard-bodied dancer. When he walks into a room, people say, 'Oh, my God!'"

What's the last thing Tickle Me Elmo receives before he leaves the factory?

Two test tickles.

Eight reasons why Santa can't possibly be a man: 1. Men can't pack a bag. 2. Men would rather be dead than caught wearing red velvet. 3. Men would feel their masculinity is threatened by being seen with all those elves. 4. Men don't answer their mail. 5. Men would never put up with their physiques being described, even in jest, as a "bowl-full of jelly." 6. Men aren't interested in stockings unless somebody's wearing them. 7. Having to do the Ho Ho Ho thing would seriously inhibit a man's ability to pick up women. 8. Finally, being responsible for Christmas would require a commitment.

A devoted blond mom is baking a cake one day when her little son asks, "Mom, can I lick the bowl?"

"No," she replies adamantly. "You must flush it like everyone else does."

Maria has just gotten married and, being a traditional Italian girl, she is still a virgin and very inexperienced with men. On her wedding night, she and her new husband are staying at her mother's house and she is very nervous when bedtime arrives.

"Don't worry, Maria," her mother says. "Tony's a good man. Go upstairs and he'll take good care of you."

So, up she goes and, when she gets there, Tony takes off his shirt and exposes his hairy chest. Maria runs back downstairs to her mother and says, "Mama, Mama, Tony's got a big hairy chest."

"Don't worry, Maria," says her mother. "All good men have hairy chests. Go upstairs. He'll take good care of you."

So, up she goes again and when she gets back to the bedroom, Tony takes off his pants, exposing his hairy legs. Again, Maria flees downstairs to her mother. "Mama, Mama, Tony's got hairy legs."

"Don't worry, Maria. All good men have hairy legs. Go upstairs and Tony will take good care of you."

So, up she goes one more time. When she gets back to the bedroom, Tony takes off his socks, and she can see that he is missing three toes on his left foot! Alarmed, she runs downstairs. "Mama, Mama, Tony's got a foot-and-a-half."

"Stay here and stir the pasta, Maria," says the matriarch. "This is a job for Mama!"

● ● ● ●

I was a goody two-shoes growing up but I hung out with all the bad girls so I could get the dangerous reputation without the rehab and the abortions.

—DEBBIE PEARLMAN, FRIARS NEW FACES OF COMEDY, 2002

● ● ● ●

Discussion between a father and his twelve-year-old son:

"Dad, I have to do a report for school. Can I ask you a question?"

"Sure, son, what's the question?"

"What is 'politics'?"

"Well, let's take our home for example. I am the wage earner, so let's call me capitalism. Your mother is the administrator of the money, so we'll call her the government. We take care of your needs, so let's call you the people. We'll call the maid the working class, and your baby brother we will call the future. Do you understand?"

"I'm not really sure, Dad. I'll have to think about it."

That night, awakened by his baby brother's crying, the boy goes to see what is wrong. Discovering the baby has soiled his diaper, the boy goes to his parents' room where he finds his mother sound asleep. He then goes to the maid's room where, peeking through the keyhole, he sees his father in bed with the maid. The boy's knocking goes totally unheeded by the busy couple, so the boy returns to his room and goes back to bed.

The next morning:

"Dad, now I think I understand politics."

"That's great son. Explain it to me in your own words."

"Well, Dad, while capitalism is screwing the working class, the government is sound asleep, the people are being completely ignored, and the future is full of shit."

It is a hot and heavy marital moment. Passions are flaring as she rolls her husband underneath her and takes control on top. Her head is spinning, she is gasping, her heart is about to burst—when the door flies open and little Tommy walks in.

"MOMMY, MOMMY!" Tommy cries, "what are you doing to my Daddy?!"

Recovering quickly, Mommy answers, "Well, sweetheart, to keep Daddy from getting too big, every now and then I bounce up and down on him to force some of the air out."

"Oh, Mommy," says the tyke, "I don't know why you even bother. The lady next door is just gonna blow him up again."

● ● ● ●

Hef has fondled more playmates than Michael Jackson.

—JEFFREY ROSS, HUGH HEFNER ROAST, 2001

● ● ● ●

A middle-aged couple with two beautiful daughters decides to try one last time for the son they've always wanted. Soon, the wife becomes pregnant, and nine months later she delivers a baby boy.

The joyful father rushes to the nursery to see his new son, and is horrified to find an incredibly ugly baby. He goes to his wife and says, "I cannot possibly be the father of that hideous child. Look at the two beautiful daughters I fathered. Have you been fooling around on me?"

"Not this time."

After a woman gives birth the doctor comes in and says, "I have to tell you something about your baby."

The woman sits up in bed, alarmed. "What's wrong with my baby, Doctor? What's wrong??"

"Well, now, nothing's wrong, exactly, but your baby is a little bit different. Your baby is a hermaphrodite."

"A hermaphrodite...what's that???"

"Well, it means your baby has the features of a male and a female."

The woman turns pale. "Oh my God! You mean it has a penis AND a brain?"

A third grade teacher says, "Okay, everybody, the word for today is 'fascinate,' and I'd like you to come up with a sentence using that word."

Little Cindy raises her hand and says, "I went to the zoo on Friday, and it was fascinating." The teacher says, "That's nice but we want to use 'fascinate,' not 'fascinating.'"

Larry raises his hand and says, "I went to a movie Saturday and I was fascinated." The teacher says, "That's nice too, but remember that we want to use 'fascinate,' not 'fascinated.'"

Johnny pipes up: "My sister has a shirt with twelve buttons on it but her tits are so big she can only fasten eight."

A Jamaican man buys a round of drinks for everyone in the bar, announcing that his wife has just given birth to "a typical Jamaican baby boy weighing twenty pounds."

Congratulations are showered him from all around, and many exclamations of "Wow!" can be heard. A woman faints due to sympathy pains.

Two weeks later, the man returns to the bar. The bartender says, "Say, you're the father of that twenty-pound baby! How much does he weigh now?"

"Fifteen pounds," answers the proud papa.

The bartender is puzzled. "What happened?"

"Mon, we had him circumcised."

A beautiful young woman wants to meet Santa Claus, so she puts on a robe and stays up late on Christmas Eve. Santa arrives, climbs down the chimney, and begins filling the stockings. He is about to move on to the next house when the gorgeous redhead says in a sexy voice, "Oh, Santa, please stay. Keep the chill away."

Santa replies, "HO HO HO, gotta go, gotta go. Gotta get the presents to the children, you know."

The girl drops her robe to reveal a sexy bra and panties, and says in her most flirtatious tone, "Oh, Santa, don't run a mile; just stay for a while..."

Santa begins to sweat but replies, "HO HO HO, gotta go, gotta go. Gotta get the presents to the children, you know."

The girl takes off her bra and says, "Oh, Santa...please...stay."

Santa wipes his brow but replies, "HO HO HO, gotta go, gotta go. Gotta get the presents to the children, you know."

She loses the panties and says, "Oh, Santa...please...stay...."

Santa, trembling, says, "HEY HEY HEY, gotta stay, gotta stay! Can't get up the chimney with my pecker this way!!!"

•   •   •   •

As a teenager Richard Belzer was so ugly he had red marks from where people touched him with a ten-foot pole.

—BILL MAHER, RICHARD BELZER ROAST, 2001

•   •   •   •

A grandfather asks his grandson what he did today.

"Today I played with my choo-choo and I fell down and got a boo-boo on my knee."

"Now, Timmy, you're a big boy. You should say, 'Today I played with my trains and I fell down and got an abrasion on my knee.' Okay?"

"Okay, I've got it. I say 'train' and 'abrasion.'"

"You're a good boy. Now, Grandpa's going to read you a story. Which one would you like?"

"How about *Winnie the Shit?*"

A young army private is home on leave. He is talking to his dad about his experience at jump school, where he learned to be a paratrooper.

"Dad, on my first jump I froze up at the door on the plane. A big black sergeant standing behind me told me that if I didn't jump, he was gonna cram about twelve inches of dick up my ass."

"Well, did you jump?"

"Just a little at first . . ."

• • • •

Poor Ben Stiller hasn't been the same since he saw his Mom go down on Señor Wences.

—Jeffrey Ross, Jerry Stiller Roast, 1999

• • • •

I t's the spring of 1957 and Bobby goes to pick up his date. He's a pretty hep guy with his own car. The girl's father answers the door and invites him in. "Carrie's not ready yet, so why don't you have a seat?" he says.

"That's cool," says Bobby.

Carrie's father asks Bobby what they're planning to do, and he replies politely that they will probably just go to the soda shop or a movie.

"Why don't you two go out and screw? I hear all the kids are doing it."

"Um ... excuse me, sir—I thought you said that we should go out and screw."

"Yeah, Carrie really likes to screw; she'll screw all night if we let her!"

Well, this just makes Bobby's eyes light up, and his plan for the evening takes a radically different turn.

A few minutes later, Carrie comes downstairs in her little poodle skirt and announces that she's ready to go. Almost breathless with anticipation, Bobby escorts his date out the front door.

About twenty minutes later, Carrie rushes back into the house, slams the door behind her, and screams at her father: "DARN IT, DADDY! IT'S CALLED THE TWIST!"

A woman has three virgin daughters and they are all getting married within a short period of time. Because Mom is a bit worried about their first experiences of sex, she makes them all promise to send a postcard from the honeymoon with a few words on it about how they are finding the physical aspect of marriage.

The first daughter sends a card from Hawaii two days after the wedding. The card says nothing but "Maxwell House." Mom is puzzled at first but then goes to the kitchen and gets out the Maxwell House jar. It says, "Good to the last drop." Mom blushes, but is pleased for her daughter.

The second daughter sends a card from Vermont one week after the wedding reading, simply, "Benson & Hedges." Mom goes straight to her husband's cigarette package and reads, "Extra Long for Extra Flavor." She is again slightly embarrassed, but still happy for her daughter.

The third daughter is spending her honeymoon in the Caribbean. Mom waits for a week but no card arrives. Another week goes by and still nothing. Finally, after a whole month, a card comes. The handwriting is shaky, and the card says "British Airways." Mom takes out a magazine and flips through it until she finds an ad for the airline. It reads, "Three times a day, seven days a week, both ways."

Mom faints.

One day a teacher decides to conduct a taste test with her students. She picks a little boy, blindfolds him, puts a Hershey Kiss in his mouth and asks, "Do you know what it is?"

"No, I don't," says the boy.

"Okay, I'll give you a clue. It's the thing your Daddy wants from your Mommy before he goes to work."

Suddenly, a little girl at the back of the room yells, "Spit it out! It's a piece of ass!"

• • • •

Richard Belzer's, like, the first person in history to actually look better on *The Simpsons*.

—JEFFREY ROSS, RICHARD BELZER ROAST, 2001

• • • •

CHAPTER 7

Over the Hill

... and deep in the woods, what the hell is granny up to with that wolf?

A•••

little old grandmother goes into a sex shop, obviously very unstable on her feet, shaking from head to toe.

"Yyyoooungg Mmmmannn," she asks the clerk, "ddddoooo you ssseeelllll vvvvibbbbrattttorssss?"

"Yes, ma'am, we do," he replies.

"Bbbbigggg ffffffluoresssssscent ooooorangggggge ones?"

"Yes, ma'am."

"Abbbboooooouttttt sssssssixxxxxxttttteennnn innnnchessss lllll-loooonggggg?"

"Yes, ma'am."

"Tttthhhhatttt ttttakkkkkke eeeeeigggggghtttttt DDDDD Cccceeeelllll bbbbbatttttteries?"

"Yes, ma'am."

"Ccccccannnn yyyyouuuu tttelll mmmmeee hhhhowwww ttttoooo ttturrrnnn tthe ffffuucccckkkkinggg tthingggg offffff?"

• • • •

My grandmother went to Atlantic City. She has this thick Italian accent and tries to speak English.

"Grandma, where'd you stay?"

"Touch my hole," she said. "Touch my hole, Vic!"

She meant Taj Mahal. It took me two weeks to figure that out.

—VIC DiBITETTO, COMEDY TONIGHT!, 2003

• • • •

A guy is driving out in the middle of nowhere, very lost. Finally he spots two farmhouses, so he goes up to the first one and looks in the doorway. He sees an old lady yanking on her boobs and an old man jerking off. He is so freaked out that he goes to the next house and says, "What's up with your neighbors?"

"Oh, that's the Robinsons," the neighbor replies. "They're both deaf. She's telling him to go milk the cow and he's telling her to go fuck herself!"

A couple is planning to go on a second honeymoon for their fiftieth wedding anniversary. The wife says, "Let's go to all the same places that we did on our first honeymoon."

"Uh huh," agrees the husband.

"We will do all the things that we did on our first honeymoon," continues the wife.

"Uh huh," agrees the husband.

"And we will make love just like we did on our first honeymoon," says the wife.

"Uh huh," says the husband, "but this time I get to sit on the side of the bed and cry 'It's too big, it's too big!'"

● ● ● ●

After a huge string of marvelous hit movies, after his incredible success on the Oscars, Billy Crystal still has time to do charitable work and be a good guy. He went to a senior citizens' home in Los Angeles and sat down beside a sweet little old lady and said, "Do you know who I am?" and she said, "No, but go to the front desk. They'll tell you who you are."

—NORM CROSBY, BILLY CRYSTAL ROAST, 1992

● ● ● ●

A man and a woman are talking about how they'd like to celebrate their fiftieth anniversary. The woman decides she will cook a nice dinner. The husband suggests that they relive their wedding night by eating at the dinner table naked. The wife agrees.

"Honey, my nipples are as hot for you as they were fifty years ago," says the wife, as they dine *au natural.*

"That's because they are sitting in your soup."

In a tiny village lived an old maid. In spite of her age, she was still a virgin and was very proud of it. As she approached the end of her life, she told the local undertaker that she wanted the following inscription on her tombstone: "Born as a virgin, lived as a virgin, died as a virgin."

Soon, the old maid died peacefully and the undertaker relayed her wishes to his stone carver. The carver began his task, but being lazy he decided that the inscription was unnecessarily long. He carved simply, "RETURNED UNOPENED."

● ● ● ●

Freddie is one of our profound thinkers. He thinks about important things like: Is performing cunnilingus on Yom Kippur technically breaking the fast?

—DICK CAPRI, FREDDIE ROMAN ROAST, 1999

● ● ● ●

A couple, both age seventy-eight, went to a sex therapist's office. The doctor asked, "What can I do for you?"

"Will you watch us have sexual intercourse?" asked the man.

The doctor was puzzled, but agreed. When the couple finished, the doctor said, "There's nothing wrong with the way you have intercourse," and charged them $50.

The following week, the pair came in again with the same request. The doctor provided the same service and charged the same amount. This happened for several more weeks without variation. Finally, the doctor asked, "Just exactly what are you trying to find out?"

"We're not trying to find out anything," said the man. "She's married and we can't go to her house. I'm married and we can't go to my house. The Hilton charges $108. The Holiday Inn charges $90. We can do it here for $50 and I get $43 back from Medicare!"

● ● ● ● ●

Hef, one of the girls explained to me why you have seven girlfriends: one to put it in and the other six to move you around.

—JEFFREY ROSS, HUGH HEFNER ROAST, 2001

● ● ● ● ●

I t's Henry's thirty-third birthday, and he goes to the post office to
collect a package. When the lady behind the counter brings out the par-
cel, Henry can't help telling her that it is his birthday.

"Oh, happy birthday!" she says. "How old are you?"

"Thirty-three," replies Henry.

"Well, have a very happy day!"

With that, Henry leaves the post office and walks to the bus stop.
Soon, an older lady joins him. Again, Henry can't resist telling her
that it is his birthday.

"Oh, happy birthday," says the lady. "Now . . . don't tell me how old
you are! I know a unique way of figuring that out, and it never fails."

"Really? What is it?"

"Well . . . it's a little embarrassing . . . but if you let me feel your balls
for about five minutes, I can tell exactly how old you are."

"I don't believe it."

"Why don't you let me prove it?"

After a couple of minutes, curiosity gets the better of Henry and he
agrees to this unorthodox technique. The lady helps herself to a good,
vigorous feel, and after five minutes she says, "You are exactly thirty-
three years old."

"How on earth could you possibly know that?" exclaims Henry, very
impressed.

"Um . . . I was in line behind you at the post office."

• • • •

You know the most popular bra size in Florida?
  38 Long.

—FREDDIE ROMAN, SALUTE TO SOUPY SALES, 2002

• • • •

An old lady in a nursing home is riding up and down the halls in her wheelchair making "revving" sounds, as if she's driving a car. As she races by his room, an old man jumps out and says, "Excuse me, ma'am, but you were speeding. Can I see your driver's license?"

She digs around in her purse a little, pulls out a candy wrapper, and hands it to him. He looks it over, gives her a warning, and sends her on her way.

Up and down the halls she goes again, and again the old man jumps out of his room and says, "Excuse me, ma'am, but I saw you cross the center line back there. Can I see your registration please?"

She digs around in her purse a little, pulls out a drugstore receipt, and hands it to him. He looks it over, gives her another warning, and sends her on her way.

She zooms off again, up and down the halls, weaving all over. As she comes to the old man's room, again he jumps out. This time, he's stark naked and has an erection!

The old lady frowns and says, "Oh no! Not the Breathalyzer again!"

An old man is sitting on a bench in the park, crying. A younger man walks up to him and asks him what is wrong.

"I am married to a sexy twenty-one-year-old who just loves sex. We have sex the minute I get home from work and right after dinner. She gives me fantastic oral sex any time I want it."

"Wow! It sounds to me like you have a great life. Why on earth are you crying?"

"I can't remember where I live!"

• • • •

All the young girls, they have the tattoo on the lower back and it's always something beautiful like a bird or a butterfly emerging from the cocoon of their butt crack, and it looks great 'cause she's twenty years old. But thirty years from now, that's gonna look like a moth that's slammed against a windshield.

—Tom Cotter, Sunshine Committee Raffle Night, 2005

• • • •

Two old ladies are standing at a bus station and they are both smoking. Suddenly, it starts to pour. One of the women takes a condom out of her purse, cuts the end off, and slips it over her cigarette.

"What are you doing?" the other woman inquires.

"I don't like it when my cigarette gets wet so I cover it with a condom."

"That's quite a handy device. Where did you get it?"

"At the pharmacy, of course."

The next day, her friend goes to the pharmacy and asks the clerk for a condom.

"What size?" asks the clerk.

"I don't know...one that will fit a Camel."

A FEW DIRTY WORDS
FROM JEFFREY ROSS

I don't ever think that I am racy. My regular act is not dirty or blue, really—it might be politically incorrect but it's not dirty. Recently, a couple told me that they weren't coming to see me with their in-laws because they didn't think they would like me. I got offended. "So, in other words, you're calling me dirty?" I was like, "What am I, a pornographer?" I just think of it as how I talk.

When I first started, I was definitely not as edgy because I think edginess comes with confidence. The edge comes when you get a little swagger to your step. In the beginning you're just trying to get on Letterman and Leno. Once you have that credit under your belt, you can stop trying to do clean jokes for TV and you can start trying to make money and do a nightclub act and do the comedy you want to do.

I didn't come from a very stuffy background. For the most part, my parents were into Cheech and Chong and stuff like that. They weren't into corny humor, they were into really cool stuff. We're in the catering business, so I grew up in a kitchen full of Brits and Scots and Haitians and people from South America and all sorts of people from all walks of life. Comedy would always be what united us. These were not classy people, these were very down-to-earth people. My grandfather was very sarcastic. It wasn't that he was dirty or blue, but he would cut deep. Nothing was off limits; he had no problem making fun of anything. That definitely stayed with me.

I never pick sides, politically. I was in Washington and you have people there from the Republican Party, from the Democratic Party—I'm right down the middle. They come to have a good time, so I check my ego and don't think too much about things. I want it to just be about laughing and having fun.

If I go on *The View* or Letterman or Leno or Kimmel—it's got to be basically TV-friendly. The thing that drives me to the Roasts is that I can be different. It's only when you get to the Roast where it becomes, "Oh boy, that guy, he's got some mouth." I find the Roasts to be liberating, like driving a race car or jumping out of a plane. A Roast is this crazy rollercoaster where you can say whatever you want and you almost can't go too far. It's like eating a big piece of cheesecake with ice cream and hot fudge, every now and then. You indulge yourself as much as you want. If I had to be that mean and that dirty every day I'd get sick of it, but because it's only a once-in-a-blue-moon type of thing, a special occasion honoring somebody you care about or respect, it's a lot of joy for me.

I don't think I ever went too far. Bea Arthur did kick my ass one time. She held me down and beat me up pretty good—no I'm only kidding. The trick is I don't try to be hurtful. I don't try to do things that would really affect people. I try to pick areas in their life or in their careers that they're really good sports about.

There was one exception—the Comedy Central Roast of Pam Anderson. Courtney Love was charging me like a rhino and the best lines, the meanest lines, I didn't think of until afterward. I mean, why couldn't somebody from PETA sedate this charging rhino? But the truth is, that was a very special case. I felt like I single-handedly took the Roast from being a sophisticated thing with a dais and tuxedos to a roller derby.

I try to find topics that other people aren't going to get to first—that's part of the challenge, finding stuff that no one else is gonna go after. No one was gonna mention Kurt Cobain that night and neither was I, actually. It was only after the way Courtney was so crazy that I let that rip. The trick is to be fast on your feet. You've got to be able to improvise and change it up. I just said, "Now folks, how is it possible that Courtney Love actually looks worse than Kurt Cobain?" You just saw the joke hit her face and then when she finally laughed it was like, boom! Euphoria. Everybody was laughing. I wouldn't have done it behind her back; I wouldn't have done it if she wasn't there.

My favorite Roast was probably when Milton Berle was poking me in the ribs during my first Roast ever. It was for Steven Seagal and every time I got a laugh he would just poke me in the ribs so only he could see. Buddy Hackett finally yelled out, "Milton, let the kid work, remember when you used to?" It's like he just kept poking me to remind me to relax 'cause I was really nervous. I'm sure he could sense that. I guess I don't need anybody to calm me down anymore.

I don't think being edgy is about boundaries or going too far. I think it's about context. I can tell a joke to a group of people at a college that is hilarious but that same joke at a charity event could be horrible. I love to jump around, I love different kinds of shows, I love making my material special for the event. I did a USO gala recently, it was a very formal black-tie affair and you don't want to be too dirty. But then I'll do a USO show in front of marines and I'll rip on Iraq and it's a totally different thing. It's for the boys; it's foxhole humor, that's where I can really let them rip. There are no subtleties in the war zone.

I think it's easier to be funny when the conditions are grim, like a lot of these shows I've done in New Orleans and Mississippi. You're in a flatbed truck, you're on a ramp in a parking lot with a makeshift microphone, makeshift stages, people sitting around, and some haven't slept in days. They're completely depressed and they've been dragging dead bodies out of buildings, and they really need to laugh. I come out and say, "This is exciting, they said if I do well here they'll get me a job running FEMA." To me, those are the best audiences there are, there's a thrill, an any-thing-goes sort of energy.

With the soldiers, you're sort of speaking vicariously for them and you can go up and make fun of the situation or goof on the general or goof on the sergeant major who has been giving them shit for days. I always try to make a few jokes about the situation. Like in the Middle East, I tell them, "If you can get some time off there is a great strip club near here that shows the whole face." I do a few jokes about Iraq and Afghanistan and then by the end of my set I've gotten them out of Iraq and Afghanistan and into New Jersey or Colorado or Tennessee or wherever they're from. I take them home for twenty minutes. I feel like that's my job.

Sometimes I like to just push it with an audience. I saw Hackett do it once. He said you can get them back. It's a little crazy but it's fun, just to see how likeable you are, like a little experiment. Even when I don't get a laugh I still think that they appreciate me pushing it. I always get them back.

●　●　●　●

I was actually walking around downtown not too long ago, and I saw Milton Berle in an antique shop—800 bucks.

—JEFFREY ROSS, STEVEN SEAGAL ROAST, 1995

●　●　●　●

An old couple is watching a religious service on television. The evangelist calls to all who wanted to be healed to place one hand on their television set and the other hand on the body part where they want to be healed. The old woman gets up and slowly hobbles to the TV set, places her right hand on it, and places her left hand on her arthritic shoulder.

Then the old man gets up, places his right hand on the set, and puts his left hand on his crotch.

His wife scowls at him and says, "I guess you just don't get it. The purpose of this is to heal the sick—not raise the dead."

A ninety-two-year-old man goes to the doctor, complaining of chest pains. A few days later the doctor sees the man walking down the street beaming from ear to ear, with a gorgeous young lady on his arm. At his follow-up visit the doctor says, "I saw you on the street last week. I guess you're feeling a lot better!"

"I'm just doing what you said, Doctor. You told me to 'get a hot mamma and be cheerful.'"

"I didn't say that! I said, 'You've got a heart murmur. Be careful!'"

O ne night, a horny old geezer decides to get himself a hooker. Since he doesn't have much money, he looks for the cheapest whore in town. He soon finds what he's looking for and spends ten dollars for oral sex and intercourse.

The next morning, the old guy wakes up and discovers he has crabs. So, he gets dressed and retraces his steps. He notices the same hooker on the street corner, so he marches over to her and says, "Listen, sister, what's the idea? You gave me crabs!"

"Hey, old man, what did you expect for ten dollars? Lobster?"

• • • •

Trump, you're lucky Don King has worse fucking hair than you. I didn't think that was possible. You realize you have turned prematurely orange? I love your hair Don. It looks like Eartha Kitt's pussy.

—STEWIE STONE, DON KING ROAST, 2005

• • • •

An elderly couple comes back from a wedding in a pretty romantic mood. The wife looks fondly at her husband and says, "I remember when you used to kiss me every chance you had."

Touched, the old man leans over and gives her a peck on the cheek.

"I also remember when you used to hold my hand at every opportunity." The old man reaches over and gently places his hand on hers.

"I also remember when you used to nibble on my neck and send chills down my spine."

This time, the old man stares blankly for a second, then gets up. As he heads out of the living room, his wife asks, "Was it something I said? Where are you going?"

"I'm going upstairs to get my teeth!"

What does an old woman have between her breasts that a young woman doesn't?

A navel.

• • • •

Eight years ago, Rob, your weight was still in triple digits. You roasted me in this very room. And for eight years I've plotted revenge, but I can see that the aging process has already beaten me to it. Abe Vigoda is here. I love Abe Vigoda. I will not say anything bad about Abe Vigoda because I was always taught to speak well of the dead. Bret Butler, I am so glad to see her. You know why she comes to the Friars? Because old Jews have narcotics with them.

—BILLY CRYSTAL, ROB REINER ROAST, 2000

• • • •

One day an eighty-five-year-old man is taking a stroll around his hometown. He's lived there his whole life, and as he passes the landmarks, homes, and streets from his youth, he starts reminiscing: "I remember helping build that bridge when I was twenty-five. I worked hard on that. But people don't refer to you as 'the bridge builder' if you do that here. No, no, they don't!

"And I remember building that house over there when I was thirty. But people don't refer to you as 'the house builder' if you do that here. No, no, they don't!

"I remember building that tavern that I still lounge in when I was just thirty-five. If you do that here, people don't refer to you as 'the tavern builder.' They just don't!

"But if you fuck one goat..."

It was the talk of the town when an eighty-year-old man married a twenty-year-old girl. One year later she went into the hospital to give birth. The nurse came out to congratulate the fellow. "This is amazing. How do you do it at your age?"

"You've got to keep that old motor running."

The following year she gave birth again. The same nurse said to the octogenarian father, "You really are amazing. How do you do it?"

"You've got to keep that old motor running," he replied again.

The same thing happened the next year. The nurse said, "Honestly, this is quite amazing."

"You've got to keep that old motor running," he said.

"Well..." said the nurse, "you had better change the oil. This one's black."

• • • •

Let me first talk about Marv Albert. I think he got a raw deal because biting during sex goes all the way back to the Founding Fathers, when they discovered splinters in Martha Washington's ass.

—BUDDY HACKETT, DANNY AIELLO ROAST, 1997

• • • •

A ninety-year-old man was having his annual checkup and the doctor asked him how he was feeling. "I've never been better!" he boasted. "I've got an eighteen-year-old bride who's pregnant with my child! What do you think about that?"

The doctor considered this for a moment, then said, "Let me tell you a story. I knew a guy who was an avid hunter. He never missed a season. But one day he went out in a bit of a hurry, and he accidentally grabbed his umbrella instead of his gun. So he was in the woods and suddenly a grizzly bear appeared in front of him. He raised his umbrella, pointed it at the bear, and squeezed the handle. And do you know what happened?"

Dumbfounded, the old man replied, "No."

"The bear dropped dead in front of him!"

"That's impossible!" exclaimed the old man. "Someone else must have shot that bear."

"EXACTLY!"

• • • •

At my age, when anyone asks me, "Did you get any?" it means sleep! I don't care about sex—regularity is more important.

—STEWIE STONE, SUNSHINE COMMITTEE RAFFLE NIGHT, 1997

• • • •

Three old guys are sitting around complaining. The first one says, "My hands shake so badly that when I shaved this morning I almost cut my ear off."

The second one says, "You think that's bad? My hands shake so badly that when I ate breakfast today, I spilled half my coffee on my toast."

"That's nothing," says the third guy. "My hands shake so badly that the last time I went to pee I came while I was taking my cock out."

How do you get four old ladies to shout, "Fuck"?

Get a fifth one to shout, "Bingo!"

• • • •

Lisa Lampanelli has been called a cross between Don Rickles and Archie Bunker, but in fairness to Lisa, she's got a much younger-looking penis. Not bigger, just younger.

—PAUL SHAFFER, CHEVY CHASE ROAST, 2002

• • • •

A knockout twenty-two-year-old woman decides she wants to get rich quick, so she finds herself a rich eighty-three-year-old man, planning to screw him to death on their wedding night. The courtship and wedding go off without a hitch, in spite of the vast age difference, and the two depart on their honeymoon. At bedtime, the woman gets undressed, and waits for the elderly groom to come out of the bathroom.

To her surprise, when he emerges, he has nothing on but a condom covering his twelve-inch erection. He is carrying a pair of earplugs and a pair of nose plugs.

Fearing her plan had gone amiss, she asks, "What are those for?"

"There are just two things I can't stand: the sound of a woman screaming . . . and the smell of burning rubber!"

A n elderly man wants to impregnate his young wife, so he goes to the doctor to check out his fertility. The doctor tells him to take a specimen cup home, fill it, and bring it back the next day.

The man comes back the next day with an empty specimen cup, the lid still in place.

"What was the problem?" asks the doctor.

"Well, I tried with my right hand . . . nothing. So, I tried with my left hand . . . nothing. My wife tried with her right hand . . . nothing. Her left hand . . . nothing. Her mouth . . . nothing. Then my wife's friend tried. Right hand, left hand, mouth, still nothing."

"Wait a minute. You mean your wife's FRIEND tried, too?"

"Yeah . . . but none of us could get the lid off of the specimen cup."

• • • •

Have you ever seen Alan King naked in the steam room?
Normally, I have to eat grass if I want to puke.

—Triumph the Insult Comic Dog, Rob Reiner Roast, 2000

• • • •

A woman is taking a walk around her neighborhood and she sees a gray-haired, toothless old man sitting in a chair on his porch, smiling serenely. "I couldn't help but notice how happy you look," she says. "What's your secret for a long, happy life?"

"I smoke three packs a day, drink a case of beer, eat fatty foods, and never, ever exercise."

"Wow, that's amazing! How old are you?"

"Twenty-six."

An elderly couple is sitting on the front porch one evening when the wife picks up her cane and whacks her husband across the shins.

"Jesus Christ, woman! What the hell was that for?" he yells.

"That's for sixty years of bad sex."

A few minutes later, the husband picks up his cane and whacks his wife across the shins! She yells, "What the hell was THAT for?"

"That's for knowing the difference."

• • • •

Hugh Hefner is an inspiration to masturbation. He's the George Washington of jacking off. I could go on and on, but what can you say about Hef that hasn't already been mumbled incoherently by a thousand young women with his cock in their mouth?

—JIMMY KIMMEL, HUGH HEFNER ROAST, 2001

• • • •

An elderly lady goes to the doctor for a checkup. Everything checks out fine. She then pulls the doctor aside and says, "Doctor, I haven't had sex for years now, and I was wondering how I can revive my husband's sex drive."

The doctor smiles and says, "Have you tried to give him Viagra?"

"Doctor, I can't even get him to take aspirin when he has a headache."

"Well, let me suggest something. Crush the Viagra into a powder. Then just stir it into his coffee and serve it. He won't notice a thing."

The old lady is delighted with the idea. A week later, she returns to the doctor.

"How did it go?" he asks.

"Terrible, Doctor, terrible."

"It didn't work?"

"Oh, it worked all right. I slipped him the Viagra and in a little while he got up and ripped his clothes off right at the table, and we made mad love right there and then. It was the best sex that I've had in twenty-five years."

"Then what is the problem?"

"Well . . . I can't ever show my face in McDonald's again."

What did one old boob say to the other?

If we don't get some support soon, they are going to think we're nuts!!

• • • •

I heard Jerry and Anne still do it, 'cause, you know, they want grandchildren.

—WENDY LIEBMAN, JERRY STILLER ROAST, 1999

• • • •

Two old ladies are sitting in rocking chairs, on the porch of the retirement home. One asks, "Do you still get horny?"

"Oh, yes!" says the other.

"What do you do about it?"

"I suck on a lifesaver."

The first lady sits there for a long while, pondering this answer. Finally she asks, "Who drives you to the beach?"

Two old ladies are sitting on a park bench outside the local town hall, where a flower show is in progress. One leans over and says, "Life is so boring. We never have fun anymore. For five dollars, I'd take my clothes off and streak through that stupid flower show!"

"You're on!" says the other, holding up a five-dollar bill.

As fast as she can, the first lady fumbles her way out of her clothes and streaks through the front door of the town hall. Waiting outside, her friend soon hears a huge commotion inside, followed by loud applause. The naked lady bursts out surrounded by a cheering crowd.

"What happened?" asks her waiting friend.

"I won first prize as Best Dried Arrangement."

What's blue and fucks old people?

Hypothermia.

• • • •

Jay Leno would have liked to have been here tonight, but he's restoring an old rod. But enough about Regis's cock. We're all here because we love Richard Belzer. In fact I haven't felt so much love in a room since Totie Fields let Alan King rub her stump.

—PAUL SHAFFER, RICHARD BELZER ROAST, 2001

• • • •

Sex Tips for Old People:

1. Put bifocals on to double-check that you're with the right partner.

2. Set alarm clock for two minutes, in case you doze off in the middle.

3. Set the mood with lighting: turn them ALL OFF!

4. Make sure you put 911 on your speed dial before you begin, just in case.

5. Write partner's name on your hand in case you can't remember what to scream out at the end.

A guy wearing just a raincoat is hiding behind the bushes at a bus stop when three really old ladies sit down together and start talking. The guy hops out of the bushes and flashes them.

The first lady has a stroke.

The second lady has a stroke.

But the third lady's arm is just too short to reach!

A lady of a certain age finds that she is lonely and decides to get a pet to keep her company—so off to the pet shop she goes. Forlornly, she searches. Nothing seems to catch her interest, until she spies this one ugly frog. As she walks by his cage he looks up and winks at her! He whispers, "I'm lonely, too. Buy me and you won't be sorry."

The lady figures what the hell, and buys the frog. As they're driving home the frog whispers to her, "Kiss me, you won't be sorry."

So, the old lady figures what the hell, and kisses the frog.

Immediately the frog turns into a gorgeous, sexy, handsome, young prince. The prince kisses her back, and you know what the old lady turns into?

The first motel she can find. (She's old, not dead!)

•   •   •   •

Before they let women in the club, the place was like Yeshiva University, where everyone majored in phlegm. I'm happy to say that now there's enough estrogen here to bring moisture back to Zsa Zsa Gabor's vagina.

—JOY BEHAR, DANNY AIELLO ROAST, 1997

•   •   •   •

Jack really takes care of his body. He lifts weights and jogs six miles every day, and always watches his diet. One morning he looks in the mirror, admiring the effect—until he notices he is suntanned evenly all over with one exception, his penis. He thinks about how to rectify this flaw and comes up with a plan.

He goes to the beach, completely undresses, and buries himself in the sand except for his penis, which he leaves sticking out.

Two little old ladies, taking their morning stroll along the beach, are startled by the sight. One of them pokes at it with her cane. She says to her friend, "There really is no justice in the world!"

"What do you mean by that?"

"Well, just look at that:

"When I was 20 . . . I was curious about it.

"When I was 30 . . . I enjoyed it.

"When I was 40 . . . I asked for it.

"When I was 50 . . . I paid for it.

"When I was 60 . . . I prayed for it.

"When I was 70 . . . I forgot about it.

"And now that I am 80, the damn things are growing wild and I am too old to squat!"

There was an old man from Nantucket

His cock was so long he could suck it

He said with a grin

As he wiped off his chin

If my ear was a cunt I could fuck it!

Don King wants to write a book about this event,
"Old Jews and the Negroes Who Frighten Them."

—DONALD TRUMP, DON KING ROAST, 2005

• • • •

An old lady thought she needed some toughening up to cope with today's world and decided to join a gang. She rocked up to the Hell's Angels bikers club and tapped on the door. "Excuse me, sirs, I'd like to join your club, if you please," she croaked in her feeble voice.

A grunt came from inside. "Ha! You got no chance, lady. We only take the toughest of the tough into our club. You can only join if you drink!"

"Oh boy, do I drink! I slam a few down every night after playing pool with the boys," she croaked back.

"Yeah? Well, you can only join if you smoke."

"Does marijuana count? Cuz I don't mind a few joints after playing pool with the boys."

"Lady... look. How can I explain it to you. The Hell's Angels is strictly for the roughest, toughest men in town. Have you ever been picked up by the fuzz?"

"Well, honestly, no. But I've been swung around by the tits a few times."

A little old couple shuffles into a McDonald's one cold winter evening. They look out of place amid the young families and couples eating there. Some of the customers look admiringly at them, obviously figuring that they've been through a lot together over many years but still enjoy a simple evening out together.

The man walks up to the counter, places their order with no hesitation, and carefully counts out the cost of their meal. The couple takes a table near the back wall and starts taking food off the tray. There is one plain hamburger, one order of French fries, and one drink. The little old man unwraps the hamburger and carefully cuts it in half. He places one half in front of his wife. Then he carefully counts out the French fries, divides them into two piles, and places one pile in front of his wife. He takes a sip of the drink, and then his wife takes a sip as the man begins to eat his few bites. The crowd looks on with a touch of sympathy.

As the old man begins eating his French fries, a young man stands up and walks to the old couple's table. He politely offers to buy another meal. The old man replies that they are just fine. They are used to sharing everything. Then the younger man notices that the little old lady still hasn't eaten a thing. She just sits there watching her husband eat and occasionally sips some of the drink. Again, the young man begs them to let him buy them another meal. This time, the lady explains that, no, they are used to sharing.

As the little old man finishes eating and is wiping his face neatly with a napkin, the young man can stand it no longer. "Ma'am, why aren't you eating? You said that you share everything. What is it that you are waiting for?"

"The teeth."

● ● ● ●

When Jerry Stiller walked into makeup I heard one make-up person say to the other, "Call your insurance company, this one's totaled!"

Dr. Ruth is here. How are you, Dr. Ruth? The last thing she said to me is, "Come on my tits"—ninety and horny, she went down on me standing up. She told me she was on the pill; I said, "What, nitroglycerin?"

—JEFFREY ROSS, JERRY STILLER ROAST, 1999

● ● ● ●

Jack decides to go skiing with his buddy, Bob. They load up Jack's station wagon and head north. After driving for a few hours, they get caught in a terrible blizzard. They pull up to a nearby farmhouse and ask the attractive lady of the house if they can spend the night.

"I'm recently widowed," she explains, "and I'm afraid the neighbors will talk if I let you stay in my house."

"Not to worry," Jack says. "We'll be happy to sleep in the barn."

Nine months later, Jack gets a letter from the widow's attorney. He calls up his friend Bob and says, "Bob, do you remember that good-looking widow at the farm we stayed at?"

"Yes, I do."

"Did you happen to get up in the middle of the night, go up to the house, and have sex with her?"

"Well . . . yes, I have to admit that I did."

"Did you happen to use my name instead of telling her your name?"

"Uh . . . yeah, I guess I did."

"Well, thanks! She just died and left me everything!"

● ● ● ●

Former Mayor Abe Beame is so short—once when he was masturbating he almost poked his eye out.

Susie Essman is a hard woman to introduce, not just because she's my lesbian lover, but because she has fucked every member of this dais. Except for Abe Beame—she went down on him.

—JOY BEHAR, FREDDIE ROMAN ROAST, 1999

● ● ● ●

A family takes their frail, elderly mother to a nursing home, hoping she will be well cared for there. The next morning, the nurses bathe her, feed her a tasty breakfast, and set her in a chair at a window overlooking a lovely flower garden. She seems okay, but after a while she slowly starts to tilt sideways in her chair. Two attentive nurses immediately rush up to catch her and straighten her up. Again she seems okay, but after a while she slowly starts to tilt over to her other side. The nurses rush back and once more right her. This goes on all morning.

That afternoon, the family arrives to see how their mom is adjusting to her new home. "So Ma, how is it here? Are they treating you all right?"

"It's pretty nice," she replies. "Except they won't let me fart."

At an old-timer's dance, there is an extremely elderly man who hasn't had any sex for a long time. He dances with all the grandmas all night, but just can't manage to score. Frustrated, he approaches one of the ladies and says, "I'm having no luck in love. How about coming back to my place for a roll in the hay? I'll give you twenty bucks!"

"You got yourself a deal, mister. Let's go."

So they go back to his place and, after a bit of foreplay; head for the bedroom. He is thoroughly enjoying himself—and can't get over how tight the old lady is, considering her age. And then it dawns on him: she must be a virgin. When they are finally done, he rolls off of her and puffs, "Wow! Lady, if I had known you were a virgin, I would have offered you FIFTY bucks."

"If I had known you were actually going to get a hard-on, I would have taken my pantyhose off!"

A little old lady goes into the headquarters of a large national bank, dragging a large bag behind her. She announces that she wants to open a savings account, but that she has to deal directly with the president of the bank because, "It's a lot of money!"

After much hemming and hawing, the bank staff finally ushers her into the bank president's office. The president asks her how much she would like to deposit. She replies, "$165,000!" and dumps the cash out of her bag onto his desk.

The president is, of course, curious as to how she came by all this cash. "Ma'am, I'm surprised you're carrying so much money around. If you don't mind my asking, where did you get it?"

"I make bets."

"Bets? What kind of bets?"

"Well, for example, I'll bet you $25,000 that your balls are square."

"Ha!" laughs the president. "That's a stupid bet. You can never win that kind of bet!"

"So, would you like to take my bet?"

"Sure. I'll bet $25,000 that my balls are not square!"

"Okay, but since there is a lot of money involved, when you show me the proof may I bring my lawyer with me as a witness?"

"Absolutely. We'll make it ten o'clock tomorrow morning."

That night, the president gets very nervous about the bet and spends a long time in front of a mirror checking his balls, turning them from side to side, again and again. He finally goes to bed reassured that there is no way his balls could be considered square. He will surely win the bet.

The next morning, at precisely 10:00 a.m., the little old lady appears with her lawyer at the bank. She asks the president to drop his pants.

The president complies. The little old lady peers closely at his balls and then asks if she can feel them.

"Well, okay," says the president. "We're talking about a lot of money, so I guess you should be absolutely sure."

Just then, he notices that the lawyer is quietly banging his head against the wall. The president asks the old lady, "What the heck's the matter with your lawyer?"

"Nothing," she answers. "Except I bet him $100,000 that at ten a.m. today, I'd have the president of this bank's balls in my hand."

● ● ● ●

Hugh Hefner is so old his first condom was made out of bark. He invented a new sexual position called the 96. You turn around and fart on the back of each other's heads.

—GILBERT GOTTFRIED, HUGH HEFNER ROAST, 2001

● ● ● ●

A man goes to visit his eighty-five-year-old grandfather in the hospital. "How are you today, grandpa?" he asks.

"Feeling fine," says the old man.

"What's the food like?"

"Terrific. Wonderful menus."

"And the nursing care?"

"Just couldn't be better. These young nurses are very kind and take great care of me."

"What about sleeping? Do you sleep okay?"

"No problem at all, nine hours solid every night. At ten o'clock they bring me a cup of hot chocolate and a Viagra tablet, and that's it. I go out like a light."

The grandson is puzzled by this last part, so he goes down the hall to question the nurse in charge. "My grandfather tells me you're giving him Viagra every night. What on earth are you doing giving an eighty-five-year-old Viagra on a daily basis?"

"Oh, yes," replies the nurse. "Every night we give him a cup of hot chocolate and a Viagra tablet. The chocolate makes him sleepy and the Viagra keeps him from rolling out of bed."

O n hearing that her elderly grandfather has just passed away, Katie goes straight to her grandparent's house to visit her ninety-five-year-old grandmother and comfort her. When she asks how her grandfather died, grandma replies, "He had a heart attack while we were making love on Sunday morning."

Horrified, Katie tells her grandmother that two people nearly a hundred years old having sex would surely be asking for trouble.

"Oh no, my dear," replies grandma. "We had a risk-proof system. Many years ago, realizing our advanced age, we figured out that the best time for us to make love was when the church bells started to ring. It was just the right rhythm. Nice and slow and even, nothing too strenuous. We simply went in on the Ding and out on the Dong." She pauses, wipes away a tear, and continues, "And if that damned ice-cream truck hadn't come along, he'd still be alive today!"

A boy is walking down the street when he notices his grandpa sitting in a rocking chair on his front porch with nothing on from the waist down. "Grandpa, what are you doing?" he exclaims.

"Well . . . last week I sat out here with no shirt on and I got a stiff neck. This is your Grandma's idea."

Mildred, ninety-three years old, is particularly despondent over the recent death of her husband, Earl. She decides that she will just kill herself and join him in the hereafter. Thinking that it would be best to get it over with quickly, she takes out Earl's old army pistol. She is determined to shoot herself in the heart—since it is so badly broken anyway. Not wanting to miss the vital organ and survive in a damaged state, she calls her doctor's office to inquire as to just exactly where the heart is located. "On a woman," the doctor says, "it is just below the left breast."

Later that night, Mildred is admitted to the hospital with a gunshot wound to her left knee.

● ● ● ●

We just put my grandfather in a rest home. Well not actually, we didn't have the money so we just went down the turnpike and put him in a rest area.

—RICH VOS, FRESH FUNNY FACES, 1999

● ● ● ●

One night, an eighty-seven-year-old woman comes home from bingo to find her husband in bed with another woman. She becomes violent and ends up pushing him off the balcony of their twentieth-floor apartment, killing him instantly.

Brought before the court on the charge of murder, she is asked if she has anything to say in her own defense. "Your Honor," she begins coolly, "I figured that, at ninety-two, if he could screw, he could fly."

CHAPTER 8

Everybody Into the Pool

A mishmash of nonsense, mayhem, and a whole pile of silly stuff.

A construction worker on the fifth floor of a building needs a handsaw. He spots a fellow hardhat on the ground floor and yells down to him, but he can't be heard—so he tries sign language. He points to his eye, meaning, "I," then points to his knee, meaning "need," then moves his hand back and forth in a sawing motion.

The man on the ground floor nods his head, pulls down his pants, whips out his cock, and starts masturbating. The fifth-floor guy gets so mad he climbs down the five stories and screams in the smart aleck's face, "What the fuck is your problem!!! I said I needed a hand saw!"

The other guy says, "I knew that! I was just trying to tell you—I'm coming!"

Three guys go to a ski lodge and there aren't enough rooms, so they have to share a bed. In the middle of the night, the guy on the right wakes up and says, "I had this wild, vivid dream of getting a hand job!"

This wakes up the guy on the left, who says, "Omigod, that is so weird! I had the same dream!"

Just then the guy in the middle wakes up and says, "That's funny, I dreamed I was skiing!"

• • • •

I voted for Bill Clinton and I have friends who hate him and I asked why. They said because he smoked pot, cheated on his wife, and didn't want to go to Vietnam. Then I realized, I'm Bill Clinton!

I hate when politicians are asked if they've ever tried marijuana—you know they're lying. They always say the same thing, "I experimented with it when I was in college." What? Did you have a lab coat on?

—SAM GREENFIELD, JIM DAVID COMEDY NIGHT, 2003

• • • •

Three friends—two straight guys and a gay guy, along with their significant others—are on a cruise. A tidal wave comes along and swamps the ship and they all drown instantly. The next thing you know, they're standing before St. Peter. First in line is one of the straight guys, with his wife in tow. St. Peter shakes his head sadly, "I can't let you in. You loved money too much. You loved it so much you even married a woman named Penny." Next comes the second straight guy. "Sorry, can't let you in, either. You loved food too much. You loved to eat so much you even married a woman named Candy!" At that point the gay guy turns to his boyfriend and whispers nervously, "It doesn't look good, Dick."

Let me ask you a question. If a Jewish guy is wearing a toupee, does he need a yarmulke?

A dwarf gets on an elevator and pushes the "up" button. Just before the door closes, a hand comes through and opens the door. In steps a very large black man. The dwarf stares and says, "You're the biggest man I have ever seen."

The man nods his head and replies, "I'm 6'9", weigh 259 lbs., and I'm packing 16 inches. I'm Turner Brown."

The dwarf faints! After coming to, the little man asks the bigger one to repeat himself.

"I said I'm 6'9", 259 lbs., and I'm packing 16 inches. My name is Turner Brown."

"WHEW! For a minute there, I thought you said 'Turn Around.'"

●　●　●　●

I believe that a Jew can always tell another Jew. It's just like black people. Black people can pick each other out of crowd like that.

—JUDY GOLD, BAD GIRLS OF COMEDY, 1998

●　●　●

A guy is horny as hell but broke. He goes to a whorehouse with five dollars and begs the madam to give him whatever she can for it.

"I'm sorry," says the madam, "but that will only cover the rent for ten minutes and none of my hookers work for free!"

So the guy gets the room but has no one to fuck. He looks out on the ledge of the building and sees a pigeon. Quietly, he opens the window, grabs the poor bird, and just fucks the living hell out of it. Satisfied, he goes home.

The next week he returns to the whorehouse with his paycheck. He says to the madam, "I got lots of money now, give me a hooker!"

"All of them are busy now... Why don't you go to the peep show and get yourself in the mood?"

The guy does as she suggests, and is enjoying the show when he turns to the guy next to him and says, "Hey, these beauties really know what they're doing, huh?"

"Yeah, but you should have been here last week. There was this guy fucking a pigeon!"

• • • •

I'm delighted to be here again, especially with Milton Berle. Milton has been suffering from a disease called Berlesheimer disease. That's where he forgets everything except everybody else's jokes.

Milton Berle: You're a prick.

Someday you'll eat those words. I'm not talking about your penis today, either, because my mother told me I should always respect the dead.

—DICK CAPRI, STEVEN SEAGAL ROAST, 1995

• • • •

An American on business in Japan hires a local hooker for the night. As they are going at it, she keeps screaming "Fujifoo, Fujifoo!!!" Not speaking any Japanese, the man can only surmise that this is an expression of pleasure.

The next day, the businessman is golfing with his Japanese clients and he gets a hole-in-one. Wanting to impress the locals, he says, "Fujifoo, Fujifoo!"

The Japanese men look at each other, confused. Finally, one of them says, "No, sir. You got the right hole."

A priest wants to raise money for his church. He hears that there is a fortune to be made in horse racing, so he decides to purchase a horse and enter it in the races. But he soon discovers that the going price for a race horse is way out of his league. He ends up buying a donkey instead. He figures that since he has it, he might as well go ahead and enter it in a race. To his surprise, the donkey comes in third! The next day the local paper carries this headline: PREACHER'S ASS SHOWS.

The preacher is so pleased that he enters the donkey in another race, and this time it wins. The paper reads: PREACHER'S ASS OUT IN FRONT.

The bishop is getting upset with this publicity, so he orders the preacher to stop racing the donkey. The paper's coverage reads: BISHOP SCRATCHES PREACHER'S ASS.

Well, this is the last straw. The bishop orders the preacher to get rid of the donkey altogether. The preacher decides to give it to a nun in a nearby convent. Next day's headline is NUN HAS BEST ASS IN TOWN.

The bishop is dumbfounded. He orders the nun to get rid of the donkey, so she sells it to a local farmer. The headline? NUN SELLS ASS FOR TEN DOLLARS.

The bishop is beside himself and orders the nun to buy back the donkey and set it out to pasture. Next day's headline: NUN ANNOUNCES HER ASS IS FINALLY FREE.

The bishop is buried the next day.

Sam goes into a clock and watch shop, and immediately spots a drop-dead gorgeous female clerk behind the counter. He walks up to her, unzips his pants, and flops his dick out onto the counter.

"What are you doing, sir? This is a clock shop!" says the outraged clerk.

"I know it is—and I would like two hands and a face put on this!"

● ● ● ●

Jewish guys don't have big cocks. I have no cock. When I take a piss it's like a turtle. I have to put a piece of lettuce there for the head to come out.

—STEWIE STONE, SMOTHERS BROTHERS ROAST, 2003

● ● ● ●

A cowboy is riding around the range one day, when off in the distance he sees a small cloud of dust. He rides closer only to find an Indian lying on the ground with his penis sticking out of his buckskin pants. "Hey, what are you doing?" he asks the man.

"Me tell time! Penis act as sundial."

"Okay, what time is it, then?"

"3:35."

"That's amazing. You're right!"

With that, the cowboy hops back on his horse and keeps going. Soon he sees another Indian in the same state. Without missing a beat, he asks this Indian the time.

The red man looks down at his one-eyed bandit and says "4:40."

The cowboy is stunned—right again! Shaking his head he hops back onto his horse and rides off.

Wouldn't you know it? A few miles across the range he spies another Indian on his back with his penis out—but this one is jerking off. The cowboy hops off his horse and says, "And what are you doing?"

"Me winding clock."

A man walks into a bank and after waiting for twenty minutes in line he goes straight to a customer service representative and says, "Hey, lady, I got this here check for deposit and I'll be goddamned if I am going to wait my ass on line anymore."

"Please," says the woman. "I won't have that kind of language in this bank."

"Well, excuse me, but this fuckin' check ain't drawing any god-damned interest with you yappin' away about my language."

"Sir, I don't have to take this abuse!"

"Well, then let's get the fuckin' manager okay? I don't have to stand here and take this shit from you."

The manager is summoned and says, "What seems to be the problem?"

"This man is using vulgar language and I won't stand for it," says the customer service representative.

"Hey! All's I'm trying to do in this goddamned bank, for Christ's sake, is deposit this fuckin' check for fifteen million dollars," says the man.

"And this fuckin' bitch won't help you?"

●　●　●　●

I thought the Hasidim came over with Moses, but it's not true. Apparently, only two hundred and fifty years ago, some guy woke up in the middle of the Ukraine and he said to himself, "Let's see, how can I serve my Lord and make a fashion statement? I know, I'll wear a big, big furry hat in the middle of August with a hot, hot woolen suit on a hundred-and-ten degree-day. It will have soup stains on it, it'll be fabulous!" And didn't it catch on? Look at the Amish; they picked right up on it. But they don't have the *payes* 'cause you don't want them to get caught in the reaping machines.

—JOY BEHAR, SALUTE TO NEIL SEDAKA, 2003

●　●　●　●

Three explorers are captured by natives deep in the Amazon jungle, and taken before the tribe's vengeful chief. The chief calls the entire tribe together. When they are all assembled, he summons the first explorer up to the altar and asks, "Death or Booka?"

Well, the explorer doesn't want to die, so he opts for Booka. The tribe starts screaming "BOOKA!" and dancing around. The chief then rips the explorer's pants off and fucks him in the ass.

The chief then calls the second explorer to the altar and asks, "Death or Booka?" Not wanting to die, he opts for Booka. The tribe again starts screaming "BOOKA!" and dancing around. The chief rips the second guy's pants off and fucks him in the ass. Finally, the chief calls the third explorer to the altar and asks, "Death or Booka?" Now, this guy is made of sterner stuff than his comrades, and though he doesn't want to die, he decides that death would be more honorable than being violated in front of his fellow explorers and hundreds of tribesman. He opts for death. The chief turns to the tribe and screams, "DEATH BY BOOKA!"

How are a highway and a woman alike?

They both have shoulders, they both have curves, and they are both slippery when wet.

Mike is trying to come up with the perfect outfit for a fancy costume party. Then he has a bright idea. When the host answers the door, he finds Mike standing there with no shirt or socks on.

"What the hell are you supposed to be?" asks the host.

"A premature ejaculation," says Mike. "I just came in my pants!"

• • • •

There is one quality that sets Billy apart from any other man and that is his ability to jerk off at will. It's uncanny, he doesn't need a *Penthouse*, he doesn't need a porno film to get him hot, this man can jerk off to a plate of kasha varnishkas. How do I know this? Let's just say he's not welcome at the Carnegie Deli anymore.

–ROB REINER, BILLY CRYSTAL ROAST, 1992

• • • •

A pirate is sitting on a bench in port, throwing peanuts to the seagulls. He has a wooden leg, a hook for a hand, and a patch over his right eye. A curious child sits down next to him, summons up his courage, and asks the pirate how he came to have a wooden leg.

"Well," says the pirate, "I was standing on the deck of me ship one day, and a wave washed me overboard. Then, a hungry shark attacked me and bit me leg off."

"Wow," says the little boy. "How did you lose your hand?"

"Many years ago, I was fighting the navy, and one of them boys cut me hand off. Me doc couldn't find a hand, so he gave me this hook."

They sit quietly for a while, and finally the boy has the nerve to ask, "How did you lose your eye?"

"Well, I was standing watch up in the crow's nest, and just as I looked up, a seagull flew over and shat right in me eye."

"But . . . how did that cause you to lose your eye?"

"It was me first day with the hook."

Joey decides to join the navy. On his first day of service, he asks another sailor to show him around the ship and help him get acclimated. "What do you guys do around here when you get really horny after months of being out at sea?"

Says the sailor, "Well, there is this barrel on the upper deck. Just pump your cock in the side with the hole."

A few days pass and Joey is getting really horny, so he climbs to the upper deck and sees the barrel. He buries his dick in the hole and starts pumping away—and it's the best feeling he has ever experienced. It is truly, deeply pleasurable.

Joey finishes up, buttons his bell bottoms, and as he is returning to his post, he sees the sailor who had clued him in about the barrel. "That barrel really was great! I could do it every day!"

"Yeah, well... every day except Thursday."

"Why not Thursday?"

"Because that's your day in the barrel."

● ● ● ●

Jerry Stiller's a great guy, a great actor, but what you might not know is that he is a good kisser. You look at the man, you might think: a little rough, probably grabs you like a pirate and just mashes his lips on you. Very affectionate, sweet kisser. You know he doesn't just ram his tongue down your throat—he just holds your hands, looks right in your eyes, soft lips. I'll be honest, the kissing was so sweet that a lot of the rough stuff took me by surprise later on.

—LARRY MILLER, JERRY STILLER ROAST, 1999

● ● ● ●

A married man goes to confession and says to the priest, "Father, I had an affair with a woman... almost."

"What do you mean 'almost'?" asks the priest.

"Well, we got undressed and rubbed together, but then I stopped."

"Rubbing together is the same as putting it in," explains the priest. "You're not to go near that woman again. Now, say five Hail Marys and put fifty dollars in the poor box."

The man leaves the confessional, says his prayers, and walks over to the poor box. He pauses for a moment and then decides to leave. The priest quickly runs over to the man and exclaims, "I saw that! You didn't put any money in the poor box!"

"Well, Father, I rubbed up against it and, like you said, it's the same as putting it in!"

• • • •

So this Mafia guy dies and you know what they put on his tombstone? "What the fuck are you looking at?"

—TONY DARROW, SOPRANOS NIGHT, 2005

• • • •

Did you hear about the new gay sitcom?

Leave It, It's Beaver.

A blind man walks into a restaurant and sits down. The owner walks up to the man and hands him a menu. "I'm sorry sir, but I am blind and can't read the menu. Just bring me a dirty fork from a previous customer, I'll smell it and order from there."

A little confused, the owner walks over to the dirty dish pile and picks up a greasy fork. He returns to the blind man's table and hands it to him.

The blind man puts the fork to his nose and takes in a deep breath. "Ah, yes, that's what I'll have, meatloaf and mashed potatoes."

"Unbelievable," says the owner to himself as he walks toward the kitchen. He tells his wife, who happens to be the cook, what has just happened.

Several days later the blind man returns and the owner mistakenly brings him a menu again. "Sir, remember me? I'm the blind man."

"I'm sorry, I didn't recognize you. I'll go get you a dirty fork."

After another deep breath, the blind man says, "That smells great, I'll take the macaroni and cheese with broccoli. Once again the owner is dumbfounded—but he is suspicious that somehow the blind man is screwing around with him. He tells his wife that the next time the blind man comes in he's going to test him.

Sure enough, the blind man returns the following week, and this time the owner sees him coming and runs to the kitchen. He grabs a fork and says to his wife, "Mary, rub this fork around your vagina before I take it to the blind man." Mary complies and hands her husband the fork back.

"Good afternoon, sir," the owner says to the blind man. "This time I remember you and I have a fork all ready."

The blind man puts the fork to his nose, takes a deep whiff and says, "Hey! I didn't know Mary worked here!"

What's the definition of trust?

Two cannibals giving each other a blow job.

• • • •

Donald Trump, Al Sharpton, and Don King. It's like the triangle of bad hair. The three of them look like the three stages of a forest fire.

Don King started out in Cleveland and then he went to prison—which, if you are from Cleveland, is called upward mobility.

—COLIN QUINN, DON KING ROAST, 2005

• • • •

Why did Frosty the Snowman pull down his pants?

He heard the snow blower coming.

Bob joins a very exclusive nudist colony. On his first day, he takes off his clothes and starts mingling. A petite, gorgeous blonde walks by and Bob immediately gets an erection. Noticing this, the pretty young thing approaches him, smiling sweetly, and says: "Sir, did you call for me?"

"No . . . what do you mean?" replies Bob.

"You must be new here; let me explain. We have a rule: If you get an erection, it means that you've called for me." She then leads him to the side of the pool, pulls him down onto a chaise longue, and has her way with him.

Afterward, Bob continues exploring the facilities. He enters a sauna, sits down, and farts. Within a few seconds a huge, horribly corpulent, hairy man with a firm erection lumbers out of the steam towards him. The man says, "Sir, did you call for me?"

"No! What do you mean?"

"You must be new here. We have a rule: if you fart, it means that you've called for me." The man then spins Bob around, bends him over the bench and has his way with him.

Bob rushes back to the colony office. He is greeted by the smiling, naked receptionist who asks how she can be of service.

"Here is your card and key back! You can keep the $500 joining fee."

"But, sir, you've only been here a couple of hours; you only saw a small fraction of our facilities."

"Listen, lady, I am fifty-eight years old, I get a hard-on twice a month, but I fart fifteen times a day. No thanks!"

• • • •

I was thinking about this, this morning as I was powdering
my balls. Those of us who know him like I do refer to him
affectionately as "the Belz." We love the Belz. So I was
thinking what makes a man the Belz?

When he was learning about the Torah as a child, his
own rabbi sucked his cock. But that's not what makes a
man the Belz. It makes him a man who has to jerk off
onto a tallis. But it doesn't make him the Belz.

Years ago we all remember that Richard landed the
coveted role in the Al Pacino film *Author, Author*—Seth,
the gay stage manager. But playing Seth the gay stage
manager is not what makes a man the Belz. To prepare
for the role of Seth the gay stage manager, Richard—and
this is the gift of foresight—went on a strict cock diet for
two months. That's not what makes a man the Belz. I
think it's staying on that diet for six months after that film
opened—that is what makes a man the Belz.

—PAUL SHAFFER, RICHARD BELZER ROAST, 2001

• • • •

A pastor explains to his congregation that the church is badly in
need of some money to repair its roof, and he would appreciate their
being more generous than usual in their donations. He adds that whoever
donates most generously will have the honor of selecting three hymns.

After the collection plates have been passed, the pastor sees that
someone has graciously offered a $1,000 bill. He is so excited that he
immediately shares his joy with the congregation, saying that he'd
like to personally thank the godly individual who placed such a generous sum into the plate.

A very prim, elderly, saintly lady in the back of the church shyly
raises her hand. The pastor asks her to come to the front, and after
protesting, she finally, slowly makes her way toward him. The pastor

thanks her warmly and asks her to pick out three hymns, as promised. Her eyes brighten as she looks over the congregation. She points to the three most handsome men present and says, "I'll take him...him...and him."

Three ladies are on a plane trip together when the captain announces, "Please prepare for a crash landing." The first lady puts on all of her jewelry. Surprised by this, the other two question her about it.

"Well, when they come to rescue us they will see that I am rich and will rescue me first."

The second lady, not wanting to be left behind, immediately takes off her blouse and bra.

"Why are you doing that?" the other ladies ask.

"Well, when they come to rescue us they will see my great tits and will rescue me first."

The third lady, an African American, doesn't want to be outdone. She takes off her pants and panties.

"Why are you doing that?" the other ladies ask.

"They always search for the black box first!"

Did you hear about the blind Moyel?

He got the sack.

A woman goes into a restaurant in a small country town. She is famished! She orders the fried chicken, and when it arrives she immediately starts wolfing it down. Soon, she finds herself choking on a chicken bone.

Two country boys in the next booth notice her distress and want to help her out. The first country boy drops his coveralls and bends over and the second country boy starts licking his butt.

The woman sees the two going at it, and she can't control her disgust—she pukes all over the place, dislodging the chicken bone from her throat.

The first country boy pulls his overalls back up and says to the other, "You're right Jimmy-Bob, that hind-lick maneuver works like a charm."

● ● ● ●

What do you say to a virgin when she sneezes?
    Goes-in-tight!
    Pat Cooper eats pasta all day long. Breakfast, lunch, dinner. He eats pasta when he's having sex. He calls it cunnilinguini.

—DICK CAPRI, FRIARS FROLICS IN HONOR OF PAT COOPER, 1998

● ● ● ●

A cop sees a car weaving all over the road and pulls it over. He walks up to the car window and sees a very attractive woman behind the wheel. He smells liquor on her breath and says, "I'm going to have to give you a Breathalyzer test to determine if you are under the influence of alcohol."

She blows up the balloon and he walks it back to the police car. After a couple of minutes, he returns and says, "It looks like you've had a couple of stiff ones."

"You mean it shows that, too?"

A FEW DIRTY WORDS
FROM JOY BEHAR

When I first started doing standup I used to talk about my hair and going to Bloomingdales and shopping; there was really nothing particularly edgy in all of that. It was very personal. Once I got comfortable with being onstage, it was natural for me to talk on stage the way I talk in real life, and to have the same kind of attitude. So I don't think that I made a huge transition while on stage.

I did a character at one time, an Italian woman who used to give news in the neighborhood, and those were jokes about people that I grew up with. I did this character on the *Steve Allen Comedy Hour*, back in the early '80s. She would say things like, "Former bodyguard Carmine Russo has become a faith healer. There's not a cripple left in the neighborhood since Carmine has been pronouncing his magical, miraculous words: 'Walk or I'll break both your legs.'"

One of those pieces mentioned that someone named Vito won the vegetable garden contest for having the biggest googootz in the neighborhood. Now, *googootz* is zucchini. They were really old-time writers there and they thought it was funny but they said it's a dick joke. I said, "No it's not, it's a zucchini." And they said, "Come on, get off of it!" It was a double entendre, and I thought it was funny and they did too, but they wouldn't put it on TV. I think it would pass now, although the FCC is on everybody's case so I don't know. I mean, I get away with stuff on *The View* that is just amazing, to tell you the truth. The things that we come out with!

I once said, "a-hole" and when I watched it on Tivo later it was bleeped. We're live but we have a seven-second delay so they can do that. The double entendres will work pretty much anywhere. I've been in front of some conservative groups, people at luncheons wearing hats at the Waldorf, all sorts of different groups, and I've never ever gotten into any trouble. The double entendre will never offend anybody because it is obvious that it's in your head. It's the old Lenny Bruce idea that it's what you're *making* of the word. So when you use a double entendre, you can pretty much say, "I meant googootz, I meant zucchini!" You're off the hook. But, if you say "fuck" or "shit" or something like that, then you can get in trouble because then it's blatant.

Sometimes, when I'm really free and funny, I will use my usual street language, and it's not that I was raised that way, either. You could not say "fuck" in front of my father. My father fought the Nazis and pulled his own teeth out because they were loose. In fact, I had an HBO special and I said "shit" and he was just furious with me. That was the only blue word that I used. He said, "Why do you have to talk that way? Nobody else does." He hasn't watched anybody else, apparently.

All audiences respond to language. If they don't respond, it's because they decided ahead of time that they are not going to respond, that they're too delicate to listen to that type of language. A lot of older-generation comics in their seventies and eighties just pooh-pooh the language of the so-called "younger comedians." You hear that all the time. I'm sure Bill Cosby says that about Chris Rock and Eddie Murphy—we all have our previous-generation censorship.

It's much more daring to use this kind of language when you're a woman. Everything that we do as comedians is daring and crazy. We're up there, putting ourselves on the line and being alone on stage in front of people who basically say, "Make me laugh." So the language is just another part of the risk. When you're a woman, it's a little bit riskier.

I don't use certain words gratuitously. Every audience is different; every audience has a different feel about it. If I can get the temperature ninety-nine percent of the time, I'll get the right reaction. I won't say something I shouldn't. You have to know how to edit, you have to know when you've crossed the line, and you have to know whether this audience is going to appreciate this particular kind of material. You have to know how to work a house.

You cannot be preceded by a dirty comic because they will lower the bar with their filthy mouth. So I don't like to follow people who are blue, I'd rather follow a squeaky-clean comedian. Even on *The View*, if we start the "Hot Topics" conversation with sex, it's very difficult to then go to Social Security.

You definitely have a conscious feeling that you're on television. If you don't, you don't belong on television. You'll see Chris Rock or Eddie Murphy or Judy Gold or Susie Essman and, when we're on television, we're different from when we're in the clubs—and we should be different. Why should you pay money to see us in a club when you can see the same thing on television?

I very, very incrementally push the envelope on *The View*. At one point, I was appearing in *The Vagina Monologues* and all of a sudden I'm talking about vaginas on television. You have to say to yourself, It's a play, I'm not saying "pussy," I'm saying "vagina." It's their problem if they can't handle the word "vagina."

I once was talking about my diet on the show and one of the girls said to me, "Are you done with your diet?" and I said, "Yes, thank you, Jesus." ABC bleeped that. And Jerry Falwell went on TV that night and spoke to a talk show host about it and he said he was on my side. He said, "The woman was testifying." I was quite taken aback by that, frankly!

I think that there are things that are not particularly funny. Rape is not funny, unless you're making fun of the rapist, maybe then you could get away with it. I don't think abortion is a particularly funny topic. Bill Maher is very edgy and very smart. Sometimes I think, am I going to get away with what I'm going to say now? And then I think, well Maher would do it. He's fearless. I totally admire comedians who are fearless.

One joke I have used is: "When I was an elementary school teacher the kids used to snitch on each other. They would say, 'Miss Behar, he said F! Miss Behar, he said F!' Finally, one day I said, 'Okay, who the fuck said F?' and I got fired." So that's a joke that has the word "fuck" in it. To me, it's a great joke because it talks about teaching, it conveys how annoying it is to have kids snitching on each other, it has the prohibited word, and it has the surprise joke at the end. It always gets a laugh.

Sometimes I have an attitude. I'm aggravated with things in the world, I'm irritated, I'm annoyed and when you're annoyed, aggravated, and irritated, sometimes you use words that are not particularly delicate and dainty. I think that there are comedians who are very funny, like Rita Rudner, who don't use language like that. But she doesn't have the same attitude that I have. She's got a different persona. It's very funny, it's hers, and it's wonderful, but it's different.

You have to be true to yourself up there. I've never heard anybody say that they thought that I was a blue comic. I don't know why, I mean, I've got the words in there sometimes. I was talking on *The View* about how I have plenty of oral sex jokes about Clinton. Then I got booked somewhere, a Jewish organization, and they called my agent up and said, "We saw her, we're scared to book her." My agent told the person what the jokes were like and they said, "Oh, that's nothing." So it made me sound scarier than I actually am.

I say "oral sex" on television and it's fine, but I say "Jesus" and I get bleeped. That's the world we live in; people get very uptight about religion. Talking about religion is probably much more edgy and much riskier than talking about sex. Nobody really cares about sex as a topic . . . but religion! Now you're talking about something that's near and dear to their hearts and very, very controversial.

I started to do material about George Bush in a room full of yuppies and they turned on me. So that happens if they don't agree with you politically sometimes. That's why politics and religion— you don't talk about those things at dinner time. Those are the two topics that make people hate you. Or love you.

Did you hear about the new *Exorcist* movie?

They got the Devil to come in to take the priest out of the child.

Fred, a devout and faithful Christian, is in the hospital, near death. His family calls their pastor to stand watch with them. As the pastor stands by his bed, Fred's condition appears to deteriorate and he motions frantically for something to write on.

The pastor lovingly hands him a pen and a piece of paper, and Fred uses his last bit of energy to scribble a note. The pastor thinks that it would be indelicate to read the note at that moment, so he places it in his pocket. With a last gasp, Fred passes away.

At the funeral, as the pastor is finishing his eulogy, he realizes that he is wearing the same jacket that he was wearing when Fred died. He says, "You know, the dearly departed handed me a note just before he died. I haven't looked at it, but knowing Fred, I'm sure there's a word of inspiration there for us all." He opens the note, and reads, "Asshole, you're standing on my oxygen tube!"

● ● ● ●

THE WRONG JERRY

We could've roasted Jerry Seinfeld or Springer, Jerry Vale or Van Dyke

Any Jerry would be better than this crabby old kike

When the Friars called me, I nearly went spastic

Any Jerry would be better than this one-note geriatric

I'll admit when I saw you on *Seinfeld*, I thought you were super

But I heard a rumor their first choice, Pat Cooper

Jerry, all jokes are aside, this thought is my last

Thanks for this chance to kiss your son's ass!

—JEFFREY ROSS, JERRY STILLER ROAST, 1999

● ● ● ●

What do parsley and pubic hair have in common?

Push it aside and keep on eating.

One Friday evening, three nuns are driving along a mountain road when a huge tractor-trailer rams into them head-on, killing them all instantly. They proceed immediately to the gates of heaven, where a sign is posted: CLOSED FOR REMODELING. The nuns start rattling the gates and out comes St. Peter.

"What are you doing here!" he says. "No one is supposed to be here! We are closed for the weekend!"

"Well, we're dead and we can't go back," says the first nun.

"All right," says St. Peter, "but we can't let you in yet. How about if we send you back for the weekend as whoever you wish to be, and then you can come back to heaven on Monday?"

All three agree.

"Okay, so who do you want to be?" St. Peter asks the first nun.

"Well, I thought her life was very interesting, especially since she gave her life to God, so I want to be Joan of Arc."

Poof! The first nun becomes Joan of Arc and vanishes back to earth.

"Okay, you're next," the saint says to the second nun. "Who do you want to be?"

"Well, I thought her life was very interesting, and she died a tragic death, so I want to become Marilyn Monroe."

Poof! The second nun becomes Marilyn Monroe and vanishes back to earth.

The third nun has been waiting patiently, and finally St. Peter turns to her and asks who she wishes to be for her last weekend on earth.

"I want to be Alice Kapippoleeney."

"Excuse me?"

"I want to be Alice Kapippoleeney!"

"I'm sorry, Sister, but we have no record of any Alice Kapippoleeney ever having existed on earth."

"There is TOO an Alice Kapippoleeney! I have proof right HERE!!!" shouts the nun, brandishing a newspaper clipping.

St. Peter takes the article and reads it. "Oh . . . um, Sister, I'm afraid that you have misread this article. It says that the ALASKA PIPELINE was laid by five hundred men in six months."

● ● ● ●

Florida's my favorite state because it looks like a penis is peeing on Cuba.

—Tom Cotter, Salute to Jackie Green, 2003

● ● ● ●

The pope has been diagnosed with a potentially fatal testicular disease, and after treatment, the papal doctors tell him that he must have sex with a woman in order to confirm that the treatment has been fully successful.

He is understandably troubled by this, and calls his cardinals together to discuss it. They insist that, as it is a life-or-death matter, the vow of celibacy should be broken.

The pope says that he will do as his doctors recommend, on four conditions. "First," he says, "the girl has to be blind so she cannot see that she is having sex with the Holy Father and reveal it to the world. Second, she must be deaf so that she doesn't recognize my voice, figure out that she is having sex with the Holy Father, and reveal it to the world. Third, she has to be dumb so that, if somehow she figures out that she is having sex with the Holy Father, she cannot reveal it to the world."

At this point one of the cardinals stands up and says, "Leave it to me, Holy Father. I know just the woman for you."

As the cardinal is about to leave, the pope says, "Wait a moment, I told you there are FOUR conditions."

"I'm sorry, Holy Father. What is the final condition?"

"Big tits!"

What do you do with 365 used rubbers?

Melt them down, make a tire, and call it a good year.

Did you hear heaven is going broke?

Yeah, Liberace is up there blowing all the prophets!

•   •   •   •

A guy comes home from work, says, "Honey, I think a guy I work with is gay. He was standing at the urinal jerking off."

"How does that make him gay?" she said.

"He was using my cock."

—JACKIE MARTLING, FRIARS CLUB COMEDY MARATHON
FOR POLICE & FIREFIGHTERS, 2001

•   •   •   •

Who is Jack Schitt you ask? The lineage is finally revealed. Many people are at a loss for a response when someone says, "You don't know Jack Schitt." Well, pay attention and you will.

Jack is the only son of Awe Schitt and O. Schitt. Awe Schitt, the fertilizer magnate, married O. Schitt, the owner of Kneedeep N. Schitt, Inc. In turn, Jack Schitt married Noe Schitt and the deeply religious couple produced six children: Holie Schitt, Fulla Schitt, Givva Schitt, Bull Schitt, and the twins, Deep Schitt and Dip Schitt.

Against her parents' wishes, Deep Schitt married Dumb Schitt, a high school dropout. After being married fifteen years, Jack and Noe Schitt divorced.

Noe Schitt later married Mr. Sherlock and became known as Noe Schitt-Sherlock. Dip Schitt married Loda Schitt and they produced a nervous son, Chicken Schitt.

Fulla Schitt and Givva Schitt were inseparable throughout their childhood and subsequently married the Happens brothers in a dual ceremony. The Schitt-Happens children are Dawg, Byrd, and Horse. Bull Schitt, the prodigal son, left home to tour the world and recently returned from Italy with his new bride, Pisa Schitt.

Now you know Jack Schitt.

Why don't witches wear panties?

Better traction when flying on the broomstick.

Two bums are talking when the first one starts bragging, "Today was the best day ever! This morning I found a brand new pack of smokes just sitting on the ground. So you know what I did? I sat and smoked every fucking one of them. Had the best day ever."

The second bum just laughs. "That's nothing. Today I was walking along the railroad tracks and I found this girl lying on the tracks. You know what I did? I fucked her all day long."

"Bullshit! You couldn't have really done it all day long!"

"Well, no, but I did it for at least a few good hours. Best day of my life."

"So did she give you a good blow job?"

"Actually, no."

"So you're saying you fucked this girl for hours and she didn't even give you a blow job?"

"How could she? She didn't have a head!"

W hat's the difference between pink and purple?

The grip!

● ● ● ●

Danny Aiello is a bisexual. Any sex the man has ever had he's had to buy.

Danny was always a very generous man. Even when he was in the navy he used to give the other sailors blow jobs. He said it was to keep up morale. He obtained the rank of semen—first class.

—RICHARD BELZER, DANNY AIELLO ROAST, 1997

● ● ● ●

A trumpeter is hired to play two solos in a movie. After the sessions, he is paid handsomely and promised by the director that he will be notified when the movie is released to the public.

Three months later, the musician receives a notice that the movie will make its debut in Times Square at a porno house. He decides to attend, but wears a dark raincoat and shades so he won't be recognized. He takes a seat in the last row, next to an elderly couple.

The film begins and, to the musician's chagrin, it is filled with explicit sex scenes of all varieties: oral sex, anal intercourse, golden showers, sado-masochism, and, near the end, the female lead even has intercourse with a dog.

Immensely embarrassed, the trumpeter turns to the elderly couple and whispers, "I'm only here because I played on the soundtrack. I just came to hear the music."

To which the elderly woman whispers in reply, "I understand. We just came to see our dog."

The pope is visiting the U.S. He and the CEO of Taco Bell are talking and the businessman says, "We will give you one million dollars if you change the wording of the Lord's Prayer from 'bread' to 'taco.'"

The pope says he's sorry but he couldn't possibly do that—his people in Rome wouldn't be happy.

"Would you do it for a billion dollars?" says the CEO.

"I don't think so, my son."

"Ok, one trillion dollars, that's my final offer."

The pope's eyes light up at the thought of all that money going into the Church coffers and he agrees to the deal.

The pope returns to Rome and says to the cardinals, "I have good news and bad news. The good news is that we made a trillion dollars; the bad news is that we lost our deal with Wonder Bread.

● ● ● ●

This is good news. Paul Shaffer is going to act in a movie. I read in *Variety* that they are doing the Abner Louima story. Paul is playing the plunger.

Ice T is coming up later; that should be fun. Ice, I don't know if this is your crowd. There were more black people in the Beatles.

Actually, I met Ice T a few years back in LA and I'll never forget the first thing he said to me: "Get out of the car, bitch, or I'll kill you."

—JEFFREY ROSS, RICHARD BELZER ROAST, 2001

● ● ● ●

Wh, at's the difference between sin and shame?

It's a sin to put it in, but it's a shame to pull it out.

A ship is sailing along the high seas one afternoon when a pirate ship appears on the horizon. The captain yells, "Everyone prepare for battle, and hand me my red jacket."

One of the crewmembers hands him the jacket, which he immediately puts on. The ship roundly defeats the pirates and continues on its voyage. Later, more pirates appear—this time in two ships.

"Men, we must go to battle again!" says the captain. "Someone get me my red jacket!" After a fierce battle, the pirates are once more defeated.

A curious young sailor approaches the captain and asks, "Why is it that every time we go into battle, you insist on wearing your red jacket?"

"It's my job to lead and inspire my men. If I should get injured, the red jacket will camouflage the blood of my wounds and the crew will not be alarmed or disheartened."

The sailor is impressed by this selfless logic.

Later that day, a massive fleet of pirate ships, ten in all, appears on the horizon. The nervous crew looks up at the captain and he yells, "Everyone prepare for battle! And hand me my brown pants!"

● ● ● ●

Don King—what a man. You have fucked more black people than Little Richard.

—STEWIE STONE, DON KING ROAST, 2005

● ● ● ●

What am I?

I am a common object enjoyed by both sexes, normally about eight inches long, with little hairs on one end and a hole on the other. For most of the day I am laying down, but I am ready for instant action. When in use, I move back and forth and in and out a warm, moist hole. When the work is finally done, a white, slushy, sticky mush is left behind, and I return to my original position. What am I? Why, I am your very own...toothbrush!

What were you thinking, you pervert?

The officer shouted orders to a nearby soldier. With considerable bravery, the GI ran directly onto the field of battle, into the line of fire, to retrieve a dispatch case from a dead soldier. In a hail of bullets, he dove back to safety.

"Private," the officer said, "I'm recommending you for a medal. You risked your life to save the locations of our secret warehouses."

"Warehouses?" the private shouted. "I thought you said whorehouses!"

A young woman enters a confessional and admits, "Last night my boyfriend made mad passionate love to me—seven times."

The priest ponders this for a while and says, "Squeeze the juice of seven lemons into a glass, then drink it."

"Will this cleanse me of my sins, Father?"

"No, but it will wipe the smile off your face."

● ● ● ●

(To the tune of *Baby Face*)

Rabbit Test, oh what a piece of shit that *Rabbit Test,* I'd rather fuck a fist than see that mess, *Rabbit Test* oh, my ass is hurtin', you ain't no Richard Burton . . .

(To the tune of *The Shadow of Your Smile*)

Throw Mama from the Train was your first smash
That frying pan and then a wad of cash
What'd you really do to earn such fame?
You simply blew DeVito till he came . . .

(To the tune of *It Had To Be You*)

You acted surprised,

When Meg rolled her eyes,

Pretending to come,

You were struck dumb,

You thought it was lies

But Janice has been doing the same

She moans and groans but she never came,

At least not with you, you're such a bad screw,

You impotent Jew.

(To the tune of *Goody Goody*)

So you met some cow and shoved your hands up her crack

CITY SLICKERS!

And you spent the night with Jack Palance on your back

CITY SLICKERS!

Even though it took a while, you finally found your smile

Now the cow loves you and Jack does too, next up it's
Gomer Pyle . . .

(To the tune of *Mr. Saturday Night*)

Mr. Saturday Night should make film history

Who'd you blow to direct it?

Oh, I forgot that was me.

Billy, you're at the top

Chaplin, Woody, now you

Janice, lock up your daughters

No tellin' what he might do!

—ROB REINER, BILLY CRYSTAL ROAST, 1992

● ● ● ●

What's the difference between oral sex and anal sex?

Oral sex makes your whole day; anal sex makes your hole weak.

Why was the woman fired from her job at the sperm bank?

For drinking on the job.

Three prostitutes live together: a mother, a daughter, and a grandmother. One night the daughter comes home looking very discouraged.

"How did you get on tonight dear?" asks her mother.

"Not too well. I only got twenty dollars for a blow job."

"Wow!" says the mother, "In my day we gave a blow job for fifty cents!"

"Good God!" says the grandmother. "In my day we were just glad to get something warm in our stomachs!"

What's the ultimate rejection?

When you're masturbating and your hand falls asleep.

During his monthly visit to the corner barbershop, Joe asks his barber for suggestions on how to treat his rapidly advancing baldness.

After a brief pause, the barber leans over and confides that the best anti-baldness treatment that he's come across is, er, female juices.

"But you're balder than I am," protests Joe.

"True. But you've gotta admit I've got one hell of a mustache!"

• • • •

I just wanna say, it's so wonderful to see this many Jews and this many blacks in one room without Al Sharpton.

—ROBIN WILLIAMS, RICHARD PRYOR ROAST, 1991

• • • •

W hat do you call an Amish guy with his hand up a horse's ass? A mechanic.

T he queen was showing the Archbishop of Canterbury around the royal stable, when one of the stallions farted so loudly it couldn't be ignored.

"Oh dear," said the queen, "how embarrassing. I'm frightfully sorry about that."

"It's quite understandable," said the archbishop. "As a matter of fact, I thought it was the horse."

T welve monks were about to be ordained. For their final test of faith, they were asked to strip from the waist down and line up in the garden, where a beautiful stripper would dance before them. Each monk was to have a small bell attached to his penis, and anyone whose bell rang would not be ordained, as he had not yet reached a state of spiritual purity.

The exotic dancer performed before the first monk, with no reaction. She proceeded down the line, getting no response, until she stood before the twelfth and final monk. As she danced, his bell rang so loudly it fell off and clattered to the ground. Embarrassed, he bent down to pick it up—and eleven other bells began to ring.

What did the banana say to the vibrator?

Why are YOU shaking? She's going to EAT me!

Two police officers, George and Mary, have been out walking the beat for only a short while when Mary says, "Damn, I was running late this morning and when I was changing into my uniform at the station house, I forgot to put on my panties! We have to go back to the station to get them."

"We don't have to go back," George says. "Just give the K-9 unit, Fido, one sniff, and he will go fetch them for you."

It was a hot day and Mary doesn't feel like heading back to the station, so she gently pushes the dog's head near her crotch. Fido immediately begins sniffing and snorting. After ten seconds he turns and sniffs the wind, and is off in a flash toward the station house.

Five minutes go by with no sign of Fido. Ten minutes pass, then fifteen, and the two cops begin to worry. After twenty minutes they hear sirens in the distance. Suddenly, followed by a dozen police cars, Fido shoots around the corner with the desk sergeant's balls in his mouth.

● ● ● ●

I'm not Jewish, I'm protestant. We don't have a rabbi, we have a golf pro.

—JIM DAVID, A NIGHT OF COMEDY, 1999

● ● ● ●

Last week a very important meeting took place among God, the pope, and Moses. They were troubled because the president of the United States had misbehaved with a White House intern and there were many people who saw nothing wrong in what he had done. They decided that the best course of action would be to create an Eleventh Commandment to get their message across. But how should they word it so that it matched the other commandments in style and holy inspiration?

After much meditation and discussion they concluded that it should say, "Thou shalt not comfort thy rod with thy staff."

A blonde is walking down the street with her blouse open. A cop happens to be walking toward her and when he is about a block away, he thinks, "Boy, my eyes must be going, it looks like that woman's right breast is hanging out." As he gets closer he realizes it's true—her breast is exposed! When he reaches her he says, "Ma'am, what on earth are you thinking? I am going to have to cite you for indecent exposure!"

"Why, officer?" she says, her eyes widening.

"Well, your breast is hanging out."

"OMIGOD! I left the baby on the bus!"

A gay man is walking through a zoo, checking out the animals. When he comes to the gorillas, he notices that the male has a massive erection. Fascinated by this, he stands and watches the beast for half an hour. Finally, he just can't bear it any longer and he reaches into the cage to touch the gorilla's penis. The gorilla grabs him, drags him into the cage, and fucks him for six hours nonstop.

When he's done, the gorilla throws the man back out of the cage. The man is immediately taken to the hospital by ambulance.

Two days later, a friend visits him in the hospital and asks, "Are you hurt?"

"AM I HURT? AM I HURT!!" he shouts. "Wouldn't you be? He hasn't called, he hasn't written...!"

When nuns are admitted to heaven they go through a special gate and are expected to make one last confession before they become angels. Several nuns are lined up at the gate waiting to be absolved of their last sins before they are made holy.

"And so," says St. Peter to the first nun in line, "have you ever had any contact with a penis?"

"Well," she says, "I did once just touch the tip of one with the tip of my finger."

"Okay," says St. Peter, "dip your finger in the holy water and pass on into heaven."

The next nun says, "Well, yes, I did once get carried away and I, you know, sort of massaged one a bit."

"Okay," says St. Peter, "rinse your hand in the holy water and pass on into heaven." Suddenly there is some jostling in the line—one of the nuns is trying to cut in front.

"Well now, what's going on here?" says St. Peter.

"Your Excellency," says the impatient nun, "if I'm going to have to gargle that stuff, I want to do it before Sister Mary Thomas sticks her ass in it."

● ● ● ●

I promised myself I would never do another Roast. I also promised myself I would never fuck another midget…but you get one in your lap and one thing leads to another…

—DICK CAPRI, FREDDIE ROMAN ROAST, 1999

● ● ● ●

How can you tell when an auto mechanic has just had sex?

One of his fingers is clean.

A devout Catholic has settled into First Class on a flight to Rome. Imagine his surprise when the pope sits down in the seat next to him! The gentleman is too shy to speak to the pontiff, but he can't keep himself from glancing over now and then.

Shortly after take-off, the pope begins a crossword puzzle.

"This is fantastic," thinks the gentleman. "I'm really good at crosswords. Perhaps, the pope will get stuck, and ask me for assistance."

Almost immediately, the pope turns to the gentleman and said, "Excuse me, but do you know a four-letter word that ends in 'unt' and refers to a woman?"

Only one word comes into the man's mind, and he knows he can't repeat that one to the pope. "There must be another," he thinks—and then it comes to him. "I think the word you're looking for is aunt.'"

"Of course!" exclaims the pope. "I don't suppose you happen to have an eraser?"

Everything has a name now. What's this Attention Deficit Disorder? Whatever happened to just stupid?

● ● ● ●

I love this country. I fought in the Gulf War. Well, not actually. I had a fight with an Iranian at a Gulf gas station.

—RICH VOS, FRESH FUNNY FACES, 1999

● ● ● ●

Fun Things to Do with Pubic Hair . . . Dye, floss, make a wig, place near fire; braid, feather, cornrow, sprinkle glitter on, or anything of that general nature; bake into delicious muffins (note: try it on your friends, it gets pretty funny); make a bird's nest; throw at a friend and yell, "Spiders!"; make a sweater, make some mittens, make some socks, make another sweater; use as a topping in a friend's sandwich.

Three gay men die and are scheduled to be cremated. Their lovers happen to be at the funeral home at the same time and they begin discussing what they plan to do with the ashes.

The first man says, "My Benny loved to fly, so I'm going up in a plane and scatter his ashes in the sky."

The second man says, "My Carl was a good fisherman, so I'm going to scatter his ashes in our favorite lake."

The third man says, "My Jim was such a good lover, I think I'm going to dump his ashes in a pot of chili, so he can tear my ass up just one more time."

Three nuns are assigned to paint a room in their church. It is a really hot day and they are starting to sweat in their heavy black habits, so they take off their clothes and continue painting in the nude. Soon they hear a knock on the door.

"Who is it?" asks one of the nuns.

"I'm the blind man."

The nuns decide to let him in since he won't be able to see them.

They open the door, the man looks around the room, and after a few minutes he says, "Nice tits, sisters, where do you want the blinds?"

Ablonde, a redhead, and a brunette are competing in the English Channel Breast Stroke Competition. The redhead wins and the brunette comes in second—but there is no sign of the final contestant. Hours and hours go by, and the crowd becomes very worried. Just as everyone is losing hope, the blonde finally arrives. She is embraced by the relieved crowd as she comes ashore.

After all of the excitement dies down, the blonde leans over to the judge and whispers, "I hate to be a bad loser, but I think those other girls used their arms."

● ● ● ●

It was traumatic when I went blond. Do you know what the maintenance is like on this thing? Every three weeks I look like a crack whore.

—DEBBIE PEARLMAN, FRIARS NEW FACES OF COMEDY, 2002

● ● ● ●

Superman is flying around really horny, when he sees Wonder Woman sunbathing naked! "They've always said I'm faster than a speeding bullet and I've always wondered what she'd be like, with all her powers," he thinks. So he zooms down and fucks her in a flash and is gone before anyone can notice.

Wonder Woman sits up and says, "What the hell was that!?!"

The Invisible Man gets off her and replies, "I don't know but it hurt like hell!"

A guy goes to hell and is greeted by the devil, who explains that his punishment will change every thousand years, and he is to select his first punishment. He is allowed to take a tour of hell and look at his options before he decides.

The first room he comes to has a young guy chained to the wall being whipped.

The next room has a middle-aged guy being tortured with fire.

The third room has a really old guy chained to the wall getting a blow job from a gorgeous blonde.

The guy jumps at the chance and selects that room. The devil walks into the room, taps the blonde on the shoulder, and says, "Okay, you can stop now—you've been relieved."

● ● ● ●

The Catholic Church doesn't recognize homosexuals —that's funny, I always can.

—PATTY ROSBOROUGH, COMEDY TONIGHT!, 2003

● ● ● ●

A woman dies and goes to heaven. While waiting in line, she hears this terrible screaming and moaning. This disturbs her, so she tracks down St. Peter to find out what is going on.

"Oh, that," he says. "That's just one of the women in front of you. They are drilling holes in her back to attach her wings."

The woman gets back into line and soon the screaming starts again, this time even louder and more bloodcurdling than before. She calls St. Peter over to find out what is happening to the woman now.

"Oh, that," he says. "They're just drilling holes in her head to attach the halo."

That's the last straw—the woman decides that she wants out! She tells St. Peter that she has changed her mind and wants to be sent to hell.

"Are you sure you want to go there?" he says. "It's a terrible place, you'll end up getting sodomized and raped and even worse!"

"That's okay," says the woman. "I already have the holes for that!"

T wo gay guys are sharing an apartment. One morning, one of them is sitting on the couch jerking off into a brown paper bag when the other walks into the room, ready to go to work.
"What the hell are you doing?!" he asks.

"I'm packing your lunch!!!"

T wo guys have just gotten divorced and they swear they will never have anything to do with women again. Since they are best friends, they decide to move up to Alaska together, as far north as they can go, just to get away from all women. They arrive in the frozen north and go to a local trading post, where they ask the proprietor for "enough supplies to last two men for one year." The trader gets the gear together, and on top of each one's supplies he lays a board with a hole in it, with fur around the hole.

"What's that board for?" asks one of the guys.

"Well, where you're going there are no women and you might need this."

"No way! We've sworn off women for life!"

"Well, take the boards with you, and if you don't use them I'll refund your money next year."

"That's a deal," they say, and leave.

The next year one guy comes into the trading post and says, "Give me enough supplies to last one man for one year."

"Weren't you in here last year with a partner?" asks the trader.

"Yeah."

"Where is he?"

"I killed him. I caught him in bed with my board!"

● ● ● ●

I'm here today because I'm the only heavyweight Don King hasn't fucked over. He tried, but I couldn't bend over to grab my ankles.

—JEFF PIRRAMI, DON KING ROAST, 2005

● ● ● ●

A woman walks into a drugstore and asks the pharmacist if he sells condoms in size Extra Large.

"Yes, we do. Would you like to buy some?"

"No sir, but do you mind if I wait around here until someone does?"

A woman sends her clothing out to the Chinese laundry. When it comes back there are still stains in her panties. The next week she encloses a note that says, "Use more soap on panties."

But when she gets her laundry back, she sees that there are still stains in her panties. This goes on for several weeks, and each week the woman encloses the same note.

Finally, she receives a note back with her laundry: "Use more paper on ass."

• • • •

Mike Tyson is the only man in America who drives a $250,000 car with license plates he made himself.

—FREDDIE ROMAN, JERRY STILLER ROAST, 1999

• • • •

A man goes into a restaurant and sits at the only open table. As he sits down, he accidentally knocks the spoon off the table with his elbow. A nearby waiter reached into his shirt pocket, pulls out a clean spoon, and sets it on the table. The diner is impressed. "Do all the waiters here carry spoons in their pockets?"

"Yes. Ever since an Efficiency Expert visited our restaurant. He determined that 17.8 percent of our diners knock the spoon off the table. By carrying clean spoons with us, we save trips to the kitchen."

The diner finishes his meal and as he is paying the waiter, he says, "Forgive the intrusion, but do you know that you have a string hanging from your fly?"

"Yes, we all do. Seems that the same Efficiency Expert determined that we spend too much time washing our hands after using the men's room. So, the other end of that string is tied to my penis. When I need to go, I simply pull the string, do my thing, and then return to work. Having never touched myself, there really is no need to wash my hands. Saves a lot of time."

"Wait a minute...How do you get your penis back in your pants?"

"Well, I don't know about the other guys, but I use the spoon."

• • • •

Pat Cooper is an angry, angry man. People would rather go Christmas fishing with Scott Peterson than hang around with Pat Cooper.

—LISA LAMPANELLI, DON KING ROAST, 2005

• • • •

Paul is ambling through a crowded street fair when he decides to stop at a palm reader's table. Says the mysterious old woman, "For fifteen dollars, I can read your love line and tell your romantic future."

Paul readily agrees. The reader takes one look at his open palm and says, "I can see that you have no girlfriend."

"That's true," says Paul.

"Oh my goodness, you are extremely lonely, aren't you?"

"Yes," Paul admits. "I'm amazed that you can tell all of this from my love line."

"Love line? No. From the calluses and blisters."

Why do so many gay men have moustaches?

To hide the stretch marks.

Late one night, an alien spacecraft lands near a deserted gas station. Soon one of the aliens comes down the ramp, looks around, and walks over to one of the gas pumps where he demands, "Earthling! Take me to your leader!"

The gas pump, of course, does not reply.

The alien becomes agitated and again demands, "Take me to your leader!" Frustrated by the lack of response, he goes back to the spacecraft where he is confronted by the captain.

"Report."

"I contacted an earthling—he would not cooperate."

"Hmmm. I will deal with this earthling myself."

"Yes, sir. Be careful, sir, I have a feeling there could be trouble."

The captain leaves the ship and approaches the gas pump. "Earthling, you will cooperate. Take me to your leader."

The gas pump remains unresponsive.

"Very well." The captain draws his blaster. "If you do not respond by the count of three, I shall be forced to fire on you. One. Two. Three." ZZZZZT. WHAM! The gas pump explodes, knocking the alien off his webbed feet. The captain jumps up and runs to the ship. "Quickly! Make ready to depart!"

"Yes. sir. What happened. sir?"

"I fired on the earthling and it responded very forcefully."

"Sorry, sir, I was afraid that might happen."

"How did you know that there would be trouble?"

"Well, sir, I assumed that anyone who can take his dick, wrap it around his feet, and stick it in his left ear is probably going to be one tough bastard."

• • • •

We should never be afraid to laugh at religion because God has a sense of humor. I realize that every time I'm naked.

—STEVEN "SPANKY" MCFARLIN, FRIARS NEW FACES OF COMEDY, 2002

• • • •

Two farm boys are hunting in the north woods when they come upon a naked woman sitting on a stump. One says to her, "Are you game?"

She smiles and says she is.

The other one shoots her!

A bandaged and badly injured turd is floating around the sewer. The turd floating next to him says, "Jeesh, you look horrible, what the hell happened to you?"

"I got rear-ended!"

Do prosthetic limbs cost an arm and a leg?

• • • •

If Richard Simmons were an insect, would he be a ladybug or a fruit fly?

—TOM COTTER, FRIARS FOUNDATION GALA, 2000

• • • •

Maria is sitting on her stoop eating a slice of pizza. Two of her girlfriends walk by and notice that she's not wearing any underwear.

"Hey, Maria," one of them calls out. "Did you take off your panties to keep yourself cool?"

"I don't know about keeping cool, but it sure keeps the flies away from my pizza!"

Why do bald men have holes in their pockets?

Because they like to run their hands through their hair.

● ● ● ●

I suppose you must be wondering out there, how we at the Friars allot the time for the speakers. Well, here's exactly how it works. If you've got a cock that's 5 inches long you do 5 minutes, 6 inches long you do 6 minutes, 7 inches long you do 7 minutes—most of this dais will only bow.

—MILTON BERLE, STEVEN SEAGAL ROAST, 1995

● ● ● ●

Jeff and Mike are in a car accident and killed instantly. Upon Jeff's arrival at the Pearly Gates, he is met by St. Peter.

"Where is my friend, Mike?" Jeff asks.

"Well, Mike was not as fortunate as you. He went in the other direction."

"Wow, that's rough. Could I see Mike one more time just to be sure he is okay?"

Jeff and St. Peter walk over to the edge of heaven and look down. There is Mike, on a sandy beach with a gorgeous, sexy blonde in a bikini, and a keg of beer.

"I don't mean to complain," says Jeff, "but Mike seems to have it pretty nice down there in hell."

"It's not as good as it looks," says St. Peter. "You see, the keg has a hole in it—and the blonde doesn't."

● ● ● ●

We cannot find Bin Laden, but we can find John Bobbitt's penis in the snow.

—Michelle Balan, Jim David Comedy Night, 2003

● ● ● ●

Two prostitutes are riding around town with a sign on the roof of their car reading TWO PROSTITUTES $150.00.

A policeman notices the car and pulls them over. He tells the ladies that they have to remove the sign or they will be arrested and taken to jail. Just then, another car passes by with a sign reading, JESUS SAVES.

"Hey mister, how come you're not pulling THAT car over?" asks one of the prostitutes.

"Well, that's a little different, since it pertains to religion."

The two ladies are furious, but they remove their sign and drive away.

The next day, the same policeman notices the same two ladies riding around town with a sign on the roof of their car, so he pulls them over again. As he approaches the car, though, he notices that the wording has been changed. The new sign reads, TWO ANGELS SEEKING PETER $150.00.

A FEW DIRTY WORDS FROM LEWIS BLACK

When I first started doing stand-up I had three or five stories about my sex life and I would tell those stories. That's all I had to talk about that was funny. I knew it was the one thing that everybody laughed at, just a few stupid stories. But you can always lose an audience with that kind of material. The one thing that I've been thinking about lately is that a lot of people will laugh at something that is considered "dirty"—which is just a ridiculous word for it—if it's done through innuendo. They'll laugh because you didn't really use the right word.

They don't to want to hear the four-letter word; they want to hear something that's equivalent to that word so that they can *think* the word in their own heads. I don't think that dirty words naturally evoke laughter. But when you do use them some people will say, "Oh, you get laughs because you said 'fuck.'" Well, that's nonsense.

My material mainly comes from what I see around me. When I see something absolutely nuts, like airline security or newspaper articles or if I watch *Meet the Press*—*Meet the Press* and *Face the Nation* usually give me one or two things a week.

I've always been pretty lucky talking about politics onstage because of both sides of the fence. For a long time now I basically try to point out that both sides are at fault. And if I feel tension from a portion of the audience, I'll say, "Look, you guys don't get it," and I'll go back and whack on the Democrats for a while just to calm them down. What's good about that is then I can say even worse than I would have said about the Republicans. The new joke that I have is that the Republicans don't think and the Democrats think too much.

It's almost overwhelming today, the wealth of material at my disposal. It's the opposite of dull. In those dull periods I think I'll never have any more material, and right now there's so much material it's almost more difficult to try to glean what it is you should do.

Talking about abortion is almost impossible. That issue is so hot that you just know if you even say the word everybody will be screaming. They won't even give me the chance to start talking about it. When the first war started in Iraq, I was upstairs watching the opening salvos and then I was supposed to go downstairs to Catch a Rising Star, in Chicago. I was sitting with friends and we were watching this thing unfold and yet it was one of those things where you don't think you can go onstage and make jokes about it because people in the audience's kids are going to be there. Sometimes it's that old axiom: tragedy over time.

The best example of facing that was Bobby Slayton. Phil Hartman had been shot by his wife and, with a particular lack of sensitivity, Bobby went onstage—legend has it, but I've heard this a couple of times—and he talked about Phil and how funny he was, and stuff that he did, and how he was a nice person, and then he paused and he went, "...and I thought I married a cunt." I thought, wow that was really, oh man! About 70 percent of the audience laughed and there's 30 percent who the word alone would have sent them around the bend.

At the yearly correspondents' dinners or the White House and Congress events, there is nothing to be gained by whacking guys personally, no matter how funny the joke is. If those people don't get it, they're not going to get it. At the correspondents' dinner, I turned my act from what it is into a series of very precise knock-knock jokes. I neutered it.

I once did a joke about Pat Buchanan in front of group of Democrats. I said, "The reason you know Pat Buchanan is insane is because, when he laughs, most people expel air, and he actually sucks it in. So when he laughs, what you're hearing is the sound of his own asshole sucking him in." With all these Democrats, nothing. I literally went, "You have got to be kidding me!" I laced into them for two minutes. I was shocked. Ann Richards was laughing, that was about it.

A comic I knew came up to me after watching me work early on and he said, "You know, I'm not angry and I'm yelling. You are angry and you're not yelling. So get up there and instead of trying to just talk about this stuff, yell about it." I did and it was like a revelation, it was really cathartic. I thought, now this stuff makes sense because I've been sitting on this anger for about five years. I finally realized what was keeping the audience at bay. They would laugh but a lot of the time it was just nervous laughter, like I was gonna shoot somebody. One of the reasons that yelling makes it work is that comedy is a release, and anger and edgy create tension. It took a long time for me to learn that.

I think coming out of the sixties adds to my style. I know it had an indelible effect on me. So many doors got open to possibilities that it seems a shame to shut them—but a lot of people do.

T wo Indians and a hillbilly are walking in the woods. One of them runs up a hill to the mouth of a small cave. "Wooooo! Wooooo! Wooooo!" he calls, and then he listens very closely until he hears an answering, "Wooooo! Wooooo! Wooooo!" He tears off his clothes and runs into the cave.

The hillbilly is puzzled and asks the other Indian what that was all about. Is the other Indian crazy or what?

"No," says the Indian. "It is our custom during mating season. When Indian men see a cave they holler, "Wooooo! Wooooo! Wooooo!" into the opening. If they get an answer back, it means there is a girl in there waiting to mate."

Just then they spot another cave. The Indian runs up to the opening and hollers, "Wooooo! Wooooo! Wooooo!" Within seconds an answer comes from deep inside the cave, so he tears off his clothes and runs inside.

The hillbilly wanders on alone, until he comes to a huge cave, the largest he's ever seen. As he looks at it in amazement he thinks, "Hoo, man! This cave is much bigger than the ones those Indians found. There must be some really big, fine women in this cave!" He hollers with all his might, "Wooooo! Wooooo! Wooooo!" Then he closes his eyes in anticipation, and sure enough, he hears the answering call, WOOOOOOOOO! WOOOOOOOOO! WOOOOOOOOO!" He races into the cave, tearing off his clothes as he goes.

The following day, the headline of the local newspaper reads, NAKED HILLBILLY RUN OVER BY FREIGHT TRAIN.

Nick the Dragon Slayer has a longstanding obsession with nuzzling the beautiful Queen's voluptuous breasts, but he knows the penalty for this will be death. One day he reveals his secret desire to his colleague, Horatio the Physician, who is the King's chief doctor. Horatio says that he can arrange for Nick to satisfy his desire, but it will cost him one thousand gold coins to arrange it. Without pause, Nick readily agrees.

The next day, Horatio the Physician makes a batch of itching powder and pours a little bit into the Queen's brassiere while she bathes. Soon after she dresses, the itching commences and grows intense. Upon being summoned to the Royal Chambers to treat this condition, Horatio informs the King and Queen that only a special saliva, if applied for four hours, will cure this type of itch. He adds that tests had shown that only the saliva of Nick the Dragon Slayer will work as an antidote.

The King quickly summons Nick the Dragon Slayer. Horatio the Physician then slips Nick the antidote for the itching powder, which he puts into his mouth, and for the next four hours, Nick works passionately on the Queen's magnificent breasts. The Queen's itching is eventually relieved and Nick leaves satisfied and touted as a hero.

Upon returning to his chamber, Nick finds Horatio demanding his payment of one thousand gold coins. With his obsession now satisfied, Nick can't care less and, knowing that Horatio can never report the matter to the King, shoos him away without paying him.

The next day, Horatio the Physician slips a massive dose of the same itching powder into the King's shorts. The King immediately summons Nick the Dragon Slayer...

• • • •

Paul Shaffer, I had no idea you were so funny. And such a sharp tongue. That must really hurt Dave's ass.

—SUSIE ESSMAN, RICHARD BELZER ROAST, 2001

• • • •

What do tight pants and a cheap motel have in common?

No ball room.

What do you see when the Pillsbury Dough Boy bends over?

Doughnuts.

A man dies and goes to hell, where he is greeted by the devil.

Devil: Hey, why are you bumming out?

Man: If you died and went to hell, you'd be bumming out, too.

Devil: Hell isn't what you think it is. It's fun down here. Say, do you drink?

Man: Sure, I love to drink. Why?

Devil: Well, you're gonna love Mondays, then. Because on Mondays, all we do here is drink. Hell, we have whiskey, tequila, rum, vodka, all the booze you want. We drink till we puke then we drink more— and no hangover, since you're dead.

Man: Wow, that sounds great!

Devil: Do you smoke?

Man: Damn right I do.

Devil: Cool! You're gonna love Tuesdays. We get the finest cigars from all over the world. Smoke all you want. You don't have to worry about getting cancer because you're already dead.

Man: No shit!

Devil: You like gambling?

Man: Hell, yeah!

Devil: Great! On Wednesdays, we have gambling night here in hell. We have slot machines, roulette, craps, black jack, horse racing, you name it. You like to get stoned?

Man: I love getting stoned! You mean...

Devil: That's right, man, Thursday is stoner night here in hell! Help yourself to a huge bowl of crack, smoke a joint the size of a nuclear sub, do all the drugs you want and you don't have to worry about overdosing because you're already dead!

Man: Awesome! I never would've thought hell was such a swinging place!

Devil: Are you gay?

Man: Uh, no.

Devil: Oooh, you're gonna HATE Fridays!

● ● ● ●

You know how you can tell a good Mexican restaurant? In the restrooms they put salt around the toilet seat.

—DICK CAPRI, SALUTE TO FREDDIE ROMAN, 2003

● ● ● ●

• • • •

The diet I liked, that was very popular in the '80s, was the Fresca, M&Ms, and Cocaine Diet. Now THAT was a great diet. But you can't do that anymore —you can't find Fresca.

—CORY KAHANEY, SALUTE TO SOUPY SALES, 2003

• • • •

*L*ife magazine sends one of its reporters to the Appalachian Mountains to gather the life stories of the locals. On the first day, the reporter climbs up a mountain and there he encounters an old man sitting in a rocking chair on the front porch of his log cabin. "Good morning, sir. I'm a reporter from *Life* magazine. I'm here to gather life stories from the folks living in this area. Do you have any memorable stories to tell?"

The old man thinks for a while and then says, "Well...I remember the day when my neighbor's sheep got lost in yonder mountains. So me and the boys went off looking for that darn sheep and we brought along some food and moonshine. When we found that sheep, we took turns humping it under the lemon tree. We had a grand time eating, drinking, and fornicating."

The reporter is dumbfounded by what he has just heard. "Um, that's an interesting story, sir, but I can't use that in the magazine. Do you have any other memorable stories to tell?"

"Let's see. Well, I remember the day when my neighbor's daughter got lost in yonder mountains. So me and the boys went off looking for that darn girl and we brought along some food and moonshine. When we found that girl, we took turns humping her under the lemon tree. We had a great time eating, drinking, and fornicating."

"Listen, sir! My magazine certainly won't allow that story to be printed. How about some sad stories? Do you have any sad stories to tell?"

"Well, I remember the day when I got lost in yonder mountains..."

Two guys go to a whorehouse. The first one goes in, and when he comes out a half hour later he says, "My wife is better."

Then the second guy goes in. When he comes out a half hour later he says, "You know what? Your wife IS better."

●　●　●　●

Some people are worried about the Orthodox Jewish community getting together with the gay community because it might spark violence. That's silly. You put gays and Jews together, you don't get violence—you get theater!

—RICK CROM, TAX RELIEF COMEDY NIGHT, 2002

●　●　●　●

By the time the sailor pulls into a little town, every hotel room is taken. "You've got to have a room somewhere," he pleads with a hotel clerk, "or just a bed, I don't care where."

"Well, I do have a double room with one occupant—an air force guy," admits the manager, "and he might be willing to share the room and split the cost. But to tell you the truth, he snores so loudly that people in adjoining rooms have complained in the past. I'm not sure it'd be worth it to you."

"No problem," the tired navy man assures him. "I'll take it."

The next morning the sailor comes down to breakfast bright-eyed and bushy-tailed.

"How'd you sleep?" asks the manager.

"Never better."

"No problem with the other guy snoring?"

"Nope, I shut him up in no time!"

"How'd you manage that?"

"He was already in bed, snoring away, when I came in the room. So I went over, gave him a kiss on the cheek, and said, 'Goodnight, beautiful'—and he sat up all night watching me."

A very pious nun went to her Mother Superior to complain about the language that the construction workers, who were working next to the convent, were using. "Sister Margaret, don't get so upset by their bad language. Those men are just people of the earth. They call a spade a spade," the mother superior explained patiently.

"Oh no they don't, Mother. They call it a fuckin' shovel!"

W hat do you get when you cross a whore with a computer?

A fucking know-it-all!

• • • •

Freddie has risen to such a position of power at the Friars that now if he wants anything he has to blow himself.

—PAUL SHAFFER, SALUTE TO FREDDIE ROMAN, 2003

• • • •

T his blonde was asked if she would like to become a Jehovah's Witness.

She said no, because she had not seen the accident.

There's a great actor who can no longer remember his lines, and when word gets out, no one will hire him. After many years he finally finds a theater that is prepared to give him a chance to shine again. The director says, "This is the most important part, but it has only one line. You walk out on stage at the opening, carrying a rose. You hold the rose to your nose with just one finger and thumb, sniff the rose deeply, and then say, 'Ah, the sweet aroma of my mistress.'"

The actor is thrilled. All day long he practices his line over and over again. Finally, showtime comes. The curtain goes up, the actor walks onto the stage, and with great passion delivers the line, "Ah, the sweet aroma of my mistress." The theater erupts. The audience is screaming with laughter, but the director is steaming! The actor looks stunned.

"You damn fool!" cries the director. "You have ruined me!"

"What happened?? I'm sure I didn't forget my line!"

"No!" screams the director. "You forgot the rose!"

INDEX